Apprenticeship in dual and non-dual systems

Studies in Vocational and Continuing Education

Vol. 19

edited by
Philipp Gonon & Anja Heikkinen

Peter lang
Bern · Berlin · Bruxelles · New york · Oxford · Warszawa · Wien

María José Chisvert-Tarazona, Mónica Moso-Diez &
Fernando Marhuenda-Fluixá (Eds.)

Apprenticeship in dual and non-dual systems

Between tradition and innovation

Peter Lang
Bern · Berlin · Bruxelles · New york · Oxford · Warszawa · Wien

Bibliographic information published by Die Deutsche Bibliothek
Die Deutsche Nationalbibliothek lists this publication in the Deutsche
Nationalbibliografie; detailed bibliographic data is available on the
Internet at ‹http://dnb.d-nb.de›.

Library of Congress Cataloging-in-Publication Data
A CIP catalog record for this book has been applied for at the
Library of Congress.

This publication is funded within the agreement signed by University
of Valencia and Bankia Foundation regarding the promotion and
cooperation around the 3rd International VET Conference 'Crossing
Boundaries in Vocational Education and Training: Pedagogical concerns and market demands' that took place on 2–3 May 2019 in
Valencia (Spain), ref. OTR2019-19288COLAB.

Fundación Bankia
por la Formación Dual

ISBN 978-3-0343-4305-3 (Print)   ISBN 9978-3-0343-4334-3 (E-Book)
ISBN 978-3-0343-4335-0 (Mobi)   ISBN 978-3-0343-4336-7 (EPUB)
DOI 10.3726/b18398   ISSN 2235-7327

This publication has been peer reviewed.

© Peter Lang Group AG, International Academic Publishers, Bern 2021
Bern@peterlang.com, www.peterlang.com

All rights reserved.
All parts of this publication are protected by copyright.
Any utilisation outside the strict limits of the copyright law, without
the permission of the publisher, is forbidden and liable to prosecution.
This applies in particular to reproductions, translations, microfilming,
and storage and processing in electronic retrieval systems.

Table of contents

List of contributors 7

Foreword 11

FERNANDO MARHUENDA-FLUIXÁ
Alternance and vocational knowledge: Reconsidering
apprenticeships and education-business partnerships from an
educational perspective 21

1. Dual systems in Europe: Reforms and modernization

SANDRA BOHLINGER
Contextualising policy transfer initiatives in the field of
vocational education and training (VET) 51

FLORINDA SAULI, MATILDE WENGER & JEAN-LOUIS BERGER
What constitutes quality in the Swiss initial vocational education
and training dual system: An apprentice perspective 79

STEFAN KESSLER & PHILIPP GONON
The disruptive potential of digitalization and the current Swiss
VET landscape 105

2. Apprenticeships in dual and non-dual systems: Adaptation and opportunities to develop

ENNI PAUL & CAMILLA GÅFVELS
Apprenticeship education and school-based vocational programmes in the Swedish upper secondary school: Different tracks towards the same goal? 135

DIETMAR FROMMBERGER, MATTHIAS PILZ, MICHAEL GESSLER
International cooperation in the field of vocational education and training: Concepts, approaches, and empirical findings from a German perspective 161

M'HAMED DIF
Apprenticeship in France: Institutional patterns, organisation, methods and performance 179

3. Dual VET and education-business cooperation in Spain

REINA FERRÁNDEZ-BERRUECO, LUCÍA SÁNCHEZ-TARAZAGA & STEPHAN HUMPL
The interest of companies in participating in higher education 209

MARÍA JOSÉ CHISVERT-TARAZONA, JAVIER VILA-VÁZQUEZ, ALICIA ROS-GARRIDO, & DAVINIA PALOMARES-MONTERO
Does the dual VET bring curriculum improvements? A normative analysis in the Spanish context 239

ANGEL DÍAZ-CHAO, MÓNICA MOSO-DIEZ, & JOAN TORRENT-SELLENS
VET, value generation and firm result: An empirical exploration from Spanish industrial firms 265

List of contributors

Jean-Louis Berger
University of Fribourg, jean-louis.berger@unifr.ch

Sandra Bohlinger
Dresden University, sandra.bohlinger@tu-dresden.de

María José Chisvert-Tarazona
University of Valencia, maria.jose.chisvert@uv.es

Angel Díaz-Chao
Fundación SEPI FSP and Rey Juan Carlos University, angel.diaz@fundacionsepi.es

M'Hamed Dif
University of Strasbourg, dif@unistra.fr

María Reina Ferrandez-Berrueco
University Jaume I, ferrande@edu.uji.es

Dietmar Frommberger
Universität Osnabrück, dietmar.frommberger@uni-osnabrueck.de

Camilla Gåfvels
University of Konstfack, Camilla.Gafvels@konstfack.se

Michael Gessler
Universität Bremen, mgessler@uni-bremen.de

Philipp Gonon
University of Zurich, gonon@ife.uzh.ch

Stefan Humpl
3s ResearchLab, humpl@3s.co.at

Stefan Kessler
University of Zurich, stefan.kessler@ife.uzh.ch

Fernando Marhuenda-Fluixá
University of Valencia, fernando.marhuenda@uv.es

Mónica Moso-Diez
Centre for Knowledge and Innovation, Bankia Foundation for Dual Training, mmoso@fundacionbankia.com/moso.monica@gmail.com

Davinia Palomares-Montero
University of Valencia, davinia.palomares@uv.es

Enni Paul
Stockholm University, enni.paul@specped.su.se

Matthias Pilz
Universität zu Köln, matthias.pilz@uni-koeln.de

Alicia Ros-Garrido
University of Valencia, Alicia.ros@uv.es

Lucía Sánchez-Tarazaga
University Jaume I, lvicente@uji.es

Florinda Sauli
Swiss Federal Institute for Vocational Education and Training, florinda.sauli@iffp.swiss

Joan Torrent-Sellens
Faculty of Economics and Business, Universitat Oberta de Catalunya, jtorrent@uoc.edu

List of contributors

Javier Vila-Vázquez
University of Valencia, javier.vila@uv.es

Matilde Wenger
Swiss Federal Institute for Vocational Education and Training, Matilde.Wenger@iffp.swiss

Foreword

Apprenticeship in dual and non-dual systems: Between tradition and innovation

This volume adds to the 'Studies in Vocational and Continuing Education' series in Peter Lang. It engages in the series ongoing discussion on the roles and conflicts around vocational education and training, and more precisely with the tensions to which apprenticeship systems are confronted in the new scenarios of production and labour market relations.

An analysis shared by the academic community suggests that a large part of the success of a VET system depends on its capacity to respond to the needs of the context in which it is developed. Bearing in mind the historical tradition of education in that country is essential, in addition to the existing relations between the production and education systems. That is why this book provides a reflexive look at the answers provided by national VET systems with different traditions, especially regarding the relationships established with the labour market. Placing emphasis on the field of education or production entails educational models that are underpinned by different rationalities.

The stability of dual systems in countries such as Germany or Switzerland is undoubtedly the result of the continuous support from social agents and governments, who acknowledge the advantages of the dual system, particularly its benefits in the effective transition from school to work. The dual system in these countries is an effective instrument to integrate young people into the labour market, as the majority of these programmes consist of work-based learning. This contributes to a low youth unemployment rate in these countries, which, on the other hand, have a healthy production fabric. The more school-based VET, which is the case of the Swedish or Spanish systems, tend towards more extensive social and education objectives, but they encounter greater difficulties to adapt to the demands of the labour market. The example of France is very rich insofar there coexist a well-developed apprenticeship system with a school VET. The future of dual VET systems depends on their capacity to help guarantee professional competitiveness, while also guaranteeing the education level of the population.

Chapter 1 reconsiders the notions of alternance and apprenticeship, claiming the former as a pedagogical arrangement and the latter as a contractual relation that favours but not necessarily results in the former. It starts with an overiew of European welfare, transition, VET and upper secondary education systems and the relations among them, with a particular focus on where do dual VET systems appear. It then provides a review of classical and modern literature on learning from experience and specifically on work experience. This allows the author to differentiate alternance and apprenticeship. Upon this differentiation, the chapter covers what sorts of vocational knowledge are needed and favoured nowadays by labour markets and how well can different vocational education and training systems equip young people with such knowledge combining the workplace and the school.

The first section in the book addresses the ways in which apprenticeships are being challenged, reformed and adapted within those countries well known for their dual system as the dominant approach towards initial VET. Examples for Germany and Switzerland are dealt with here. The nature and scope of current challenges seems to be diverse and extends to different areas of the dual VET systems: the institutional (and its public VET policies), the educational (and the underlying quality of the dual) and the socio-technological (and new technologies) one. The review of these very diverse issues, but at the same time so interconnected, gives us a refreshing view of the 'current homework' for the modernisation and advancement of the dual systems that are most advanced. These challenges are basically three. First, it tackles the German challenge of modelling public policy on IVET and its potential transferability to other countries (as progress in the positioning of certain models and their underlying educational regimes), which will be dealt with in Chapter 2. A second challenge is ensuring quality which, although not new, still lacks validated and harmonised assessment schemes, and therefore requires further work, as pointed out in Chapter 3. Finally, the challenge of new technologies and how they could be assimilated in VET systems is discussed, especially concerning disruptive technologies, where the time vector is key to the effectiveness of VET system modernisation, as noted in Chapter 4.

In Chapter 2 Sandra Bohlinger contributes with 'Contextualising policy transfer initiatives in the field of vocational education and training,' which seeks to enlarge the ongoing discussion on VET policy transfer in the scientific literature. The author aims at linking the field of policy borrowing and lending with policy transfer initiatives in the context of VET and apprenticeship training in the German-speaking countries. To this end, the chapter delivers an in-depth review of the state of the art of comparative analysis of education systems and public policy transfer approaches, on which to critically reflect on the strengths and weaknesses of existing theories of educational policy transfer and to align them with initiatives to reform or implement VET and apprenticeship training. By contextualising findings, the author proposes a comprehensive framework to understand the design of educational policy transfer with a focus on VET. This extensive and thorough analysis of the scientific literature on the transfer of education policies is a refreshing approach to educational comparative studies, including issues related to power relations and the subject of coercive decision-making.

In Chapter 3 Florinda Sauli, Matilde Wenger and Jean-Louis Berger present 'What Constitutes Quality in the Swiss Initial Vocational Education and Training Dual System: An Apprentice Perspective' which focuses on an important and discussed topic, namely quality in initial VET (IVET). Authors provide a wide overview on the Swiss context, both in terms of VET system and VET policy, framing the subsequent quantitative analysis on perceptions of IVET quality from apprentices enrolled in a dual IVET program. The quantitative study is conducted on a sample of 320 apprentices from the Swiss Dual system, considering two occupational fields, technical and retail ones. A thematic analysis was performed on data collected through open-ended questions. Results revealed that the quality of IVET was multi-layered and complex. Apprentices' perceptions of high and low quality were grouped into three different levels of a more comprehensive system. The levels included elements referring to the learning objects, the social learning environment, and the IVET context. Differences in the perceptions of quality between learning sites and occupational fields were also highlighted, confirming the multifaceted dimensions of quality in IVET, the role of subjective perceptions, the differences among school- and company-environments, and sectoral differences.

In Chapter 4 Stefan Kessler and Philipp Gonon present 'The Disruptive Potential of Digitalisation and the Current Swiss VET Landscape,' which seeks to discuss the disruptive potential of digitalisation in the current Swiss VET context. On the assumption that digitisation is regarded as having an extensive impact on the world of work and hence, affects vocational education and training, authors discuss on three levels: debates and concerns, politics and practices. Firstly, it presents a brief overview of the key aspects of digitalisation as discussed in the literature, regarding the future of work and the performance of VET as a training model. Secondly, authors argue that the level of educational practice is a promising field of study in assessing the disruptive potential of digitalisation, especially in dual training systems. To this end, authors examine four brief case studies where digitalisation has had some effect on the nature of work or the learning process, highlighting that VET providers (both schools and firms) take different courses of action with respect to digitalisation. Thirdly, digitalisation emerges to a focal point in the present political agenda. Besides the promises and premises of a fundamentally changing VET landscape, digitalisation primarily takes place as a gradual process of change. In conclusion it is argued that rather than a radical disruption, digitalisation represents an evolutionary development with core aspects of the system remaining largely the same.

The second section covers the ways in which different countries that are not known for having a dual system have introduced apprenticeships, as well as the efforts taken by dual systems, particularly the case of Germany, to make them available in third countries, as an example of globalisation of VET as a market product.

Chapter 6 opens the section and deals with international efforts to spread dual systems world-wide, in an attempt not driven by international institutions or European policies, but rather focusing upon efforts taken by a country like Germany, well positioned in the global competition. Dietmar Frommberger, Matthias Pilz and Michael Gessler, three prestigious professors at German universities and with extensive experience in the internationalisation of VET, provide a historical and critical review regarding the debates on the export and transfer of the German dual VET system. They clearly describe how Germany organises the cooperation to development of dual VET in other countries, analysing the generation of structures from a coordinated approach both at a political and academic level. Readers access a theoretical-conceptual as well as a practical analysis, in which the role of companies and the context is enhanced. The end of the chapter shows the difficulties of transferring the dual VET model to a greater extent than its advances.

This guiding thread takes us to Chapter 7, written by M'Hamed Dif, where there is a detailed explanation of how an apprenticeship system has coexisted in France, a country not usually identified as a dual system, in proper coexistence with a school-based VET system. More efforts should be taken to analyse and understand this coexistence in the light of the beginning chapter of the section. This chapter gives an in-depth description of the historical background of the VET System in France, the coordination promoted by the legislation between companies and education centres, as well as the instruments that make this possible. One of the main outcomes of this research confirms that apprenticeship obtains the best results from its education system with regards to access to employment. A system that is undergoing changes and updating, raising new questions about the benefits of the liberation of apprenticeship provision market through the Reform Act of the 5th September 2018.

Chapter 5 studies the school traditions of dual VET in greater depth. Based on an ethnographic case study, the interactions of students from two national upper secondary VET programmes in the Swedish context are analysed: The child and recreation programme and Transport and vehicle programme in the school environment and in the business environment. The authors, Enni Paul and Camilla Gåfvels, mention the contrast between tacit knowledge and embodied experience, accessible in the business context, and theoretical and propositional knowledge, more typical of the school context. They express deep concern for curriculum and assessment and argue that the latter shows theoretical apprenticeship to a greater extent. Aware of the limitation of the case study to develop generalisations, they aptly propose dialogue with previous research that provides similar results. This chapter invites reflection and among its conclusions it recovers the initial assumption: Swedish apprenticeship education is still a school-based apprenticeship education adhering to a school logic.

The third and final section deals with the way in which education-business partnerships have evolved recently in Spain, addressing the complexities of trying to implement a dual model in a strongly rooted school-based system, where companies are used to demand and complain about the labour market. Nevertheless, the involvement of companies in educational policies and practices, as well as investment in VET, has not been a landmark of the entrepreneurial culture of the country so far.

Chapter 8 is a joint contribution by Fernández-Berrueco and Sánchez-Tarazaga, both working at the University Jaume I, and Humpl, managing director of 3s Unternehmensberatung. Despite being a contribution on Spain, it is enriched by the perspective of someone from abroad who has extensive knowledge in the role of companies in training young people both at VET as well as in Higher Education. The chapter portrays data from a survey prepared and conducted by the authors to cover the interest of companies in contributing to Higher Education, by getting involved into it in different ways. Not being a chapter on VET in itself (it addresses ISCED levels 6 to 7), it provides important inputs on the reasons, interests and needs that Spanish companies, particularly small companies, have to contribute to the education of the future generations, as well as on the obstacles they face in order to do this. The study contextualises the manifold aspects why a company might engage in providing a placement for university students together with the regulations that legally frame their involvement. From here, the authors move into a review of the literature about the benefits that this engagement, under the shape of collaboration in the initial education of university graduates, adds to the policies of the company. Of course, recruitment, saving costs and productivity are reasons addressed here, like the corporate image. Nevertheless, there are other benefits like innovation, which may become part of the culture of the company through engaging in learning provision, as well as developing a business strategy that becomes more adaptive, out of traditional ways of facing changes in the market. Third, the authors provide an empirical framework shaped by innovation, economic effects, social image, social corporate responsibility as well as strategic planning that is the result of their empirical work conducted among a small sample of Spanish companies. The final part of the chapter points to the limitations of this research but also to its potential, through the interpretation of results as well as the suggestion of hints to improve the links between companies and higher education institutions.

Chapter 9 is written by Chisvert-Tarazona, Vila-Vázquez, Ros-Garrido and Palomares-Montero, who contribute with a curriculum-based analysis of the introduction of a dual model of VET within a school-based system that already embeds internships in real workplaces as part of the mandatory curriculum of all VET qualifications. They draw upon the requirements posed by the loose regulations upon dual VET in order to explain to what extent learning provided by this type of VET improve the knowledge base of the workforce. Dual learning, the focus of the book, is addressed here with caution, not mainly because of the limited impact in terms of numbers (less than 3 % of all VET students are enrolled in a dual modality, even if the enrolment in IVET has almost double along the last decade), but because of how duality does not affect the prescribed curriculum.

Building upon curriculum theory, the authors develop a framework to analyse regulations upon dual VET, drawing upon curriculum in itself, assessment of learning and the organisational arrangements of apprenticeship. They rely upon their previous work as well as that produced by the academic community since the introduction of dual VET in school-year 2012–2013, and they discuss the difficult balance between state-wide framework and regional regulations, that allow up to five different modes to introduce what is called dual VET, in many cases without the proper status of apprenticeship. They also point to the fact that such a way to implement dual VET, almost in an experimental way, allows companies to select their students and therefore resulting in the best academic students able to access to dual VET, this implying the risk of dual VET being an elitist alternative to ordinary IVET. Such a conclusion puts serious limits to consider dual VET as a successful mode because access to dual VET has a strong impact upon its result and, second, because the chances to expand such a mode of VET to the whole system will not be able to apply this selection requirements and will also face the hardships to engage all those companies where training is not highly valued, as expressed in the previous chapter. The authors look towards Germany, whose effort in introducing dual VET in Spain has been clear through the German Chambers, BiBB and Bertelsmann Foundation, in order to consider what organisational arrangements happen there and what is the involvement of the companies in order to improve the quality of dual VET in Spain as it attempts to spread out. They finally conclude that, without relevant changes in the adaptation of Dual VET in Spain, it hardly adds value to the school-based system.

Díaz-Chao, Moso-Díez and Torrent-Selles have contributed with Chapter 10: 'VET, value generation and firm results: An empirical exploration from Spanish industrial firms,' in a quantitative analysis of data in the past decade that has been supported by the SEPI foundation, which has recently incorporated VET-related items in their annual panel survey of industrial manufacturing companies. The authors provide a synthetic overview of the productive system in the country and the landscape of manufacturing industry within it. Taking upon the capacity building system and the human capital policies of companies as well as their potential for innovation, the authors study the contribution of initial VET to this landscape, detailing the different levels of qualification as well as the growing dual VET model implemented in the regions. They also compare graduation of VET students with those in other European countries to consider how different the skills match result according to the qualification of the workforce. Therefore, they also refer to continuing VET. Upon such a contextualisation, the chapters deepens into the quantitative analysis of the Business Strategy Survey run by the Ministry of Industry and the SEPI Foundation, with the support of the Bankia Foundation for Dual Training, the most representative survey in this field in the country. The authors provide an overview of the workforce qualification in the manufacturing companies, touching upon accreditation, R&D+I activities both in general as well as in particular subsectors. In order to do this, they use a three-dimensional framework where efficiency, learning and innovation are the focus of the strategies that they analyse in relation to VET and qualifications (ISCED levels 3/5). The reader will find useful information, well-structured and able to provide a thorough overview to understand why companies with VET qualified workers tend to be more competitive than those which do not behave so. No matter how simple this conclusion may be, it is relevant to make it explicit to understand the way in which business have often ignored the worth of VET and how different Spain is yet from its neighbor countries. The chapter ends with several recommendations that are worth taken into account not only by policymakers, but mainly from business-people themselves, if they want to compete better in the global market.

We invite the reader to enjoy the different sections and chapters and actively engage in the debates portrayed here: scholars, practitioners and policy-makers are confronted to new ways of dealing with work and to address labour relations that are being rapidly redefined. While we write this foreword, the Covid-19 pandemia has extended to all continents and it has already had an impact (beyond the humanitarian and medical aspects that are the most important with no doubt) upon issues like tele-working, suspension of face-to-face activities, both educational and productive, and different national instructions upon what is considered 'necessary,' among which education and vocational education, also under the shape of apprenticeship, do not seem to belong. Whether that pandemia will lead the humankind to reconsider the way we live, work, interact and educate remains to be seen. Anyhow, vocational education will still be subject to controversial expectations and aspirations: those of individual students and apprentices, teachers and trainers, employers; but also of institutions like unions and employer representatives. These are a rich field of study for social sciences and one in which educationalists and academics have engaged since the right to education and to vocational education was first claimed and more recently acknowledged.

Before closing the foreword, we want to make explicit our acknowledgement and thanks to Prof. Philipp Gonon who first welcomed the idea of this publication, to him and Prof. Anja Heikkinen for accepting it in the Peter Lang series; as well as to the authors of the chapters for their care and patience. We want to thank Bankia Foundation for Dual Training for sponsoring this publication, which is one more collateral effect of the Crossing Boundaries Conference that was held in Valencia in May 2019[1]. The support of Bankia Foundation for Dual Training[2] to this publication is part of its objective to promote research in the field of VET and its dual modality. To this end, it has set up its Knowledge

---

1 https://vetnetsite.org/conferences/crossing-boundaries/2019-valencia/
   https://zenodo.org/record/2644069#.XnuiiS1DmfU
2 https://www.dualizabankia.com/es/centro-de-conocimiento/publicaciones/

and Innovation Centre, which is responsible for producing and coordinating studies that provide systemic and prescriptive analyses of VET in Spain with the aim of contributing with useful data and evidences for its improvement in terms of quality, inclusiveness and innovation.

Last but not least, we thank all reviewers: without them, their effort, time and professional expertise this book would not have been possible. Thanks therefore to L. Deitmer, S. Khoza, J. Li, O. Melnyk, C. Nägele, P. Nardi, V. Wedekind as well as other reviewers who remain anonymous.

Fernando Marhuenda-Fluixá, María José Chisvert-Tarazona and Mónica Moso-Díez
Valencia – Madrid (Spain), March 2020

FERNANDO MARHUENDA-FLUIXÁ

Alternance and vocational knowledge: Reconsidering apprenticeships and education-business partnerships from an educational perspective

Abstract: Both vocational education as well as apprenticeship (one of the shapes it takes in several countries), are undergoing a process of review and update. National differences show up in terms of upper secondary education, vocational education, transitions from education into employment and from youth into adulthood as well as different welfare systems providing a variety of structures to become adults, workers and citizens. Despite the literature tends to deal with apprenticeship as a synonym to alternance, our view is that the latter is a pedagogical device that builds upon work-based learning, a form of experiential learning itself, in order to set up bridges upon several crossroads: theory and practice, school and work, democracy and productivity and, more importantly, individual and shared knowledge. Learning on the workplace, in its different arrangements, gives place to different understandings of vocational and professional knowledge. These are the topics discussed in this chapter, in an attempt to frame developments in apprenticeship schemes portrayed in this volume.

Keywords: work-based learning, alternance, dual VET, experiential learning, education-work relations, education-business partnerships, apprenticeship

Introduction

Well into the 21st century, a decade after the global financial crisis of 2008, Vocational Education and Training systems are demanded to respond to changes in the world of work. These are affected by smart specialization, as Brown and Lauder (1992) explained towards the end of the 20th century; they are also fundamentally affected in several fronts (OECD, 2010), like continuing innovation, increasing digitalization, crucial sustainability or aiming at entrepreneurship. European institutions like Cedefop (2017) have been and are still working on the impact of all of these upon VET and looking for strategies appropriate for the different expected scenarios while at the same time they perceive opportunities for European VET in the new global competition (Cedefop, 2018). Some countries are trying to take a stand for this competition (Vroonhof, 2017; Deutsche Gesellschaft für Internationale Zusammenarbeit, 2019), Germany being one of them, as it is addressed in two of the chapters in this volume.

Furthermore, the International Network on Innovative Apprenticeships (Deitmer et al., 2013; Deißinger et al., 2019) has been describing and analyzing the evolution of apprenticeship since 2006, addressing several changes and challenges: the introduction of artificial intelligence, the digitalization of jobs, and the growing academization of the vocational offerings among others. Furthermore, changes in the organization of work, labor relations and the increasing dualization and segmentation of the labor market must also be considered (Orteu, 2017). Echoing the views of Standing (2013) on the growing precarization and the loss of security for the worker, we understand neologisms such as flexicurity that have not been able to cover properly and that are having an impact upon the way a career may be understood nowadays. In this regard, Jammulamadaka (2019) has recently edited an enlightening volume on informal work in the global economy that reminds us that what we consider typical employment in Europe was not the dominant work even in the world in the 20th century (OIT, 2016).

In this chapter, I will first address the role apprenticeship plays in shaping different vocational education and training systems and how these portray and define expectations upon education-work relationships. This is relevant, in terms of the book ahead, as its three sections cover different systems all of which are adapting apprenticeships to current production needs: the first section deals addresses challenges of Switzerland and Germany adapting to post-industrial demands; the second section shows apprenticeships in Sweden and France coexisting with school-based systems as well as German attempts to make its dual system better known throughout the world; and the final section deals with dual attempts and education-business partnerships in a country with a strong school-based tradition such as Spain. No matter how different they are, all of them take apprenticeship into account, certainly with considerable differences among them.

Second, I will draw upon classical and contemporary literature about learning from experience and, particularly, about learning on the workplace as a form of experiential learning. Much has been written on the issue, even though this is not an approach exclusive from vocational education: experiential learning was part of the debates around the massification of schooling in the early 20th century, and relevant educationalists of the time contended for a school where the academic weight (or the relevance of school subjects based upon scientific disciplines) did not overcome the importance of personal and social dimensions in people's everyday lives, that the universalization of the school system has nevertheless ignored for too many years and it still does in many countries. Furthermore, learning from experience was always the ground of adult education, that has historically showed more respect for the learner as a subject carrying on a life of its own than most child- and youth-education practice. A third approach that favors experiential learning is, without doubt, all practice of popular education in communities, so common in America Latina, Africa and some South-East Asian countries since the early 1960s. VET literature can also learn from these traditions.

Third, I will try to address the confusion between apprenticeship and alternance and I will contend that the second is possible even without the first, as they belong to different domains: apprenticeship lies under labor relations, where training and learning is embedded; while alternance lies under pedagogical relations, requiring an intentional intervention that goes beyond the limits of what apprenticeship provides. By this, I do not want to disregard apprenticeship at all: it is a very valuable source of vocational learning that goes well beyond the acquisition of technical skills. Apprenticeship is a way to socialize the future generations of workers, to hand over the cultural tradition of an occupation, to equip the young person with an occupational identity; all of which were indeed relevant in the 20th century in the industrial era. However, I will take the effort to differentiate apprenticeship from alternance and I will try to highlight the added value that alternance brings to apprenticeship, insofar it adds a planned educational surplus that experience itself does not guarantee.

The paper finishes by debating whether the knowledge generated and acquired through apprenticeship and alternance is the same and what vocational knowledge is worth fostering in the current times. This will be an attempt, my attempt, to claim that vocational knowledge was never confined to the acquisition of technical competences and that a sense of a working culture is something worth developing even nowadays, when many occupations seem to vanish in an indistinctly blurring de-professionalization or even to disappear as they are replaced by smart machines. Vocational knowledge as a notion itself is and can be the result of intentional educational practice, where the vocation acts as a driver and knowledge attempts to embed cognitive, practical, emotional and social dimensions of the worker. Vocational knowledge also claims for a collective background where learning is not just an individual accumulation of skill: it becomes part of a tradition shared by a community of people that are not only workers but who also share an identity as citizens. Vocational knowledge could then be a right for all who expect to have an occupation or a profession, as well as the responsibility they have to show for the society in which they are trained and in which they will work. If apprenticeships are to survive to the smart-production model, as they did along the past centuries as society moved from an artisan into an industrial one; they will have to engage in knowledge production and become smart apprenticeships too.

Vocational education and training systems: Relations between education and employment

If there is some agreement in vocational education, that is the fact that every country has dealt with education-work relations in socio-historical ways that have resulted in a particular landscape so that many solutions have been found to such relations (Stenström and Lasonen, 2000; Heikkinen, 2004; Brunet and Moral, 2017; Marhuenda-Fluixá, 2018). Even in a global world 'national' companies outsourced to third countries have opted for bringing their own VET tradition with them, adapting it to the national context of the receiving country (Langthaler, 2015; Pilz, 2016; Gessler, Fuchs and Pilz, 2019). In this book, apprenticeships and education-work relationships are examined in countries as varied as Spain, Germany, Switzerland, Sweden or France; each of them trying to stick to their own VET traditions while also looking at innovations in other countries. No country intends to get rid of its identity, while all of them look out to ways for a proper update and to remain competitive: continuity and change belong to national education systems, to which vocational education belongs.

Vocational education has distinguished itself from academic education not just in the aims, but also and mainly in the way it is delivered, the use it makes of experience, and how it allows real life to be part of the educational process. These do not necessarily rely upon didactical arrangements customary in academic education.

Welfare and VET

Vocational education was also a relevant piece in the social contract in the 20th century in Europe, with a significant social meaning well beyond its educational purpose. In this regard, welfare regimes as portrayed by Esping-Andersen (1993) provide an appropriate framework to understand and interpret the role of vocational education within the social contract of each society or country. Considering vocational education as the access of the working classes to universal education, even if segregated, as well as a way to promote social progress, different countries have approached this according to the role they attribute to their vocational education system and to their graduates within adult society.

Liberal countries (the United Kingdom, Ireland, the USA, Canada and Australia and, to a large extent, also Switzerland), favor the market above the State as a way to regulate social relations and the context within which people can find the appropriate place in society. Social democratic countries (like Norway, Sweden, Netherlands, Denmark, Austria, Belgium and Finland) stress the regulative role of the State, whose intervention can contribute to avoid discrimination subject to market operations, and hence stressing equality of opportunities for all. There are countries with a Christian democratic approach to welfare, where the State steps aside and civil society rather than the market is invited to take the role of distributing social justice. Among these we find Germany and Italy, France, Portugal and Spain and, to a certain extent, also Austria.

It is worth considering, in the context of this chapter and volume itself, that there are countries with apprenticeship systems (dual approaches to VET) in all three welfare regimes. This exemplifies the ability of apprenticeships to adapt and survive in different political circumstances, probably for its compromised and agreed nature, involving private and public actors in different ways and regards. Another issue worth considering, of course, is the size of the country in terms of demography, its wealth in terms of GDP, as well as its political structure and governance systems: all of those are factors that help us understand differences in what there exists already as well as in what is possible for the success of changing trends or introducing and adopting reforms in vocational education. Large countries and economies such as Germany, France, Italy or the United Kingdom are pretty different to the small and wealthy Nordic countries as well as other smaller countries as varied as the Netherlands, Switzerland, Austria or Belgium.

Transition and VET

Transition regimes (Gallie and Paugam, 2000) are contextualized within welfare regimes. Empirical research (Walther, 2006) has identified four distinct regimes of transitions: (1) liberal economies (Britain and Ireland) which are often weak; (2) the Nordic countries (Sweden and Denmark) where there is a universalistic approach, high support and comprehensive policies (youth, housing, employment); (3) employment-centered (France, Netherlands and Germany) which are representative of continental Europe, despite being unequal in societal terms; and (4) sub-protected and family-supported (Italy, Portugal and Spain), rather weak and very incomplete in terms of what it is involved within transitions from youth into adulthood. Again, we find a couple of dual systems operating in different regimes, once more reinforcing the idea that dual systems are flexible and ready to adapt to whatever the circumstances.

In universalistic regimes secondary education is not selective, the State plays a relevant role in social security, female employment is high and transition policies rely upon activation of individuals, who despite their youth are considered full-right citizens. In liberal regimes, school is neither selective, training shows low standards and female employment is also high; the stress is upon individual employability and young people are somewhat dependent of their families. Employment-centered regimes have selective school systems, training is highly standardized and recognized, people adapt to social positions and transitions rely upon vocational training. In sub-protective countries, where female employment is low, the labor market is often segmented and dualized.

Upper secondary education and VET

VET systems are part of upper secondary education systems and, as such, they have to be considered as initial vocational education. Two major comparative studies at the turn of the century pointed to this fact. First, the report edited by Green, Wolf and Leney (1999). Second, the volume published by the Finnish Institute of Educational Research, at the University of Jyväskylä (Lasonen and Young, 1998). This was the result of European comparative projects that studied post-16 education in the frame of an increasingly globalized economy featuring what at the time was labeled as post-Fordism.

Four kinds of parallel developments were identified at the time, in four different trends. These marked the ways in which different countries were reacting to similar demands from the productive system based upon their existing systems of vocational education; in an interesting exercise of the relations between markets and policies, demands and expectations, that usually shape educational reforms as complex processes. The first trend was labeled unification, merging academic and vocational upper secondary education. The Nordic countries (Sweden and, to a lesser extent, also Norway and Finland) seemed to be going down that line together with Scotland, whose educational policy was trying to detach from the English one (perhaps as part of a larger project of national development). Second, linkage strategies that were identified in countries like England, France or Spain. Here, connections, bridges and recognition were developed between two parallel tracks of academic and vocational post-compulsory pathways. Third, countries that stressed the value of vocational education as a system of its own, segregated from the rest of upper secondary education. This allowed relevant management and control tools to non-educational actors such as the Chambers, companies and unions; here we find countries with a dual (vocational) system. Finally, a fourth trend was inspired by Norway and Finland, which seemed to keep two different tracks, academic and vocational, that could enrich each other mutually. Different strategies demand different solutions in terms of, at least, the following:

- Education of vocational teachers and trainers
- Relations between companies and schools
- Apprenticeship regulations within the labor market
- Role of careers guidance staff
- Learning vocational knowledge and skills
- Tensions among specialization, general knowledge and core and soft skills
- Educational policies to upskill the qualifications of the workforce
- Career expectations and upper mobility

Of course, these trends cannot be properly understood without considering the structure and demands of lower secondary education and to what extent segregation or comprehensiveness are fostered.

Models and systems of VET and apprenticeships

At the turn of the century, Greinert and Hanf (2002) differentiated three models to approach vocational education; and more recently Busemeyer and Trampusch (2012) have offered us a seminal work on what they have named collective skill formation regimes. The former named the first of them the liberal one, well rooted in the market economy, meritocracy being a high principle, assuming that career planning is a rational individual election that relies upon the existence of a market, in which companies provide the training they demand and where the

State intervention has to be reduced to its minimum. Ireland and the United Kingdom are good examples, and Vossiek (2018), who worked with Christine Trampusch, has recently updated and analyzed these and others. A second model is the bureaucratic one, where academic qualifications are the key for political planning, vocational qualifications are universally regulated and controlled and planned by the State, which intervenes in the offer and demand of the provision of qualifications. France and Spain lie under such a model, despite the differences between their systems. A third approach is the dual one, where there is a social contract behind the recognition of vocational qualifications; qualified jobs are acknowledged in terms of income, working conditions and career possibilities; and responsibility over the provision of qualifications is shared by the State and the companies, with the necessary contribution and management of the Chambers. Of course, Germany, Austria, Switzerland and Denmark belong to this model.

In all three models, there is a different involvement of social actors, governance is conducted differently and has found its ways throughout history, as the result of struggles and tensions among the different actors and the power they were able to conceit in certain moments. Vocational schools and vocational teachers have therefore different roles, commitments, expectations and responsibilities within vocational provision, and students are given a different status: trainees, apprentices, students, interns ... These are not only different names but also different social understandings of what they can expect from vocational education and society, as well as what is expected of them.

Systems can be traced at national level, and they provide institutional coverage to their traditional way of understanding vocational education. Types, on their side, are specific and contingent arrangements of vocational education that are possible within, around and at the margins of systems. Types have therefore a rather limited scope, even though they are able to survive and coexist with systems of a different kind.

A well-known classification of systems is that of Greinert (2004), who named four of them: Nordic countries, integrated by Norway, Sweden and Finland; dual systems, among which Germany is the best-known and shaped differently in Austria, Switzerland and Denmark; school-based systems, with Italy, Portugal and Spain, as well as France despite the fact that it coexists with a well-developed apprenticeship system[1]; and finally the so-called de-regulated systems, a weird expression indeed, as regulation is somewhat intrinsic to a system: here we find the United Kingdom and Ireland.

Of course, most of this comparative work refers to formal initial vocational education, without considering that some countries make available alternatives under the shape of non-formal vocational training for the unemployed. These alternatives often lack entry requirements related to previous qualifications or educational achievements, and they sometimes lack proper assessment systems, which results in the non accredited qualifications for those who attend them.

Another issue to be considered here is the connection between initial and continuing vocational education, something relevant in terms or careers and professional development.

However, it is often the case that initial and continuing vocational education are disconnected and act, as a matter of fact, as different systems in many countries, reflecting the tensions between the administrations of employment and education, the educational system and the productive system, the public and the private provision of vocational education and training. Whether those enrolled in CVET or having attended CVET might get more involved in the provision of IVET on the job is something worth considering.

No matter what the system looks like, all of them welcome the idea that apprenticeship should be fostered as a means to improve quality of provision of vocational education, employability of workers and better transition from education into work, not to mention a potentially significant reduction in youth unemployment rates. This is so even despite criticisms have been raised for long (Kruse, 1991; Collier, 1992).

Learning from experience and learning from work experience

Experiential learning, practical learning, learning from experience, these are all names given to a way to acquire knowledge that often differs from what the school offers. Activity is considered a source

---

1 See Diff in this volume for a better understanding of its complexities.

of learning, and real activity seems often a better way to learn than teaching practice, where simulation or passive roles are encouraged. Whether activity remains as mere practice or also embeds further forms of knowledge like reflective and critical thinking is not so clear.

Work, as a form of activity and socially regulated practice, is also a source of learning and a kind of experience where effective and efficient or competitive production is expected while learning may occur as a by-product. Whether reflective and critical thinking are possible in the workplace depends on the kind of job and the type of organization for which one works. Furthermore, there is a moral dimension to work, as a labor relation, that demands attention when considering learning on the workplace.

Experience is an educational principle, claimed as a crucial dimension in educational practice back in 1938 by John Dewey (1967), to make it meaningful and relevant, to give it an educational purpose not only for what is to come but for the very educational practice as it happens. From this perspective, educational experience is able to overcome dichotomies like general *vs.* vocational education, basic *vs.* technical knowledge, knowledge *vs.* skill or theory *vs.* practice. Educational experience is the source of further education, as it embeds a transformative potential of the individual as well as the society with which the individual interacts. Habit and interaction are the two principles underlying experience, in a way that fosters continuity or contributes to provide an identity. Educational experience also lies behind the more recent notion of situational learning (Lave and Wenger, 1992) and its wider notion of communities of practice as developed by Wenger (1999), where the notion of experience is replaced by practice. Other recent approaches such as Engeström's (2001) activity theory have also been criticized by Langemeyer and Roth (2006). To these we come back in the final section in the chapter.

Already in 1912, Georg Kerschensteiner (1934, 1964) offered his view on the value of experience and work as means for an educational purpose. This is far beyond from qualification (Marhuenda-Fluixá, 2017), rather connected to the moral development of citizens (Gonon, 2009), within a much wider educational attempt that García Moriyón (2011) has also analyzed for the case of Spain. The education of citizens is an education for democracy, which becomes relevant at a time when either the State or the Capital are gaining increasing power in ruling human relations: that was the case in the early 20th century and it is again the case at the beginning of the 21st, while the second half of the last century remained a time of increasing equality.

Experience may and may not be educational. An educational use of experience if indeed possible, even in case the experience proves negative, insofar it is embedded in a formative (training-learning) processes. This is relevant when it comes to the use of experience within a vocational education program, particularly of in-company experience, whatever the name and shape it takes. Whether apprenticeship is a form of experiential learning is something we will examine in the next section.

The notion of experiential learning is strongly rooted in certain traditions within the field of adult education, where its input and value in the educational process is given credit instead of considering the educational institution as the only or main source of possible knowledge and information.

Dealing with experience in an educational way consists in acknowledging work experience as knowledge produced in a given context of practice. Own experience, as well as the experience of others, are sources of knowledge which is both contingent and provisional. In this sense, working upon experience contributes to show the links between production of personal knowledge and shared meaning, as well as the understanding of the conditions of the workplace. By doing so, experiential learning fosters the analysis of differences and similarities, historicity and contradictions, hence dealing with the workplace as a socially defined space.

Of course, one may choose among possible educational uses of experience; varying from the highest level of reflection and understanding to an instrumental use by which one may learn specific skills related to a job without attempting to go any further. The difference lies, among others, in a collective or individual use of experiential learning, one that is shared with others who take part of the experience in different ways, and one which remains in the realm of the individual, as personal acquisition of skills and awareness. Boreham (2004) has addressed the collective dimension of competencies at work, challenging the dominant notions of competence as something an individual possesses disregarding the context in which it is acquired and employed.

An individual though reflective approach was explained long ago by Argyris and Schön (1974), who invited both self- as well as critical reflection, approaching professional education to the domain of personal development. In a step forward, Mezirow (1990) suggested the chance to use learning as a process of production of interpretation and of giving meaning to real life, in contrast with mere production in itself: reworking our own reference frameworks as we grow up as adults is a relevant part of the educational process, as it is upon these frameworks that we address our own experience and through them that we interpret it, as well as how we use it in order to give meaning.

David Kolb (1984) is well-known for having developed a theory of experiential learning even if, like many others (Eraut, 1994; Mc Kee and Eraut, 2012), he has focused his work upon higher education rather than vocational education. Kolb takes upon the circle of experience developed by Kurt Lewin, considering it in relation to the model of cognitive development of Jean Piaget. This is in an attempt to link learning to knowledge structures, giving way to learning styles that stress different dimensions of experience.

Eraut has worked extensively on learning on the workplace and learning from experience at work; first around the notion of competence and more recently shifting towards a more comprehensive and holistic view of knowledge (2007), which he named learning trajectories. I turn back to these in the final section of the chapter.

The extent to which experiential learning will adapt to the new circumstances of virtual reality and artificial intelligence, where experience happens before a smart machine, is something to reconsider. Without doubt, the use of simulation in learning processes due to the expansion of gamification is something worth considering too, as these are becoming working tools in many different production sectors.

Apprenticeship and alternance as different ways to address learning on the workplace

Apprenticeship has always been seen as the exemplary form of work-based learning, and it has been used indistinctly as a way to refer to dual systems of VET, where apprenticeship was the main source of knowledge and the school played a subsidiary role. Even if apprenticeships take upon a tradition going back to the medieval guilds, they found their way to adapt to the industrialization and, in the past two decades, there are significant efforts not only to revitalize them but also to consider them as the most appropriate way in which a VET system can deal with the current challenges of production. Apprenticeships have a long historical tradition (Bonoli, 2017; Juul, 2017) and they were already modernized in Germany in the second half of the 20th century (*Berufsbildungsgesetz*, 1969), rebirthed as Modern Apprenticeships in the United Kingdom in the mid 1990s (Steedman, 2011), or attempted in Spain in present times disguised as dual VET (Marhuenda-Fluixá, 2015). The INAP conferences as well as the efforts recently taken by the European Commission (2017) as a way to face global competitiveness are also pointing in this direction.

However, we must not confound apprenticeships with alternance. These are not synonyms, even if the literature tends to use both as if they were. Alternance is the combination of school and work guided by the school and allowing for the student to prepare the experience, enjoy it, then reflect upon it; both in individual as well as in collective sessions. It demands backward and forward movements and it requires an investment of time in these processes as well as activating the different cognitive processes involved in experiential learning. Apprenticeship, on its side, consists of work-based learning where the school is a supplement aside from what is learned in the workplace, under the assumption that these are different forms of knowledge that do not necessarily relate to each other.

Alternance between school and the workplace relies upon the educational principle of activity, where experience, learning by doing, demands not only the guide of an experienced worker but also a didactical preparation of the experience where there is room for both observation and reflection: the circle of experience evolves upon certain pedagogical arrangements. Within alternance, the learner is a student that enjoys the chances offered by the workplace, where learning happens and it is afterwards reconsidered and analyzed inside the school, upon proper critical and even collective reflection[2].

Apprenticeship, on its side, does not require alternance. It relies upon a role of its own, that of the apprentice, no longer a student, not yet a full worker, but someone playing a transitional function that is subject to the rationale of the labor market and only subsequently to the educational system, given that the accreditation to which the apprenticeship leads is still missing. Accreditation and, therefore, assessment, are keys to apprenticeship, competence rules and learning lies behind, as so do training processes that are, in a way, irrelevant: it is practice upon a time base.

Hamilton (1990) described apprenticeship as a way to improve transitions itself, as part of the transition system in fact. Apprenticeship, therefore, underlies an occupational identity, one in which the person is socialized. In order to accomplish this, a well-defined occupational profile is required, a sense of collective belonging, even certain political awareness of the vocation, call and occupation to which one commits. In the industrial and Fordist times, this meant a sense of working class and a sense of community strongly linked to one's identity and social status. Whether that is still alive should also be considered.

In apprenticeship systems, the school often plays a subsidiary role towards the industry, while in alternance schemes, schools are in charge and take the lead of the educational process. We dare to suggest that alternance is part of an educational policy while apprenticeship is part of a labor policy. Whether both are able to merge depends on the weight one is allowing to the other, keeping in mind that labor policy has more chances to become the winner.

---

2 Of course, companies may provide such a reflection, and this might happen more frequently in the coming future due to the blurring borders between production and knowledge. Furthermore, it may be the case that schools do not procure such a reflection process. Nevertheless, in the current context where the distinction and separation between the educational and the production process still exist, I consider valid the statement behind this footnote.

The issue, therefore, is whether they are that different and whether apprenticeship needs to be part of an alternance scheme or not. This is not a new debate, but something already discussed in the early 1980s in Europe by Cedefop commissioned experts (Jallade, 1982; Murray, 1984). The emphasis at that time was laid upon alternance, as a way to improve the preparation and qualification of the workforce, although apprenticeship was used as the legal basis for alternance to happen.

Two principles lie behind alternance: first, the combination of theoretical knowledge and the chance to put it in practice in a reciprocal way. Second, the combination of roles, production and learning. This implied combining a productive and an educational rationale, where mistakes are understood differently; as well as allowing for transfer of knowledge that may happen in a twofold direction, and this is relevant too.

Alternance allows for developing a joint core of knowledge, while apprenticeship tends to keep both learning sites as separate (Gessler, 2017), there is no need for coordination, therefore allowing different kinds of knowledge to be developed as well as to be applied. Apprenticeship does not need proper planning, while alternance requires it. Apprenticeship proves useful in individual terms, while alternance may be individual as well as collective, insofar it allows the chance to different students to learn from the experiences of their mates.

From the perspective of inclusive education (Olmos, 2017), while apprenticeship applies the selective rationale of the labor market, alternance may favor the introduction of affirmative action within vocational education, hence facilitating new and more opportunities to those who need them more. This is worth noting nowadays, when most dual systems are promoting school-based VET as the way to provide education to those who are left behind and do not have access to apprenticeship contracts; while the scarce apprenticeships available in school-based VET systems are occupied by students whose employability is already outstanding, particularly in countries with high unemployment rates.

Apprenticeship consists of two kinds of learning and knowledge, while alternance is one that evolves upon two different sources, the company and the school. It is no surprise, therefore, that alternance can be perceived as an institutional principle able to structure learning around work (Jallade, 1982).

Apprenticeship is of course valuable, both in terms of learning as well as in terms of transition and access into employment. Alternance adds value to apprenticeship, and it also applies to school-based systems where there is no apprenticeship but there exists a work placement, internship, practice period or on-the-job period (Marhuenda-Fluixá, 2019); even if none of these can be considered apprenticeship as there is no legal regulation, no working contract, no status as trainee nor apprentice. Alternance helps overcoming the limits that apprenticeships have. Alternance demands cooperation, and this goes beyond competition in the workplace and across qualification levels, as Eraut (2007) and Mc Kee and Eraut (2012) have shown. Alternance, therefore, becomes a pedagogical artifact, and to this I turn in the final section of the chapter.

Before doing so, however, let me consider one more aspect where alternance adds value to apprenticeship. Apprenticeships are always a form of initial VET, while alternance is a very appropriate way to handle continuing vocational education, where existing practice is enriched by education, training and theory to facilitate ways to observe, analyze and reflect upon practice, as well as to explore new alternative ways to handle practice. Therefore, in a context in which lifelong learning seems to be gaining increasing attention, alternance should be fostered as a way to combine work and education. In this regard, apprenticeship remains in the domain of initial education.

Vocational learning and vocational knowing: What is pedagogically possible and what is expected by the labor markets

The final section of this chapter engages in the discussion of vocational knowledge and how vocational education contributes to it. At a time where knowledge seems replaced by skills (Kämäräinen, Attwell and Brown, 2002) or competence (Mulder, 2017), where expertise and professionalism force vocational curricula to shift towards learning outcomes instead of focusing on input-defined contents, it is relevant to consider whether vocational education and training systems keep their educational orientation. The question is, therefore, whether vocational education can foster the acquisition of knowledge in a wide sense. Of course, this is not a debate that will be solved in this section, but it deserves attention in a book addressing challenges and innovations in dual and non-dual systems: no matter what, both systems are expected to deal with knowledge in a way different to the past two centuries.

One concern behind all ways to deal with vocational education is what one can learn and what one can know about a certain occupation, about an occupational domain and about work in itself (Simon, Dippo and Schenke, 1991). A second concern is what can be learned more efficiently and effectively in the workplace, what in the school, and what in the combination of both, keeping in mind that one site is devised for producing while the other site is devised for learning, even if learning while working is both possible and valuable. A third concern, then, is whether apprenticeship provides a different kind of competence or knowledge that the school is not able to and, if so, what is the role of alternance, if any.

All of the previous questions refer to how we can arrange pedagogically the provision of teaching and training so that people acquire occupational competence and knowledge in a way both secure and efficient. Is there something like a vocational didactic that can be applied to different occupational areas or are vocational didactics dependent upon every specific occupations or occupational domains? Is there a vocational pedagogy embedded in a vocational system?

I claim that there is a pedagogy of alternance; that we can refer to it; and that such pedagogy is able to enhance the vocational learning by bridging the workplace and the school sites. This can be done in a way that contributes to help classmates benefit from the learning achieved by an apprentice while on the workplace, and to help workmates in the company benefit from what an apprentice brings from the school. Such processes, however, do not happen accidentally, as if one were exposed like an old photo machine and then imprinted by what lies before him/her. Either we do something (a didactical arrangement) to share learning and develop knowledge collectively or all the benefits of an apprenticeship remain in the individual domain. Stenström and Tynjälä (2009) have clearly argued in favor of organizational learning and Gruber and Palonen (2007) have demanded participation of the

Alternance and vocational knowledge 39

learner and others. The latter have also contended that there is a collective dimension behind learning culture, motivation and responsibility. Moving beyond individual learning can be achieved through processes like learning from errors, discussing about informal learning, boundary objects and boundary crossing in multi-professional negotiation. These can be achieved by considering apprentices as well as workers as subjects with emotional competence that lie behind their expertise. Here, we also find a way to connect initial to continuing vocational education, in a process hardly explored so far.

Of course, any pedagogical arrangement has to deal with the curriculum, the device that teachers and trainers design and develop and make possible the transmission and acquisition of knowledge in an educational environment. The implications for the curriculum and the organization of VET were already tackled by Nijhof, Heikkinen and Nieuwenhuis (2002) in a volume addressing flexibilization of VET and touching upon its implications on issues like career planning and development, professionalism as well as the institutional demands in a leaning economy, where innovation demands not only a technical but also a social organization. Their claim for flexibility in VET is not just to respond to labor market demands, but also to facilitate a greater consciousness among workers of current working conditions and to make the world of work more human, despite the trends it already showed at the beginning of the century.

Such an attempt has been carried along by Heikkinen and Kraus (2009) through a meaningful title such as 'reworking vocational education, where they take a look at the growing internationalization of VET[3] and how it can be accountable not just in terms of performance but also of inclusiveness and cooperation. Such an attempt implies dealing with global immigration, older workers and the growing focus upon employability and competence, moving away from employment and knowledge. In their book, they warn us about how soft pedagogy (and apprenticeship may fall under this category) can be serving the needs of soft capitalism. Again, such claims drive our attention towards efforts to keep vocational education and training as a collective and

---

[3] An issue addressed twice in this volume, by Bohlinger and Frommberger, Pilz and Gessler.

educational system where individuals are invited to cooperate rather than to compete.

Their message is a constant in many of the books in the Peter Lang series on Continuing and Vocational Education, like the volume edited by Weil, Koski and Mjelde (2009), where vocational curriculum is studied in relation to social relations and their moral implications: mobile workplace, literacies and skills, tacit knowledge and students' engagement. Again, here we find a manifesto in favor of knowledge as a cornerstone of vocational education, where technical issues mingle with identity and morality, fostering vocational literacy as part of humankind, recovering the almost lost notion of permanent education that has been lately replaced by continuing education and lifelong learning. Those are issues that Gonon, Kraus, Oelkers and Stolz address (2008) when rethinking the relations between apprenticeship and professionalism, taking upon the German notion of *Beruf* as the crux upon which the dual system was set up, implying not only a personal call but also a collective identity and social recognition.

The possibilities to integrate work and learning have been addressed by Stenström and Tynjälä (2009) and they also claim to move beyond the individual learning experience into organizational development and networked learning. In this regard, the work by Boreham, Fischer and Samurcay (2004) is also a relevant contribution. Mulder and Sloane (2004) have also provided insights into the new demands put upon VET that can be addressed in a pedagogical way, supported upon constructivism and reconsidering the value of theoretical learning not to let it disappear into work-based learning understood as practice. In this regard, addressing language and intercultural competences goes beyond the workplace itself and together with transfer of knowledge, both are stressed as relevant features within vocational education.

As Guile and Unwin (2019) have recently argued, VET, like HRD, are subject to a political economy that is now played in a global contest where the notion of occupation itself is at stake. Something similar has happened to other traditional concepts in education and work relations such as career or collective bargaining, both relevant highlights of typical industrial relations of the 20th century. Vocationalism and professionalism are not just individual capabilities but features subject to education, as Young and Muller (2014) argue in ways compatible with those of Eraut (2007) and McKee and Eraut (2012). Dimensions beyond performance, such as awareness, personal development, academic knowledge and skills as well as teamwork, decision making or judgement (Eraut's learning trajectories) are appreciated features in many jobs nowadays. Such demands exceed the value of a qualification under the assumption that the workplace is a social environment where people with different levels of qualification and even occupations have to interact in order to provide a good service. Malloch, Cairns, Evans and O'Connor (2011) have shown how theory on learning in the workplace is perhaps more advanced than current practice. Even though theory has still more questions; what practice reveals in itself and through research is that individual approaches to learning and limited views on apprenticeship or other kinds of internship are dominant, while alternance is often missing. That is perhaps the challenge ahead of us.

Biographical note

Fernando Marhuenda-Fluixá is Chair in Didactics and School Organization at the Faculty of Philosophy and Educational Sciences at the University of Valencia (Universitat de València), Spain. He coordinates the interdisciplinary research group Transitions (GIUV2013–093) from education into work for vulnerable populations. His research interests are in vocational education and training (VET) and its relation to social inclusion, education policy, comparative education, and social pedagogy. His current research addresses the vocational pedagogical model of second chance schools as well as the role of Third Sector Organizations in vocational training and access to employment.

References

Argyris, C. and Schön, D.A. (1974). Theory in practice: increasing professional effectiveness. San Francisco: Jossey-Bass.

Bonoli, L. (2017). An ambiguous identity: the figure of the apprentice from the XIX century up to today. In Switzerland. F. Marhuenda-Fluixá (ed.) Vocational education beyond skill formation (pp. 31–49). Bern: Peter Lang.

Boreham, N. (2004). A theory of collective competence: challenging the neo-liberal individualisation of performance at work. *British Journal of Educational Studies*, 52, 5–17.

Boreham, N., Fischer, M. and Samurcay, R. (eds.) (2004). Work process knowledge. London: Routledge.

Brown, P. and Lauder, H. (eds.) (1992). Education for economic survival. London: Routledge.

Brunet, I. and Moral, D. (2017). Origen, contexto, evolución y futuro de la Formación Profesional. Tarragona: URV.

Busemeyer, M. and Trampusch, C. (eds.) (2012). The political economy of collective skill formation. Oxford: Oxford University Press.

CEDEFOP (2017). The changing nature and role of vocational education and training in Europe. Luxembourg: Publications Office, vols. 1–5.

CEDEFOP (2018). Globalisation opportunities for VET. How European and international initiatives help in renewing vocational education and training in European countries. Luxembourg: Publicacions Office.

Collier, H. (1992). Training tomorrow's labor force: the new Germany's big challenge. The Economist Intelligence Unit, European Trends 1, 53–58.

Deißinger, T., Hauschildt, U., Gonon, Ph., Fischer, S. (eds.) (2019). Contemporary apprenticeship reforms and reconfigurations. Münster: Lit Verlag.

Deitmer, L., Hauschildt, U., Rauner, F. and Zelloth, H. (eds.) (2013). The architecture of innovative apprenticeship. Dordrecht: Springer.

Deutsche Gesellschaft für Internationale Zusammenarbeit (2019). New work and its impacts on vocational education and training in German development cooperation. Proposition paper. Frankfurt: GIZ.

Dewey, J. (1967). Experiencia y educación. Buenos Aires: Losada.

Engeström, Y. (2001). Expansive learning at work: toward an activity theoretical re-conceptualization. *Journal of Education and Work*, 14, 1, 133–156.

Eraut, M. (1994). Developing professional knowledge and competence. London: Falmer Press.

Eraut, M. (2007). Learning from other people in the workplace. *Oxford Review of Education*, 33, 4, 403–422.

Esping Andersen, G. (1993). Los tres mundos del Estado de bienestar. Valencia: Alfons el Magnànim.

European Commission (2017). European Alliance for Apprenticeships – Assessment of progress and planning the future. Final report. Luxembourg: European Comission.

Gallie, D. and Paugam, S. (eds.) (2000). Welfare regimes and the experience of unemployment in Europe. Oxford: Oxford University Press.

García Moriyón, F. (2011). El troquel de las conciencias. Una historia de la educación moral en España. Madrid: De la Torre.

Gessler, M. (2017). The lack of collaboration between companies and schools in the German dual apprenticeship system: historical background and recent data. *International Journal for Research in Vocational Education and Training*, 4, 2, 164–195.

Gessler, M., Fuchs, M. and Pilz, M. (Hrsg.) (2019). Konzepte und Wirkungen des Transfers Dualer Berufsausbildung. Wiesbaden: Springer.

Gonon, P. (2009). The quest for modern vocational education – Georg Kerschensteiner, between Dewey, Weber and Simmel. Bern: Peter Lang.

Gonon, P., Kraus, K., Oelkers, J. and Stolz, S. (eds.) (2008). Work, education and employability. Bern: Peter Lang.

Green, A., Wolf, A. and Leney, T. (1999). Convergence and divergence in European education and training systems. London: Institute of Education.

Greinert, W.-D. (2004). Los 'sistemas' europeos de formación profesional: algunas reflexiones sobre el contexto teórico de su evolución histórica. *Formación Profesional*, 32, 18–26.

Greinert, W.-D. and Hanf, G. (2002). Towards a history of vocational education and training in Europe in a comparative perspective. Luxembourg: Cedefop.

Gruber, H. and Palonen, T. (eds.) (2007). Learning in the workplace – new developments. Turku: Finnish Educational Research Association.

Guile, D. and Unwin, L. (eds.) (2019). The Wiley hanbook on vocational education and training. New York: Wiley.

Hamilton, S.F. (1990). Apprenticeship for adulthood. Preparing youth for the future. New York: The Free Press.

Heikkinen, A. (2004). Evaluation in the transnational 'Management by Projects' policies. *European Educational Research Journal*, 3, 2, 486–500.

Jallade, J.P. (1982). Alternance training for young people: guidelines for action. Luxembourg: Office for Official Publications of the European Communities.

Jammulamadaka, N. (ed.) (2019). Workers and margins: grasping erasures and opportunities. Singapore: Palgrave.

Juul, I. (2017). The twin aspiration of Danish craftsmen to maintain their traditional privileges and be accepted as respectable members of the emerging bourgeois society, in F. Marhuenda-Fluixá (ed.). Vocational education beyond skill formation (pp. 85–108). Bern: Peter Lang.

Kämäräinen, P., Attwell, G. and Brown, A. (eds.) (2002). Transformation of learning in education and training. Key qualifications revisited. Luxembourg: Office for Official Publications o the European Communities.

Kerschensteiner, G. (1934). La educación cívica. Barcelona: Labor.

Kerschensteiner, G. (1964). La escuela del trabajo. In L. Luzuriaga (ed.) Ideas pedagógicas del siglo XX (pp. 123–132). Buenos Aires: Losada.

Kolb, D.A. (1984). Experiential learning: experience as the source of learning and development. Englewood Cliffs (NJ): Prentice Hall.

Kruse, W. (1991). Formació professional dins de l'empresa: un potencial de modernització? El sistema dual a la RFA. *Temps d'Educació*, 5, 57–74.

Langemeyer, I. and Roth, W.M. (2006). Is cultural-historical activity theory threatened to fall short of its own principles and possibilities as a dialectical social science? *Outlines: Critical Practice Studies*, 8, 20–42.

Langthaler, M. (2015). The transfer of the Austrian dual system of vocational education to transition and developing countries. Vienna: OFSE.

Lasonen, J. and Young, M. (1998). Strategies for achieving parity of esteem in European upper secondary education. Jyväskylä: Institute of Educational Research.

Lave, J. and Wenger, E. (1992). Situated learning: legitmate peripheral participation. Cambridge: Cambridge University Press.

Malloch, M., Cairns, L., Evans, K. and O'Connor, B.N. (eds.) (2011). The SAGE handbook of workplace learning. London: SAGE.

Marhuenda-Fluixá, F. (2015). Vocational education abused: precarisation disguised as dual system. In A. Heikkinen and L. Lassnigg (eds.). Myths and brands in vocational education (pp. 59–77). Newcastle upon Tyne: Cambridge.

Marhuenda-Fluixá, F. (ed.) (2017). Vocational education beyond skill formation. VET between civic, industrial and market tensions. Bern: Peter Lang.

Marhuenda-Fluixá, F. (2018). La formación profesional dual en los sistemas europeos. In M. Valcarce, M.J. Diz, A.F. y Rial (eds.). A formación profesional dual: Dúos ou duetos? (pp. 17–36). Santiago de Compostela: USC.

Marhuenda-Fluixá, F. (ed.) (2019). The school-based vocational education and training system in Spain. Achievements and controversies. Singapore: Springer.

McKee, A. and Eraut, M. (eds.) (2012). Learning trajectories, innovation and identity for professional development. New York: Springer.

Mezirow, J. (1990). Fostering critical reflection in adulthood. San Francisco: Jossey-Bass.

Mulder. M. (ed.) (2017). Competence-based vocational and professional education. Bridging the worlds of work and education. Singapore: Springer.

Mulder, R. and Sloane, P.F.E. (eds.) (2004). New approaches to vocational education in Europe. The construction of complex learning-teaching agreements. Oxford: Symposium.

Murray, J. (1984). Alternance training. Training contracts or young people in the European Community. A comparative analysis of contents and the associated legislation. Luxembourg: Office for Official Publications of the European Communities.

Nijhof, W.J., Heikinnen, A. and Nieuwenhuis, L.F.M. (eds.) (2002). Shaping flexibility in vocational education and training. Dordrecht: Kluwer.

OECD (2010). Learning for jobs. Paris: OECD.

OIT (2016). El empleo atípico en el mundo: retos y perspectivas. Ginebra: OIT.

Olmos, P. (2017). The role of VET into social participation and self-determination of disabled people as full citizens. In F. Marhuenda-Fluixá (ed.). Vocational education beyond skill formation (pp. 183–201). Bern: Peter Lang.

Orteu, X. (2017). Desafíos en un Mercado laboral en transformación. Barcelona: UOC.

Pilz, M. (2016). Training patterns of German companies in India, China, Japan and the USA: what really works? *International Journal for Research in Vocational Education and Training*, 3, 2, 66–87.

Simon, R., Dippo, D. and Schenke, A. (1991). Learning work. A critical pedagogy of work education. New York: Praeger.

Standing, G. (2013). The precariat: the new dangerous class. London: Bloomsbury.

Steedman, H. (2011). The State of Apprenticeship in 2010: International Comparisons – Australia, Austria, England, France, Germany, Ireland, Sweden, Switzerland. A Report for the Apprenticeship Ambassadors Network. Paper No' CEPSP22.

Stenström, M.-L. and Lasonen, J. (2000). Strategies for reforming initial vocational education and training in Europe. Jyväskylä: Institute for Educational Research.

Stenström, M.-L. and Tynjälä, P. (eds.) (2009). Toward integration of work and learning. Strategies for connectivity and transformation. Singapore: Springer.

Vossiek, J. (2018). Collective skill formation in liberal market economies? Bern: Peter Lang.

Vroonhof, P. (coord.) (2017). Business cooperating with vocational education and training providers for quality skills and attractive futures. Luxembourg: Publications Office of the European Union.

Walther, A. (2006). Regimes of youth transitions. *Young*, 14, 2, 119–139.

Weil, M., Koski, L. and Mjelde, L. (eds.) (2009). Knowing work: the social relations of learning and working. Bern: Peter Lang.

Wenger, E. (1999). Communities of practice. Learning, meaning, identity. Cambridge: Cambridge University Press.

Young, M.F.D. and Muller, J. (eds.) (2014). Knowledge, expertise and the professions. New York: Routledge.

1.
Dual systems in Europe: Reforms and modernization

SANDRA BOHLINGER

Contextualising policy transfer initiatives in the field of vocational education and training (VET)

Abstract: This chapter contributes to the field of policy transfer in vocational education and training (VET). It aims at linking the field of policy borrowing and lending dominated by an Anglosphere perspective with policy transfer initiatives in the context of VET and apprenticeship training in the German-speaking countries.

Contextualising findings from both research strands provides a comprehensive framework to understand the design of educational policy transfer with a particular focus on VET. Moreover, it attempts to strengthen the international approach to (vocational) education transfer, to critically reflect on the strengths and weaknesses of existing theories of educational policy transfer and to align them with initiatives to reform or implement VET and apprenticeship training.

The contribution aims at enlarging the ongoing discussion on VET policy transfer seen from a German-speaking country's perspective by considering additional, non-German research findings rather than reviewing all existing literature on 'exporting' the German VET system.

Keywords: education policy, policy transfer, comparative education,

1. Introduction

Numerous studies point at the strengths and weaknesses of Public-Private-Partnership models in VET and see it as a role model to integrate young people into the labour market. One of the models that has gained substantial attention is the German apprenticeship model ('dual apprenticeship scheme') and certificates such as the Master craftsmen certificates regulated at national level which are strongly interlocked with the apprenticeship model and are a building block of continuing VET (e.g. Canning et al., 2000; MacLean and Lai 2011, 5).

Advocates of the German dual apprenticeship model emphasise the country's low unemployment rate, its strong linkage with labour market needs, the strong involvement of social partners and a sound fundament built on mutual trust and shared responsibilities. A vast body of literature has elaborated the numerous elements and preconditions of the system guaranteeing its stability and its public acceptance and distinguishing it from other modes of VET. Among those elements that constitute a VET system per se and the German apprenticeship model in particular are legal frameworks, financing structures, responsible bodies, standards (including occupational standards as well as teaching and training standards for learners, teachers and trainers), the contractual status of learners (apprentices or students), the mode of training (on the job, off the job, combination of both), the connection of theory and practice, that is, the linkage between work-based learning and learning in the classroom, and co-operation between stakeholders (e.g. Deissinger 2015; Deissinger and Hellwig 2005; Euler 2013b; Pilz 2016).

While the intention of this article is not to summarise and review all findings resulting from this research, it is important to understand that one of the core features of the German apprenticeship model, is, however, its century-old tradition – a fact that cannot be transferred at all. The factor dominating most discussions, however, is the low youth unemployment rate which often results in what Phillips and Ochs (2003; 2011) call 'cross-national attraction': a model that promises an adequate solution for solving unemployment-related problem, that seems to guarantee labour market-relevant skills and a shift of responsibilities towards employers – an issue of particular relevance with respect to financing VET and remuneration of apprentices.

Against this background, this paper is built on the theoretical framework of policy borrowing and lending as developed by Dolowitz and Marsh (2000) and adapted to the field of education by for example, Phillips and Ochs (2003) or Phillips and Schweisfurth (2011). It focuses on core assumptions and characteristics of policy borrowing in the context of VET including the level of coercion indicating the conditions under which the 'transfer' is developed (Philipps and Schweisfurth 2011, 17). This framework allows for analysing the policy cycle of transfer initiatives including their underlying epistemological positions and methodological approaches. Moreover, this framework provides the opportunity to align findings from the German-speaking 'VET transfer community' with previous approaches to policy borrowing, most of them deriving from the Anglosphere and documented in for example, in the Yearbook of Education or reports from international stakeholders (e.g. Steiner-Khamsi 2004).

To understand the linkage between these two strands of research I will first provide examples of VET policy transfer in Germany that derive from past and present initiatives by the German government to 'export' its apprenticeship system to Mediterranean, Northern African, Latin American and Asian countries (e.g. Clement 1999; Greinert et al. 1997; Stockmann and Kohlmann 1998). Taking Germany as a case study seems relevant as this country is the most prominent bilateral donor *country* with respect to VET policy transfer world-wide (next to international and multilateral international organisations; Heitmann 2019, 107). Second, I will focus on a more general understanding of comparative (vocational) education research and educational policy transfer. I will then turn to the question how to identify appropriate cases for international comparisons and find the 'right' cases for policy transfer. In an additional step, all these elements will be allocated in the process ('cycle') of policy transfer. The contribution ends with identifying challenges for policy transfer and conclusions for future research and action in this field.

2. Examples of German VET policy transfer initiatives

VET policy transfer initiatives from Germany to elsewhere (mostly towards emerging nations) and initiated during the past 60 years were much imprinted by a number of policy documents published by the Ministry for Economic Cooperation and Development (BMZ) in 1969, 1986, 1992, 2005, and 2012 (for an overview see e.g. Heitmann 2019; Stockmann 2019). In this period, the German government mainly supported policy transfer initiatives that aimed at implementing the dual apprenticeship model or elements of it to emerging and developing countries in Northern Africa, Latin America and South-East Asia. Since the launch of the first initiatives in the 1960s, the mere '1:1' transfer idea was replaced by a stronger focus on systemic change including poverty reduction, gender equality, peace building and a stronger linkage with active labour market policies and business development. Today, many initiatives aim at applying a value chain model developed for VET transfer including (a) governance structures, (b) funding, (c) information systems for VET planning, (d) qualifications and curricula, and (e) training partnerships (e.g. Heitmann 2019; Stockmann 2019).

Moreover, in recent measures by the German Government and its subordinated governmental units (for an overview see Bundesregierung 2019), evaluation and monitoring turned out key factors that – however – have been implemented as mandatory elements of such initiatives only recently and still need much attention to be run systematically (Bormann and Stockmann 2009, 90–91; Stockmann 2004, 275; Wiemann et al. 2019, 13–15).

Today, numerous studies and evaluation reports emphasise the importance of the policy transfer process and contrast policy learning against policy borrowing and policy transfer. Models of policy transfer have gained much attention and cross-national attraction or decision-making in policy transfer are considered core elements of most initiatives. Policy transfer as a service implies its understanding it as a value chain model and presupposes strengthening the role of evaluating and monitoring transfer initiatives. All in all, VET transfer and VET policy transfer has crossed the border between aid and trade as it is now publicly declared a market (Euler 2013b; Fraunhofer MOEZ 2012; Posselt et al. 2018) that clearly needs professionalisation. In this context, several meta-evaluations have identified drivers and obstacles of policy transfer in VET by differentiating between several dimensions of policy transfer in VET. For example, a meta-analysis of 49 German VET transfer initiatives identifies drivers and obstacles at policy level (e.g. co-ordinated support by political stakeholders, incompatibility with existing education system), at societal level (e.g. low acceptance of vocational education or development of learning units), and at economic level (e.g. lack of technical infrastructure or lack of linkage with labour market needs) (Fraunhofer MOEZ 2012).

In 2011, *Stockmann and Silvestrini* published a meta-analysis based on 23 single VET policy transfer initiatives and two meta-evaluations across 11 countries. For identifying both, drivers, and obstacles, they apply a matrix based on and four levels of analysis (levels of application, target groups, institutions, and system) and five core evaluation criteria (relevance, effectiveness, impact, efficiency, sustainability). One of the core findings points at key factors for sustainability for VET transfer projects which cover 'ownership' (acceptance by all partners), flexible governance, staff and system compatibility (Stockmann and Silvestrini 2011, 141). Among the many findings one seem key to pushing forward the agenda of research on policy transfer in education: the authors find that the project partners' body of knowledge on policy transfer is insufficiently considered when it comes to evaluating and drawing lessons from policy transfer (Stockmann and Silvestrini 2011, 68) – a finding that points at an enormous 'treasure' of experience that should be revealed for future research.

Next to initiatives to transfer German VET to emerging nations there are a number of studies addressing the question if the German apprenticeship scheme could be a role model for further European countries (e.g. Bohlinger and Wolf 2016; Deissinger 2015). With respect to such initiatives Deissinger summarises: 'The 'best solution' for Europe – if anything like this does exist at all – ought to be based on the question whether the different national modes of delivery in vocational training open up stable career opportunities for young people' (Deissinger 2015, 564).

These examples indicate the difficulty of comparing such initiatives and deriving future action from it. Moreover, they point out that VET policy transfer is shifting from aids initiatives towards an export good (Euler 2013b). While VET policy transfer initiatives used to be run under the auspices of the Ministry of Economic Cooperation and Development, it has been only recently that the German Ministry of Education intensified its initiatives to support VET transfer as a field of research and service good. This trend goes along with two shifts, one of which is the (ablegen) of the idea of dismantling and deconstructing the German VET system into its elements, then transferring the elements and reconstructing them elsewhere (Euler 2013b, 11–19). The other one includes a shift towards

- a more systemic perspective of VET
- its interplay with other societal subsystems (labour markets, health, welfare)

- including a stronger focus on financing and (local) stakeholders and
- raising awareness that 'less is more,' that is, that only single elements (ideas, methods) of the VET system can be borrowed rather than transferred – if at all.

Moreover, these examples indicate that the amount of research on the specifics of the German VET system including attempts to transfer it to emerging countries is huge. However, the discussion has paid little attention to the underlying processes of cross-national attraction and 'borrowing' educational ideas, structures, elements and policies from elsewhere (Barabasch and Wolf 2012; Bohlinger and Wolf 2016; Pilz 2017). Indeed, policy borrowing and lending is closely related to the field of both comparative education and (education) policy. In this field, shaping education policies and addressing reform needs are often perceived as a quest to achieve a 'world class' education system through a process of identifying and transferring the practices and structures of those systems that seem to perform best in terms of a particular aspect – for example with respect to providing smooth transitions into the labour market. Thus, education policy *making* demands for comparative studies across countries and regions, labour market and educational sectors, academic disciplines and fields of policy.

At the core of this field is the question to what degree one can learning anything from other countries' education systems, how to compare them and borrow at least parts of them (Zymek and Zymek 2004, 25). However, comparing (vocational) education systems across borders harbours the risk of focusing on the macro level of education systems and/or 'picking cherries' and thus neglecting the system environment and history (for overviews see e.g. Arnove and Torres 1999; Nóvoa and Yariv-Mashal 2003). This applies particularly to vocational education and training where the notion of 'system' is either inadequate or covers only parts of the overall landscape of providers, programs, stakeholders and learning settings.

Against this background, it seems relevant to re-address the notion of policy transfer in educational contexts to provide a better understanding of the complexity of VET policy transfer.

3. Comparative (vocational) education research and policy transfer

Much has been written about the notion of comparative education in general and comparative (VET) research in particular (e.g. Hans 1967; Kubow and Fossum 2007; Noah and Eckstein 1998 for the German-speaking countries see e.g. Gonon 2012; Lauterbach 2003; Pilz 2016). Though there is no clear answer to what precisely is meant by these terms the motivation to actually *do* comparative (vocational) education research is similar across definitions: It aims at better understanding one's educational system ('home system') and thus provides a baseline for decision-making processes with respect to educational reforms. However, comparative educational research is determined neither by any particular theoretical or methodological framework nor by a clear-cut set of empirical methods. Instead, it seems that 'the comparative study of education is not a discipline: it is a context' (Broadfoot 1977, 133).

Against this background, it is obvious that comparative education (research) is rarely an aim in itself. In fact, it builds a fundament for policy transfer in education which spans a large set of activities for initiating, implementing and evaluating changes to education systems and involves numerous stakeholders including governmental bodies and their representatives, teachers, trainers, learners etc.

The notion of policy transfer is closely related to similar concepts including *policy borrowing, policy lending, policy diffusion* (particularly in the EU context; for the German VET context see e.g. Bender et al. 2014), *policy learning, (educational) transfer, assimilation* or *import/export* (Phillips and Ochs 2003, 251). Additionally, in the German-speaking community, the notions of *(VET) policy transfer* (e.g. Pilz 2017; Welfens 2016) and *export* (e.g. Euler 2013a; Krekel and Walden 2016) have recently dominated the field.

However, developing a clear-cut definition for each of these notions seems realistic for analytical purpose only and the numerous concepts are distinct in view of their underlying purpose. While *policy transfer* refers to processes 'by which knowledge about policies, administrative arrangements, institutions and ideas in one political system (past or present) is used in the development of policies, administrative arrangements, institutions and ideas in another political system' (*Dolowitz and Marsh* 2000, 5),

policy learning focuses on a mutual learning process – ideally involving all stakeholders. Moreover, some authors emphasise the distinction between *policy borrowing* and *policy lending* on the one hand and *policy learning* on the other (Portnoi 2016; Raffe and Spours 2007). Policy *borrowing* (and *lending*) refers to the international search for easy-to-transfer good practice that hardly needs any adaption (buying off-the-shelf policies). Policy *learning*, in contrast, refers to developing individual, 'tailor-made' solutions based on findings ('lessons learnt') from elsewhere (Raffe and Spours 2007; Rose 1991). Ideally, a mix of policy borrowing and mutual learning leads to an improved (mutual) understanding of the education system and thus increases the chances to jointly develop reforms, anticipate and evaluate reform effects, their impact and sustainability. In sum, the core difference between these concepts is the *perspective* from which the process is observed and analysed which is summarised in the following table:

Tab. 1: Modes of policy transfer.

Concept	Focus on...
policy transfer	...the process of identifying and looking at lessons learnt elsewhere and then transferring and adopting it in other contexts. Basically, this concept does not provide any statement about the intention of the process; however, it is often reduced to the idea that policies can be transferred to national, regional or situational preconditions without amendments.
policy borrowing and policy lending	...the 'donor' country (institutions, government etc.) (policy lending) or the receiving country (policy borrowing)
policy learning	...the process of mutual learning and understanding while adopting (or transferring) policies
policy diffusion	...the ways in which policies are spreading in a particular context or across countries and continents.

As indicated, these distinctions are primarily relevant for analytical purpose while in practice, the use of these notions is ambiguous and depends on the aims, intentions and agendas of those (legal, administrative, cultural, technical, and educational) bodies and stakeholders involved in the process. Moreover, the underlying intentions of educational policy transfer and comparative education research have changed over the years: they range from an early period of travellers' tales (Noah and Eckstein 1998, 15) through the intended borrowing of educational policies in the 19th century (Hans 1967) to an era of international cooperation starting in the early 20th century driven by the wish for of an in-depth (mutual) understanding and providing capacity building (Arnove and Torres 1999). Though the intentions have changed over time, what has remained is the fact that

> 'the degree to which there has been a reciprocal relationship of sharing between countries [...] is questionable with each country making decisions in light of what is best for development in its own nation' (*Kubow and Fossum* 2007, 8).

More pointedly, Nóvoa and Yariv-Mashal (2003) summarise the evolution of policy transfer as evolving from *knowing the other* (1880s), to *understanding the other* (1920s) followed by *constructing the other* (1960s) and culminating in *measuring the other* (2000s); they assume that the increasing influence of international institutions such as the OECD and the World Bank is at the core of the trend towards 'constructing and measuring the other.' Moreover, their findings provide a paradigmatic example of the difficult distinction between education research and policy transfer: both involve the more or less systematic comparison of education systems and structures. In contrast, the core difference is that comparative education research does not necessarily imply policy transfer while conversely, policy transfer presupposes comparing education systems or – at least – systems' elements.

The discussion on policy transfer *per se* is extensive, and this is even more the case with the criticism levelled at it. For example, Crossley (2009) or Crossley and Watson (2003) question the uncritical adoption of Western educational ideas, models and approaches without any obvious added value for those countries that implement them either with or without adaption. Lingard (2010) criticises the insufficient or total lack of willingness to learn anything from the receiving country and/or from the transfer process, with the latter one mostly referring to donor organisations or exporting countries. As a consequence, educational contexts and conditions are more likely to be adapted to the transfer model rather than vice versa (Ozga et al. 2012), a risk that is higher in VET than in any other educational field: Given the high number of stakeholders, institutions, (legal) frameworks and standards, VET-related policy transfer initiatives need a more context-sensitive implementation and building up of ownership than those in any other field of education (McDonald 2005).

I will now address two more issues that seem highly relevant for (vocational) education policy transfer. The first one refers to the identification of cases for comparison and thus the identification what is best practice while the second one refers to the process ('cycle') of policy transfer.

4. Identifying the 'right' cases for comparison

A precondition to develop individual, 'tailor-made' solutions for VET policy transfer is to understand what constitutes a 'good' VET system and how to compare a foreign system with the one at home.

However, VET structures vary between countries, countries interested in adopting a VET system similar to the German one are likely to only opt for the German system, their search for the 'best' VET system is likely to start with comparing their system with the what they consider 'good' VET systems. Thus, any such comparison starts with identifying cases to be compared, be it by questioning their commonalities or their differences. In this context, comparative politics has provided numerous analytical reference frameworks for (educational) policy transfer, among them an approach to identify cases for comparison (Caramani 2010; Lijphart 1971, 1975[1]):

---

[1] Lijphart himself (1971) and Meckstroth (1975) explicitly point out that Lijphart's approach harks back to the inductive method of concomitant variations developed by John Stuart Mill.

(1) The *Most Similar Systems Design* (MSSD, so-called method of difference) draws comparisons between cases (more precisely: between variations of variables across cases) that are as similar as possible. The core idea is to analyse why the results vary between such objects or cases. In trying to apply this approach to countries, the core problem is obvious: first, there is only a limited number of countries in the world to be compared. Secondly, as a result, the items to be examined (*factors of explanation*) cannot be kept constant and, therefore, operating with for example, controlled variables in country studies is as impossible as identifying large numbers of variables that can reveal similarities in the system comparison.

(2) The *Most Different Systems Design* (MDSD, so-called method of agreement) compares cases that are as different as possible. To qualify for this design country examples are selected on a least similar principle (as far as this is feasible, see MSSD) with the one precondition that they share at least one dependent variable. This precondition allows treating all other conditions found in the contrasting cases as independent variables. In other words, the MDSD design focuses on at least one commonality across cases to eliminate other explanations.

As both, comparative education research and (VET) policy transfer are based on (system) comparisons, the question of cross-spatial similarities and differences is key to identifying and comparing cases as it addresses the question 'Do we address the important questions? Are we certain that it is cross-country differences that are the most relevant problem to analyse? The danger is that our approaches do not allow us to decide objectively' (Caramani 2010, 39). Steiner-Khamsi (2014), following Berg-Schlosser (2002, 2430), adapted the MDSS/MDSD design to educational contexts. She elaborated on result variations discriminating between a results dimension ('very similar results' and 'very different results') and a relevance dimension ('irrelevant' and 'even in...', 'transatlantic transfer' and 'contrastive analysis'), with the results shown in the following table:

Tab. 2: Implications from (educational) policy transfer (Steiner-Khamsi 2014; Berg-Schlosser 2002, 2430).

	Results of comparison	
	(Very) similar results	**Very different results**
Very similar system	Irrelevant: Even if, from a scientific perspective, a (VET) policy transfer and corresponding analysis seem to be the most promising, this constellation is usually less interesting for research as challenges and solution are too similar to be attractive for comparison and reform ideas.	Transatlantic transfer: when transferring credit point systems in higher education, for example, from the Anglosphere to other countries, systems that seem quite similar can develop completely different and develop completely different solutions (e.g. with respect to associate degrees in most European continental countries).
Very different system	Even in...: Despite significant differences in systems, (very) similar solutions and reforms result. Of all cases, this is the most difficult one to understand as it implies similar results from very different system environments (as is the case e.g. with outcomes-based education).	Contrastive analysis: Though this case is not relevant for policy transfer due to the (massive) difference of systems and results, it is of relevance to comparative educational research to contrast and compare educational systems, understand their impacts and their societal environments.

Though the MSSD/MSDS designs and typical conclusions drawn from their application are relevant to identify cases for comparison it is not likely to anticipate all risks harboured in comparing educational systems.[2]

With respect to the ongoing discussion of transferring educational policies from the Global North to the Global South it seems quite problematic that some countries and regions are assumed superior to and more advanced than others. Similar assumption are often underlying VET policy transfer: For example, taking the German apprenticeship scheme as a role model for an 'advanced' VET system due

---

[2] For example, the requirement to consider control groups, the debate over quantitative country studies versus case studies, etc.

to the country's low youth unemployment rates ignores the relatively low image and poor attractiveness of the system – both, in Germany and elsewhere. This bias seems even more relevant with respect to the unit(s) of analysis and comparison, if, for example, federal states are compared with centralised states, individual US states are compared with Great Britain or very small and 'successful' states (as e.g. Switzerland or Iceland) are compared to large and/or emerging nations (e.g. India or Brasil) etc. (Bray and Thomas 1995; Bray et al. 2007).

Difficulties with identifying adequate and relevant units of analysis and cases for comparison can arise from insufficient consideration of cultural contexts,[3] language and translation problems,[4] or so-called 'cherry-picking' pointing at the idea of 'picking, shaking and mixing' educational elements from various contexts without respecting their (original) preconditions, environments and contexts.[5] Additional risks with identifying the 'right' cases for comparison and the right 'role models' to be adopted stem from neglecting the relevance of stakeholders and their acceptance of reforms that are key to national or regional VET systems including, for example, teachers, trainers, teacher trainers, training providers, NGOs or regional/national/sectoral authorities. Moreover, reform ideas are often insufficiently adapted to local contexts, and policy makers or experts involved

---

3   For example, a typical problem in the classification of VET models applied in the German-speaking countries ignores the importance of context factors: The classification developed by Greinert (1998; 2000) distinguishes four types of models (the company and market-based model, the school-based model, the dual model, and the informal model). In comparison, research by for example, Walther (2006) or Walther et al. (2013) emphasises the role of *welfare regimes* (referring to social-state structures and the culturally specific status of youth) and VET prestige that impact not only on individual career choices but also on the structure of VET systems and school-to-work transition regimes.
4   For example, middle school in China refers to the secondary level, while in England it designates the bridging level between primary and secondary education. In Bavaria, it refers to one of three school types at lower secondary level.
5   An example of cherry picking is the German so-called Excellence Initiative in higher education. This initiative is geared to the Anglosphere's logic of top and elite universities while maintaining traditional salary and access structures which prevents universities from actually being able to attract the best international students and researchers.

with the transfer process may lack basic information and/or a solid understanding of national, regional and cultural contexts relevant to VET (Bohlinger and Wolf 2016, 349; McDonald 2012).

All of these factors condense into what is known as the 'process' or 'cycle' of (educational) policy transfer which I will turn to in the next section.

5. The process of educational policy transfer

Among the numerous models of policy transfer the one developed by Phillips and Ochs (2003) is among the most often applied ones in educational research. This model includes – regardless of context – four stages: (1) cross-national attraction, (2) decision, (3) implementation and (4) internalisation/indigenisation. At the first stage, an assumed or actual problem in the 'home' system is identified and stakeholders start seeking for what they think are similar problems and relevant solutions elsewhere. The decision-making stage usually involves several visits to countries that appear to have an adequate solution for what is assumed an 'identical' problem. Back home again, problem solutions are drafted based on what was observed in the other countries, frequently with serious misinterpretations of what was observed in the host country. Such misinterpretations may result from ignoring existing research findings, contextual aspects and/or relevant empirical data. As a consequence, linkages between reform needs (and solutions) in the home country and what seems a similar challenge (and its solution) in the other country are often hard to prove or simply do not exist once an in-depth analysis of both systems has been run (Morris 1998). Moreover, insufficient attention is often paid to questions of who takes decisions on what (legal) grounds and in line with which interests. It is precisely with respect to this aspect that Phillips and Ochs (2011, 17) distinguish five levels of coercion in the context of educational transfer:

- imposed policy in totalitarian or authoritarian regimes;
- policy transfer required under constraints in occupied or defeated countries;
- policy transfer that is negotiated under constraint and required by bilateral or multilateral agreements;
- policy transfer that is borrowed purposefully and aims at intentionally copying policies/practices observed elsewhere;
- policy transfer that is introduced through influence and includes for example, educational ideas, methods, practices etc.

These levels of coercion are built on several forms of policy transfer whose boundaries are blurring. It is particularly policy transfer deriving from and in (post-)colonial contexts that involves high levels of coercion. This type of transfer has had and still has a massive impact on education systems and is at the core of many discussions in postcolonialism (e.g. Tikley 1999).[6] However, little is documented in this context with respect to Germany and that is, its colonial schools or the attractiveness of its early welfare system (Briggs 1961; Hoffmann 1980).

In current discussions on VET policy transfer, however, it seems that a less-coercive 'dissemination' of reform ideas is dominating the field. With respect to Germany, for example, there are numerous examples describing the transfer (and its failure) of the dual apprenticeship model to other countries (e.g. Clement 1999; Greinert et al. 1997; Stockmann 1996). Other examples of such 'travelling reforms' (Steiner-Khamsi 2006, 665) – beyond the scope of VET – include the Bologna process, the learning outcomes orientation or qualifications frameworks (Alderson and Martin 2007; Allais 2014; Wheelahan 2011). Introducing such instruments often results from the strive for greater (cost) efficiency, more competitiveness and 'better' (stronger) links between the education system and the labour market. Unsurprisingly, such *policy diffusions*, *travelling reforms* and *policyscapes* (Steiner-Khamsi and Waldow 2012, 337) are often massively

---

6 Tikley (1999, 605) refers to postcolonialism as a term '(that) is used to describe a global 'condition' or shift in the cultural, political and economic arrangements that arise from the experiences of European colonialism both in former colonised and colonising countries. Importantly, it is used to describe not just specific developments or events related to colonialism and its aftermath but also to signify an epistemological shift in the way that these events are described and interpreted.'

promoted by international organisations since they finance the reforms (Jakobi 2011, 2012).

The following table provides examples of such travelling reforms and indicates when and by which region or by which particular institution it began spreading across the globe:

Tab. 3: Examples of the origin and spread of 'travelling' educational reforms.

Reform	Originating from	Period
Apprenticeship education ('dual' apprenticeship model)	German-speaking countries	since the late 1960s
Outcomes-based education	New Zealand	since the 1980s
Qualifications frameworks	(France) Scotland	since the late 1980s
Three cycles of higher education, credit point systems	United Kingdom, Canada, USA	starting in the early 1960s; massive spread since the late 1990s
Large Scale Assessments (e.g. PISA, PIAAC)	OECD (based on a UNESCO idea)	since the 1990s

Another mode of policy transfer is based on publicly available, predominantly negative results from (international) assessments or monitoring. The results of the first PISA study furnish the most prominent example of this phenomenon. In many countries, they triggered a search for best practice to improving education systems – linked to syndromes like the 'PISA shock' or 'teaching to the test.'[7] Similarly, while there is as yet no large scale assessment in VET,[8] indicator-based reporting and

---

7   The PISA shock refers to the unexpectedly poor results by German students in the first PISA survey in 2000 and the subsequent massive reform efforts. *Teaching to the test* refers to the often criticised 'method' of teaching towards the passing of tests as practised, for example, in the PISA context.

8   There actually were German efforts to implement a vocational PISA, the so-called VET-LSA (Vocational Education and Training – Large Scale Assessment). However, it was rejected mainly by the OECD because the OECD's own design for an international large scale assessment for all adults (PIAAC) covers a much larger population sample than would have been the case with an assessment limited to VET (see BMBF 2009 for the final report).

monitoring (such as *Education at a Glance* or the progress reports of the European Commission for achieving the *Europe 2020* educational objectives) have become common in reforming education systems.

As these examples indicate, the levels of coercion provide a helpful instrument to analyse the purpose of a transfer process. However, they do not address the more fundamental question which policies, reforms, and solutions have proved successful or have at least a realistic chance of being implemented sustainably. To answer this question, one needs to consider the socio-economic context of the other (education) system in detail – along with all its educational structures, transition pathways between for example, higher and vocational education, financing mechanisms, involvement of social partners and co-operation between governmental and non-governmental bodies, private companies and training providers. Against this background, it is obvious that a one size fits all (or mere 'export-import-model') is impossible and that

> 'there are no absolute answers in such decisions, any more than there is an absolute answer to what constitutes an ideal society. The question is one of efficiency – what inputs into the system will give maximum output of the educational products (skills, knowledge and attitudes) identified as desirable in a particular society' (*Broadfoot* 1977, *134*).

Kingdon's concept of *policy formation* as result of a coincidence seems crucial (Kingdon 1995, 19). He assumes that three simultaneously converging phenomena play a major role in actually initiating policy changes. This 'flow of three streams' (Guldbrandsson and Fossum 2009, 434) which became known as *policy windows* or *windows of opportunity* include the *problem stream*, that is, the recognition of a problem; the *policy stream,* which refers to the availability of (realistic) solutions; and the *politics stream*, that is, changes in the political environment that refer to for example, changes of administration, upcoming elections or changes in public opinions etc.

Steiner-Khamsi (2014) adapted this approach to educational reform contexts to analyse why some educational ideas, approaches and countries serve as reference models while others do not. This so-called *externalisation framework* (Steiner-Khamsi 2004, 2014) addresses the question how policy transfer is realised and under what conditions it is initiated. While Steiner-Khamsi focuses on policy transfer from the Global North to the Global South, in many cases it also involves

> 'quasi-market, neo-liberal, or hyper-liberal reforms that originated during the Thatcher-Reagan era. Initially, they were borrowed from New Zealand and Australia, adopted in the UK and in the US, and then disseminated to every corner of the world. Precisely because they were introduced so long ago, policy makers in late-adopter countries refer to them as "international reforms", without explaining where they originated' (*Steiner-Khamsi* 2014, *160*).

Despite these constraints, (VET) policy transfer was and still is highly attractive and beneficial to policy makers (and researchers) – both, for the foreign system and for the home system given that it can have a 'salutary effect on protracted policy conflict' (Steiner-Khamsi 2014, 156). Research has pointed out that educational policy transfer can be seen as a coalition builder as it 'enables opposed advocacy groups to combine resources to support a third, supposedly more neutral, policy option borrowed from elsewhere' (Steiner-Khamsi 2014, 156; see also Steiner-Khamsi and deJong-Lambert 2006).

In that sense, policy transfer serves as a source of legitimisation. It is a symbolic certification for what seems the most obvious (and relevant) answer to an educational reform need rather than it provides necessarily the best possible solution:

> 'Local actors reach out and grab the arm of the octopus that is closest to their particular policy agenda, and thereby attach (local) meaning to a (global) policy' (*Steiner-Khamsi* 2014, *155–156*).

Thus, the risk harboured in 'grabbing the arm of the octopus' lies in the salutary effect promised by (international or foreign) stakeholders, organisations or governments. For example, large scale assessments such as PIAAC or PISA, global monitoring and evaluations such as the Unesco's realisation of 'Education for All' or the OECD's 'Education at a Glance' all imply an increasing governance of a political field that is – traditionally – deeply rooted in national contexts. Moreover, reaching out for the arm of the octopus labelled 'global education and international competition' poses a risk that international stakeholders, donors and reform pacemakers take the reins to govern national VET systems by their (international) agendas, benchmarks and indicators (Nóvoa and Yariv-Mashal 2003, 426).

While none of these findings provides answers to the question how to run best an educational policy transfer they all indicate that the decision to adopt a particular (vocational) education policy can derive from considerations far from the system's attractiveness in its home country and that is rarely considered in research on (vocational) educational policy transfer.

6. Conclusions

Policy transfer has a long-standing tradition in many fields, including education. Developing, implementing, assessing and evaluating education policies is a contested field of both, policy making and research.

Though German VET policy transfer initiatives have been dominated by the idea of 'exporting' the dual apprenticeship model, additional transfer ideas have found access to this arena as well. Such ideas include for example, qualifications frameworks, the learning outcomes orientation, inclusive education, credit point systems or validation of prior learning. In comparison with the 'traditional' VET-related policy transfer initiatives, the newer ones, however, were more related to 'importing' reform ideas from elsewhere while the dual apprenticeship model is still considered the dominating export service in education.[9]

The ongoing internationalisation of VET in the sense of transferring it to other countries and supported by the German government is reflected in current initiatives such as GOVET[10], the national initiative 'International Vocational Training Cooperation from a Single Source'[11] or the national 'Strategy for the Internationalisation of Education, Science and Research.'[12] Compared with previous national strategies, however, it seems that the latest initiatives put a stronger focus on actually

---

9 With the exception of the above-mentioned Vocational Education and Training-Large Scale Assessment (VET-LSA) which was never realised.
10 Central Office of the Federal Government for International Vocational Training Cooperation at BIBB, cf. https://www.bibb.de/govet/de/index.php.
11 https://www.bmbf.de/de/internationale-zusammenarbeit-in-der-berufsbildung-322.html.
12 https://www.bmbf.de/de/internationalisierungsstrategie-269.html.

developing reforms with receiving countries and developing sustainable initiatives and ownership rather than 'exporting and selling' services and aid. Moreover, VET policy transfer has re-gained attention in the wake of the 2008 economic crisis and researchers have emphasised the need for a stronger linkage between international and national initiatives to strengthen VET policy transfer and exchange experience and best practice. In this context, there is a need to further develop VET policy transfer theories and provide research on exogenous influences on the evolution of the 'home' education system including the role of developing ownership and fostering mutual learning. Next, little is known about the above-mentioned policy windows, and those opportunities and constellations under which policy transfer can succeed. Systematic research that is beyond anecdotal evidence is needed to identify appropriate and feasible policy transfer measures providing answers to key questions such as 'is it adequate? If so, for whom? And: is it sustainable?'

Also, tracing back roots and re-addressing the fundamental issue of why do we do educational policy transfer could be of help. This question allows for both, ex-post and ex-ante evaluations to identify 'successful' (VET) policy transfer and pave the way (back and) forward to the origins of comparative educational research and facilitate reflection on what is actually relevant for the (further) development of (vocational) education and training from the perspectives of those affected by it (learners, teachers, trainers, etc.).

Additional aspects to be considered for future research include diffusion pathways and the role of international stakeholders as well as a critical reflection of existing models of policy transfer. Other issues are well known to be of importance; however, it is unclear how to address them methodologically. For example, windows of opportunity much depend on individual key figures and the level of coercion by which a reform is adopted. Even though interrelations between countries may be strong, and reciprocal sharing between countries may be common, this is not necessarily an indicator for adopting foreign policies. Other examples include, for example, phony policy borrowing (i.e. policy transfer as lip service without actual reforms), travelling reform ideas and their impact on the country of origin as well as policy transfer as a niche for professionalisation (who is providing training, expertise and consultancy in this field?). Last not least, in some cases, the core question may be even more basic and refer to the right 'size' of an initiative or to the question 'what if apprenticeship training was not the right answer to the reform need?'.

Those findings may sound simple and logical; however, for a very long time they emerged in parallel and decoupled from similar international experience with educational policy transfer. Bringing together research on policy borrowing (in education and beyond) with VET research is an opportunity to point at black box issues and pave the way forward for a better understanding of this issue.

Biographical note

Sandra Bohlinger is Full Professor of Adult Education and Director of the Institute of Vocational Education at Dresden University (Technische Universität Dresden), Germany. Her research interests are in adult education, vocational education and training (VET), education policy, comparative education, and skills development. Her current research includes governance of adult and vocational education in the European Union, policy borrowing in vocational education and training (VET), and improving teacher education in South Asia.

References

Alderson, A.; Martin, M. (2007). Outcomes based education: Where has it come from and where is it going? *Issues in Educational Research*, 7(2), 161–182.

Allais, S. (2014). *Selling out Education. National Qualifications Frameworks and the Neglect of Knowledge*. Rotterdam, Boston, Taipei: Sense.

Arnove, R.F.; Torres, C.A. (1999): *Comparative Education: The Dialectic of the Global and the Local*. Lanham, MD: Rowman & Littlefield Publishers.

Barabasch, A.; Wolf, S. (2012). Policy Transfer in der Berufsbildung in den Ländern China und USA. *Die Berufsbildende Schule*, 64(5), 161–166.

Bender, K.; Keller, S.; Willing, H. (2014). *International Policy Learning and Policy Change: Scientific Inputs for the Dialogue on Social Protection with Global Partners. The Role of International Policy Transfer and Diffusion for Policy Change in Social Protection.* IZNE Social Protection Working Paper 14/1. Bonn, Rhein-Sieg.

Berg-Schlosser, D. (2002). Comparative studies: Method and design. In: Smelser, N.J.; Baltes, P.B. (eds.). *International Encyclopedia of the Social and Behavioural Sciences*. Vol. 4. Amsterdam: Elsevier, 2427–2433.

BMBF (2009). *Feasibility Study VET-LSA. A Comparative Analysis of Occupational Profiles and VET Programmes in 8 European Countries – International Report*. Bonn: BMBF.

Bohlinger, S.; Wolf, S. (2016). Zwischen Dynamik und Stagnation. Politiktransfer kooperativer Berufsausbildung als Weg aus der Jugendarbeitslosigkeit in Südeuropa. *Zeitschrift für Pädagogik*, 62(3), 340–357.

Bray, M.; Adamson, B.; Mason, M. (2007). *Comparative Education Research. Approaches and Methods*. Hong Kong: Springer.

Bray, M.; Thomas, R.M. (1995). Levels of comparison in educational studies. *Harvard Educational Review*, 65(3), 472–490.

Briggs, A. (1961). The welfare state in historical perspective. *Archives Europeennes de Sociologie*, 2(2), 221–258.

Broadfoot, T. (1977). The comparative contribution – A research perspective. *Comparative Education, Special Issue: Comparative Education, Its Present State and Future Prospects*, 13(2), 133–137.

Bundesregierung (2019). *Strategie der Bundesregierung zur internationalen Berufsbildungszusammenarbeit*. Berlin. https://www.bmbf.de/files/137_19_Strategie_Bundesregierung.pdf.

Canning, R.; Deissinger, T.; Loots, C. (2000). Continuity and change in apprenticeship systems: A comparative study between Scotland

and Germany. *Scottish Journal of Adult and Continuing Education*, 6(2), 99–117.

Caramani, D. (2010). Of differences and similarities: Is the explanation of variation a limitation to (or of) comparative analysis? *European Political Science*, 9(1), 34–48.

Chakroun, B. (2010). NQFs: From policy borrowing to policy learning. *European Journal of Education*, 45(2), 199–216.

Clement, U. (1999). *Politische Steuerung beruflicher Bildung. Die Bedeutung unterschiedlicher Entwicklungslogiken für die Berufsbildungspolitik in den Ländern der Dritten Welt am Beispiel Chile.* Baden-Baden: Nomos.

Crossley, M. (2009). Comparative education and research capacity building: Reflections on international transfer and the significance of context. *Journal of International and Comparative Education*, 1(1), 4–12.

Crossley, M.; Watson, K. (2003). *Comparative and International Research in Education. Globalisation, Context and Difference.* London and New York: Routledge.

Deissinger, T. (2015). The German dual vocational education and training system as 'good practice'? *Local Economy*, 30(5), 557–567.

Deissinger, T.; Hellwig, S. (2005). Apprenticeships in Germany: Modernising the dual system. *Education and Training*, 47(4/5), 312–324.

Dolowitz, D.P.; Marsh, D. (2000). Learning from abroad: The role of policy transfer in contemporary policy-making. *Governance*, 13(1), 5–23.

Euler, D. (2013a). Die deutsche Berufsausbildung – ein Exportschlager oder eine Reformbaustelle? *Zeitschrift für Berufs- und Wirtschaftspädagogik*, 109(3), 321–331.

Euler, D. (2013b). Germany's dual vocational training system: A model for other countries? Gütersloh: Bertelsmann Stiftung. https://www.bertelsmann-stiftung.de/fileadmin/files/BSt/Publikationen/GrauePublikationen/GP_Germanys_dual_vocational_training_system.pdf.

Fraunhofer (MOEZ) (2012). Treibende und hemmende Faktoren im Berufsbildungsexport aus Sicht deutscher Anbieter. Leipzig.

https://www.imw.fraunhofer.de/content/dam/moez/de/documents/Gruppe_Bildung/Studie_TH_2012_07_03.pdf.

Gonon, P. (2012). Policy borrowing and the rise of a vocational education and training system: The case of Switzerland. In: Steiner-Khamsi, G.; Waldow, F. (eds.). *World Yearbook of Education: Policy Borrowing and Lending*. London: Routledge, 191–206.

Greinert, W.-D. (1998) *Das 'deutsche System' der Berufsausbildung. Tradition, Organisation, Funktion*. Baden-Baden: Nomos.

Greinert, W.-D. (2000). *Organisationsmodelle und Lernkonzepte in der beruflichen Bildung. Analytische Grundlagentexte*. Baden-Baden: Nomos.

Greinert, W.-D.; Heitmann, W.; Stockmann, R.; Vest, B. (1997). *Vierzig Jahre Berufsbildungszusammenarbeit mit Ländern der Dritten Welt*. Baden-Baden: Nomos.

Guldbrandsson, K.; Fossum, B. (2009). An exploration of the theoretical concepts policy windows and policy entrepreneurs at the Swedish public health arena. *Health Promotion International*, 24(4), 434–444. https://doi.org/10.1093/heapro/dap033.

Hans, N. (1967). *Comparative Education: A Study of Educational Factors and Traditions*. London: Routledge.

Heitmann, W. (2019): 60 Jahre internationale Förderung der Berufsbildung im Überblick. In: Gessler, M.; Fuchs, M.; Pilz, M. (eds.). *Konzepte und Wirkungen des Transfers Dualer Berufsausbildung*. Wiesbaden: Springer VS, 59–118.

Hoffmann, W.K.H. (1980). *Vom Kolonialexperten zum Experten der Entwicklungszusammenarbeit: Acht Fallstudien zur Geschichte der Ausbildung von Fachkräften für Übersee in Deutschland und in der Schweiz*. Saarbrücken u.a.: Breitenbach.

Horn, S. (2011). *Wirkungsorientierte Evaluation nichtstaatlicher deutscher bilateraler Berufsbildungszusammenarbeit in Ghana*. Dissertation an der Technischen Universität Dresden.

Jakobi, A.P. (2009). *International Organizations and Lifelong Learning. From Global Agendas to Policy Diffusion*. Houndmills: Palgrave.

Jakobi, A.P. (2011). International organizations and policy diffusion: The global norm of lifelong learning. *Journal of International Relations and Development*, 15(1), 31–64.

Jakobi, A.P. (2012). Facilitating transfer: International organizations as central nodes for policy diffusion. In: Steiner-Khamsi, G.; Waldow, F. (eds.). *World Yearbook of Education: Policy Borrowing and Lending*. London: Routledge, 391–407.

Kingdon, J. (1995). *Agendas, Alternatives, and Public Policies*. 2nd edition. New York, NY: Longman.

Krekel, E.M.; Walden, G. (2016). Exportschlager Duales System der Berufsausbildung? In: Bellmann, L.; Grözinger, G. (eds.). *Bildung in der Wissensgesellschaft*. Marburg: Metropolis, 55–70.

Kubow, P.K.; Fossum, P.R. (2007). *Comparative Education. Exploring Issues in International Context*. Upper Saddle River and Columbus: Pearson.

Lauterbach, U. (2003). *Vergleichende Berufsbildungsforschung. Theorien, Methodologien und Ertrag am Beispiel der Vergleichenden Berufs- und Wirtschaftspädagogik mit Bezug auf die korrespondierende Disziplin Comparative Education/Vergleichende Erziehungswissenschaft*. Baden-Baden: Nomos.

Lijphart, A. (1971). Comparative politics and the comparative method. *The American Political Science Review*, 65(3), 682–693.

Lijphart, A. (1975). The comparable-cases strategy in comparative research. *Comparative Political Studies*, 8(2), 158–177.

Lingard, B. (2010). Policy borrowing, policy learning: Testing times in Australian schooling. *Critical Studies in Education*, 51(2), 129–147.

MacLean, R.; Lai, A. (2011). Editorial – the future of technical and vocational education and training. *International Journal of Vocational Research*, 9(1–2), 2–15.

McDonald, B.L. (2005). Training impact: Maximising aid projects. In: Sanga, K.; Chu, C.; Hall, C.; Crowl, L. (eds.). *Re-Thinking Aid Relationships in Pacific Education*. NZ, He Parekereke, Victoria University ,143–160.

McDonald, B.L. (2012). Educational transfer to developing countries: Policy and skill facilitation. *Procedia Social and Behavioral Sciences*, 69, 1817–1826.

Meckstroth, T.W. (1975). 'Most Different Systems' and 'Most Similar Systems': A study in the logic of comparative inquiry. *Comparative Political Studies*, 8(2), 132–157.

Morris, P. (1998). Comparative education and educational reform: Beware of prophets returning from the far east. *Education 3 to 13*, 26(2), 3–7.

Noah, H.J.; Eckstein, M.A. (1998). *Doing Comparative Education: Three Decades of Collaboration*. Hong Kong: Springer.

Nóvoa, A.; Yariv-Mashal, T. (2003). Comparative Research in Education: A Mode of Governance or a Historical Journey? *Comparative Education*, 39(4), 423–438.

Ozga, J.; Seddon, T.; Steiner-Khamsi, G. (2012). Introduction. In: Steiner-Khamsi, G.; Waldow, F. (eds.). *Policy Borrowing and Lending in Education*. New York: Routledge, xvii–xx.

Phillips, D.; Ochs, K. (2003) Processes of policy borrowing in education. *Comparative Education*, 39(4), 451–461.

Phillips, D.; Schweisfurth, M. (2011). *Comparative and International Education*. New York, London: Continuum.

Pilz, M. (2016). Typologies in comparative vocational education: Existing models and a new approach. *Vocations and Learning*, 9, 295–314.

Pilz, M. (2017). Policy borrowing in vocational education and training (VET). In: Pilz, M. (ed.). Vocational Education and Training in Times of Economic Crisis: Lessons from Around the World. Cham: Springer, 473–490.

Portnoi, L. (2016). *Policy Borrowing and Reform in Education. Globalized Processes and Local Contexts*. New York: Palgrave Macmillan.

Posselt, T.; Salameh, N.; Preissler, A.; Hudak, S. (2018): Treibende und Hemmende Faktoren im Berufsbildungsexport aus Sicht deutscher Anbieter. Leipzig: BMBF and DLR

Posselt, T.; Abdelkafi, N.; Radić, M.; Preissler, A. (2019). Berufsbildungsexport: Zentrale Bausteine der Geschäftsmodellentwicklung. In: Gessler, M.; Fuchs, M.; Pilz, M. (eds.). *Konzepte und Wirkungen*

des Transfers Dualer Berufsausbildung. Wiesbaden: Springer VS, 163–196.
Raffe, D.; Spours, K. (2007). *Policy-Making and Policy Learning in 14–19 Education.* Bedford Way Papers. London: ULIE.
Rose, R. (1991). What is lesson-drawing? *Journal of Public Policy,* 11(1), 3–30.
Steiner-Khamsi, G. (2004). *The Global Politics of Educational Borrowing and Lending.* New York, NY: Teachers College Press.
Steiner-Khamsi, G. (2006). The economics of policy borrowing and lending: a study of late adopters. *Oxford Review of Education,* 32(5), 665–678.
Steiner-Khamsi, G. (2013). What is wrong with the 'What-Went-Right' approach in educational policy? *European Educational Research Journal,* 12(1), 20–33.
Steiner-Khamsi, G. (2014). Cross-national policy borrowing: understanding reception and translation. *Asia Pacific Journal of Education,* 34(2), 153–167.
Steiner-Khamsi, G.; deJong-Lambert, W. (2006). The International Race over the Patronage of the South: Comparative and International Education in Eastern Europe and the United States. *Current Issues in Comparative Education,* 8(2), 84–94.
Steiner-Khamsi, G.; Waldow, F. (2012). *Policy Borrowing and Lending. World Yearbook of Education.* London and New York: Routledge.
Stockmann, R. (1996). *Die Wirksamkeit der Entwicklungshilfe. Eine Evaluation der Nachhaltigkeit von Programmen und Projekten der Berufsbildung.* Opladen: Westdeutscher Verlag.
Stockmann, R. (2004). Evaluation staatlicher Entwicklungspolitik. In: Stockmann, R. (ed.). *Evaluationsforschung. Grundlagen und ausgewählte Forschungsfelder.* Opladen: Budrich, 375–410.
Stockmann, R. (2012). Von der Idee zur Institution. Institut für deutsche Entwicklungsevaluierung gegründet. *Zeitschrift für Evaluation,* 11(1), 85–93.
Stockmann, R. (2019). Ziele, Wirkungen und Erfolgsfaktoren der deutschen Berufsbildungszusammenarbeit. In: Gessler, M.; Fuchs, M.; Pilz, M. (eds.). *Konzepte und Wirkungen des Transfers Dualer Berufsausbildung.* Wiesbaden: Springer VS, 121–162.

Stockmann, R.; Borrmann, A. (2009). *Evaluation in der deutschen Entwicklungszusammenarbeit*. Band 1 Systemanalysen. Münster: Waxmann.

Stockmann, R.; Kohlmann, U. (1998). *Transferierbarkeit des Dualen Systems*. Berlin: Overall.

Stockmann, R.; Silvestrini, S. (2011). Synthese und Meta-Evaluierung Berufliche Bildung. Saarbrücken.

Tan, C.; Ng, P.T. (2012). A critical reflection of teacher professionalism in Cambodia. *Asian Education and Development Studies*, 1(2), 124–134.

Tikley, L. (1999). Postcolonialism and comparative education. *International Review of Education*, 45(5/6), 603–621.

Walther, A. (2006). Regimes of youth transitions. *Young*, 14(2), 119–139.

Walther, A.; Stauber, B.; Pohl, A. (2013). Support and success in youth transitions: A comparative analysis on the relation between subjective and systemic factors. In: Mínguez, A.M. (ed.). *Family Well-Being. European Perspectives*. Dordrecht: Springer, 225–243.

Welfens, N. (2016). Transfer durch Krise? Frankreichs Berufsbildungssystem zwischen Pfadabhängigkeit und deutschem Modell. In: Schmid, J.; Amos, K.; Schrader, J.; Thiel, A. (eds.). *Internationalisierte Welten der Bildung: Bildung und Bildungspolitik im globalen Vergleich*. Baden-Baden: Nomos, 97–119.

Wheelahan, L. (2011). Beware Anglophone countries bearing gifts. In: Bohlinger, S.; Münchhausen, G. (eds.). *Recognition and Validation of Prior Learning*. Bielefeld: Bertelsmann, 36–86.

Wiemann, K.; Li, J.; Wiemann, J.; Fuchs, M.; Pilz, M. (2019). 'Lost (in) VET': Zum Stand der Transferforschung in der internationalen Berufsbildungszusammenarbeit aus Sicht verschiedener Wissenschaftsdisziplinen. In: Gessler, M.; Fuchs, M.; Pilz, M. (eds.). *Konzepte und Wirkungen des Transfers Dualer Berufsausbildung*. Wiesbaden: Springer VS, 13–57.

Zymek, B.; Zymek, R. (2004). Traditional – National – International. Explaining the inconsistency of educational borrowers. In: Phillips, D.; Ochs, K. (eds.). *Educational Policy Borrowing*. Oxford: Symposium, 25–35.

FLORINDA SAULI, MATILDE WENGER & JEAN-LOUIS BERGER

What constitutes quality in the Swiss initial vocational education and training dual system: An apprentice perspective

Abstract: In Switzerland, the promotion of quality of initial vocational education and training (IVET) is stated in law. However, little is known about what characterizes this quality, especially from the perspective of the main actors of IVET. This study investigated the perceptions of IVET quality from 320 apprentices enrolled in a dual IVET program. Two occupational fields were considered: technical and retail. A thematic analysis was performed on data collected through open-ended questions. Results revealed that the quality of IVET was multilayered and complex. Apprentices' perceptions of high and low quality were grouped into three different levels of a more comprehensive system. The levels included elements referring to (1) the learning objects, (2) the social learning environment, and (3) the IVET context. Differences in the perceptions of quality between learning sites and occupational fields were also highlighted.

Keywords: initial vocational education and training, Switzerland, quality of education, dual system,

1. Introduction

1.1. The relevance of quality in initial vocational education and training

The quality of initial vocational education and training (IVET) has been acknowledged as a key factor in explaining apprentices' motivation and learning, helping them sustain their efforts and acquire the necessary skills for their future occupation (Ebbinghaus, Krewerth,

Flemming, Beicht, Eberhard, & Granato, 2010). Also, over the last few decades, the quality of education and training has gained a considerable role in educational policies and political discourse, as revealed by other studies in the international community (for an exemple, see the works of the project EQAVET funded by the European Commission; EQAVET, 2019). In Switzerland, it has been enshrined in the Federal Act on Vocational and Professional Education and Training of 13 December 2002 (= VPETA; CC[1] 412.10). More specifically, Article 8 on quality development states, "Education and training providers within the VPET[2] system shall be responsible for ensuring the constant improvement of quality" (par. 1) and that, "The Confederation shall promote quality development, establish quality standards and monitor compliance" (par. 2). In addition, in Article 24, it was specified that quality shall be formally monitored both in professional practice and in school education. Moreover, in the mission statement for Vocational and Professional Education and Training 2030 developed by the State Secretariat for Education, Research and Innovation (SERI), one of the strategic guidelines refers to the establishment of qualitative standards (SERI, n.d.). This demonstrates that maintaining and increasing quality in IVET remains a major challenge for Swiss institutions. Although the topic of quality is directly mentioned, it is not specified how to concretely develop it. This task is left to the stakeholders directly involved in the implementation of IVET, such as the vocational schools or the training companies. However, no shared understanding of what characterizes a high- or low-quality education exists (Wittek & Kvernbekk, 2011). A better understanding of what characterizes the quality of IVET from the perspective of its main actors is therefore necessary. The current study represents an effort to investigate what constitutes quality from the viewpoint of the recipients of IVET: the apprentices.

---

1 Classified compilation.
2 Vocational and Professional Education and Training.

1.2. The Swiss dual system: Different learning sites, different logics

In Switzerland, IVET is the most prevalent educational track after compulsory school: two out of three young people follow an apprenticeship (Swiss Federal Statistical Office, 2017). The majority of IVET is organized according to a dual system, where programs alternate between two main learning sites: the professional school and the training company. Therefore, apprentices attend classes at school on a basis of one to two days per week and spend the remaining days at a training company under the supervision of a trainer. IVET is composed of certificates and qualifications obtained in a two, three, or four years education and training program. This dual training system—praised abroad and frequently used as an example of optimal IVET—allows apprentices to learn a trade by focusing on the practical aspect of it, while acquiring the necessary theoretical and general knowledge at school. To enable apprentices to learn in a dual manner, two learning sites are fundamental: the vocational school and the training company. These learning sites have, in principle, the same general goal: training apprentices in a trade. However, they differ in their methods to attain it: vocational schools offer vocational and general knowledge, whereas training companies provide the opportunity to develop professional skills. Hence, even though vocational schools and training companies are formally connected and cooperate in the IVET system, specific and distinct logics exist within each learning site (Prenzel & Drechsel, 1996). In fact, at vocational schools, apprentices evolve a learning logic, whereas at training companies, a production logic is prevalent. Teachers at the vocational school and trainers at the company have different profiles and pedagogical preparation. They also have separate and distinctive visions of apprentices, with teachers seeing them as pupils at school and trainers seeing them more as workers at the training company. These two logics lead apprentices to experience two different forms of training in the two learning sites (Alves, Gosse, & Sprimont, 2010; Gurtner, Gulfi, Genoud, de Rocha Trindade, & Schumacher, 2012; Tynjälä, 2008). First, even if there are specific aims at the training company, the level of formality is much lower as the curriculum is less detailed and formalized than at the vocational school. Problems are real at the training company, whereas they are artificial or created at the vocational school. Regarding the knowledge produced, it is implicit, tacit, and situation specific at the training company, whereas it is explicit and generalized at the vocational school (Tynjälä, 2008). Different methods are used to demonstrate the knowledge acquired from the two learning sites: at school, vocational knowledge is assessed by tests or exams, whereas procedural knowledge acquired at training companies is assessed in practical situations "in action" (Gurtner, Furlan, & Cattaneo, 2018). Moreover, apprentices view the utility and the attractiveness of their training at the vocational schools more skeptically than at the training company (Gurtner et al., 2012). Often, a reason to choose IVET is to start working and leave the school; for instance, because of negative school experiences. Due to organizational conditions, teaching at vocational schools cannot provide individualized feedback to the same extent as the training company (Prenzel & Drechsel, 1996). These differences lead to learning processes, notably motivations, which are specific to each learning site. In other words, apprentices attribute different values and expectations to the two sites and are differently motivated in the two learning sites during their training (Gurtner et al., 2012; Krapp & Lewalter, 2001). Based on these observations, this study focused on the apprentices' perceptions of quality of their training at school and at the training company across two occupational fields—retail and technical occupations.

2. Prior research related to IVET quality

2.1. What is quality in education?

Despite an explicit willingness of the authorities to guarantee a certain level of quality in IVET, no shared understanding of what characterizes a high or low quality exists. In the scientific literature related to quality in education, the term is under debate, and it is considered to be multidimensional (Behrens, 2007; Griffin, 2017). Quality can be seen as an ideal towards which every actor should aspire to but which is not known in advance (Bouchard & Plante, 2002). Quality is also seen as "fitness for purpose" and "fitness of purpose" (Wittek & Kvernbekk,

2011). Quality as fitness for purpose is defined through its adequacy to an objective. For example, "Does the education match the requirements of the occupation?". Quality as fitness of purpose refers to the adequacy of the objective. For example, "Do the objectives match with the requirements of the profession?". Additionally, quality can be considered either in an objective or in a subjective manner or according to Stake and Schwandt (2006), as "Quality-as-Measured" and "Quality-as-Experienced." When quality is treated in an objective manner, it can be decomposed in specific and measurable parts called "indicators" (Bouchard & Plante, 2002). Indicators are used in a comparative way to verify whether predefined standards are attained; for instance, by a training program (Wittek & Kvernbekk, 2011). According to objective approaches, quality can be measured, for instance, through students' performances (e.g., using the Programme for International Student Assessment—PISA), teaching or teacher effectiveness (Gates Foundation, 2013), or the attainment of certain standards by an educational organization (e.g., based on Quality Management Systems; Moreland & Clark, 1998). The appeal of such approaches lies in their apparent objectivity given that the indicators are measurable. However, the objective approaches tend to vanish the subjective perceptions of some key actors involved in the educational system, such as the students and the teachers (Behrens, 2007). In addition, the increasing emergence in the past few decades of standardized measures of quality and of international comparisons has led to a shift in the way quality is defined: quality has become primarily defined by its results (e.g., students' test scores), rather than by the elements that determine it (e.g., the teaching practices). It is thus relevant to consider the notion of quality in education as subjective and based on actors' perceptions. Based on the literature reviewed, we offer the following definition of IVET quality:

> The quality of initial vocational education and training is the subjective conception of an ideal towards which training should aim. This ideal may differ according to the actors of the training and according to the professional field concerned. The notion of quality is based in particular on judgments of fitness for purpose and fitness of purpose in relation to personal expectations and needs. Quality has many aspects related to the places of training and the levels of the ecosystem in which the apprentice operates. If quality is not directly measurable, perceptions of quality are; these perceptions play a major role in learning processes, motivational beliefs and well-being.

2.2. Some empirical evidence about quality in initial vocational education and training

Some studies have indicated the necessity of considering the perceptions of the multiple stakeholders acting at different levels of the educational system, such as apprentices, teachers, in-company trainers, and professional associations (Griffin, 2017; Sappa & Aprea, 2014; Tremblay, 2012). According to these studies, quality is context- and purpose-specific (Griffin, 2017). Other studies conducted in the German IVET dual system—which is largely similar to the Swiss one—attempted to identify what characterized quality (Ebbinghaus et al., 2010; Velten & Schnitzler, 2012). In the study of Ebbinghaus et al. (2010), a large group of apprentices in several occupations was asked to assess a predefined set of quality criteria. The criteria considered the most important by the apprentices were the following: (a) contents, methods, and training environment at the training company (e.g., diversity of the tasks and apprentices' autonomy) and (b) eligibility and behavior of trainers and teachers (e.g., trade-specific and pedagogical skills of trainers, willingness to supervise, recognition of apprentices' work, feedback, etc.). Similarly, Velten and Schnitzler (2012) developed the instrument *Inventar zur betrieblichen Ausbildungsqualität* (IBAQ, Inventory of in-company training quality) to study quality at the training company from the apprentices' perspective. Eight dimensions of quality were stressed: diversity and demand of the work tasks, task importance for the company, autonomy/flexibility, trainer assistance, trainer professional skills, feedback, time overload, good relationship and integration with colleagues. This framework did not consider elements referring to the institutional context in which the IVET occurred or concerning the organization of IVET. Quality was therefore mainly linked to the apprentices' tasks, interpersonal and relational aspects, and the trainers' skills.

In the Swiss context, studies have approached the topic of IVET quality from a macro perspective. For example, some studies have analysed how the IVET's quality can be related to major reforms in the apprenticeship system (Gonon, 2017) or highlighted some success factors of the Swiss IVET dual system (Wettstein, Schmid, & Gonon, 2018). Taking a more micro perspective, Stalder and Carigiet (2014) focused on the quality of Swiss IVET from the apprentices' perspective. Drawing on organizational psychology literature, they identified certain elements that might constitute a framework for the quality of IVET. These elements included the following: (a) education and training conditions, (b) learning possibilities and teachers and trainers skills, (c) education and training satisfaction, (d) premature contract termination and nonlinear training histories, and (e) completion of training. This framework shared some similarities with the quality aspects found in the German literature (Ebbinghaus et al., 2010; Velten & Schnitzler, 2012).

The studies by Sappa and colleagues conducted in the Swiss IVET context focused on the connections between learning sites from different stakeholders' perspectives including apprentices (Sappa & Aprea, 2014; Sappa, Aprea, & Vogt, 2018). Even though the studies did not focus directly on quality, they might indirectly inform regarding conceptions and success factors in fostering the connections between learning sites, which are considered as crucial components of IVET quality (Mulder, Messmann, & König, 2015). Four conceptions, from a superficial to a deeper connection across learning sites, were identified: (a) separate learning experiences, (b) complementary learning experiences, (c) mediation by an intercompany center, (d) school-centered integration (Sappa & Aprea, 2014). Three factors that foster the connections between learning at school and at the workplace were uncovered: (a) collaboration and communication disposals (e.g., teachers' and trainers' experiences across the different sites), (b) curriculum development (e.g., parallelism/alignment between content), and (c) instructional factors (e.g., connected training at the workplace) (Sappa, Aprea, & Vogt, 2018). These conceptions might be reflective of the quality of the connections between learning sites and the factors fostering such connections as diverse levers to act on this aspect of quality.

In the case of apprentices in the retail field (i.e., one of the populations considered in the current study), the quality of social relationships within the training company and with customers appears crucial in helping apprentices face highly demanding working conditions (Duemmler & Caprani, 2017). This brief overview on the literature reveals that a multitude of factors can play a role in the definition of IVET quality.

2.3. Research questions

Based on prior research, three research questions were investigated by this study:

(a) According to apprentices, which elements characterize, both positively and negatively, IVET quality at school and at the training company?
(b) To what extent do the connections between the school and training company play a role in IVET quality?
(c) Do the apprentices' perceptions of quality differ between the two occupational fields considered (i.e., the technical and retail fields)?

3. Methods

3.1. Participants

The participants included 320 apprentices enrolled in a Swiss dual IVET program (M_{age} = 18.70; SD = 3.15; see Tab. 1 for more details). Two occupational fields, each of them in a different school, were considered: technical (e.g., IT technicians and electronic engineers) and retail. Apprentices were spread across different training years: over three years for retail (1st year = 34.8 %; 2nd = 32.6 %; 3rd year = 32.6 %) and over four years in the technical occupations (1st year = 20.7 %; 2nd = 25.5 %; 3rd year = 31.4 %; 4th year = 22.3 %). The company size, as reported by apprentices, varied from small (up to 49 employees, 45 %) to medium (from 50 to 249 employees, 15 %) and large companies (more than 250 employees, 36 %). Four percent of the respondents did not note their company size.

Tab. 1. Sample features.

	Retail	Technical
Number of apprentices	132	188
Mean age	18.65	18.76
% Females	64.1 %	10.5 %
Training year	1st–3rd	1st–4th
% Apprentices who completed compulsory education in a section allowing access to high school[a]	32.1 %	54.8 %
% Apprentices who started or completed another training or school before their apprenticeship[b]	20.4 %	33.5 %

[a] 3 apprentices out of 320 did not answer the question.
[b] 18 apprentices out of 320 did not answer the question.

3.2. Procedure

Participants were invited to complete a questionnaire, including both closed and open-ended questions during 20–30 min of class time. The survey was administered by the research team in ten retail classes and fourteen technical classes. In this study, only the open-ended questions were considered when collecting the apprentices' perceptions of quality of education and training at school and at the training company. More specifically, apprentices were asked to provide, for each of the two learning sites, at least three answers about the following: (a) what they like ("What do you like in your education at school/the training company?") (b) the positive aspects of their training ("What are the positive aspects of your education at school/the training company?"), and (c) the aspects they would like to see improved ("What could be improved in your education at school/the training company?").

The answers to the open-ended questions were transcribed and imported in the Nvivo 11 software for coding. For the data analysis, the answers to the three questions related to the vocational school were analysed separately from the answers to the three questions related to the training company. Moreover, for the coding procedure, no difference was made between the positive and the negative aspects.

In the first stage, the corpus of data was analysed using an inductive approach, which involved not imposing predefined theoretical constructs unto the data but rather allowing the data to reveal new insights and conceptual directions. A list of meaning units—defined as a data segment that contains one idea that is comprehensible when read outside its context (Tesch, 1992)—was generated and it constituted the basis for code generation. Each sentence was used to segment the data into coding units. This segmentation criteria was chosen due to the nature of the data (short, structured sentences). Among all meaning units, thematic similarities were identified in order to identify a preliminary set of codes, one referring to the school and another referring to the training company. The different codes were then discussed within the research team in order to reduce interpretation bias and to establish links with theories in education and psychology. This approach resulted in a preliminary workable coding scheme. In the second stage, the data were analysed both in an inductive manner (keeping in mind the codes found in the previous step) and in a deductive manner (considering the existing theories discussed among the research team; Saldaña, 2013). The coding scheme was refined over several rounds and the overlap between the codes were reduced. Each code was assigned a clear label with a definition, a description that explained when it was likely to occur in the data, inclusion and exclusion criteria, and coding examples, following the example of Saldaña (2013).

Eventually, a total of 3,713 coding units were coded: 1,872 referred to quality at school (using 17 codes) and 1,841, at the training company (using 18 codes). Intercoder agreement based on 5 % of the statements was satisfying (school: Cohen's κ = .782, company: κ = .735), which allowed us to proceed to analysis.

4. Results and discussion

4.1. What characterizes IVET quality according to apprentices

For most of the codes, similar themes reflecting the perceived quality at school and at the training company were found (see the Appendix for the complete list). Inspired by Bronfenbrenner's (1977) *Ecological systems theory*, which distinguishes several nested environmental systems that individuals interact with, all codes were further categorized according to their level in the system: (a) *micro-level* ("learning object") codes, referring to the main activities realized at school (classes) or at the training company (tasks) (e.g., diversity of the classes/tasks); (b) *meso-level* ("social learning environment") codes, referring to the direct or indirect involvement of persons influencing the perceptions of IVET quality (e.g., the pedagogical skills of teachers or trainers); and (c) *exo-level* ("IVET context") codes, referring to the organization of the IVET and the educational programs (i.e., the institutional and decisional levels) (see Fig. 1).

In Fig. 1, the left side of the schema refers to the elements of quality at school, whereas the right side, to the elements of quality at the training company. The majority of elements were found both for the school and for the training company, even if the labels given to the codes sometimes slightly differed (e.g., "Autonomy support" and "Apprentices' autonomy"). Four elements, indicated in italic in the schema, applied only to the training company: skills acquisition, contacts with customers, salary and training management.

Tab. 2 summarizes the most cited aspects related to high and low quality at school and at the training company according to apprentices' perceptions. The elements mentioned constitute approximately 50 % of all codes for each location. *Social relationships* and *links between school and training company* were considered as aspects of high quality both for the school and the training company. A detailed analysis of the links between school and training company follow in the next section. *Time management* and the *pedagogical skills of the teachers and trainers* appeared to reflect both the positive and negative aspects of quality. The pedagogical skills were the most frequently indicated among all the teacher and/or trainer skills[3]: they represented two-third of these codes for the teachers and three-fourths for the trainers. These results confirm the importance, for the apprentices, of their teachers'

---

3 Teachers' and trainers' skills include the following codes: "Pedagogical skills," "Trade-specific skills," "Social skills and intrinsic motivation of teachers and trainers," and "Teachers (not specified)."

and trainers' pedagogical skills and their central place in perceived IVET quality (Stalder & Carigiet, 2014). Hence, a pedagogical preparation of teachers and trainers can be beneficial to assure quality training.

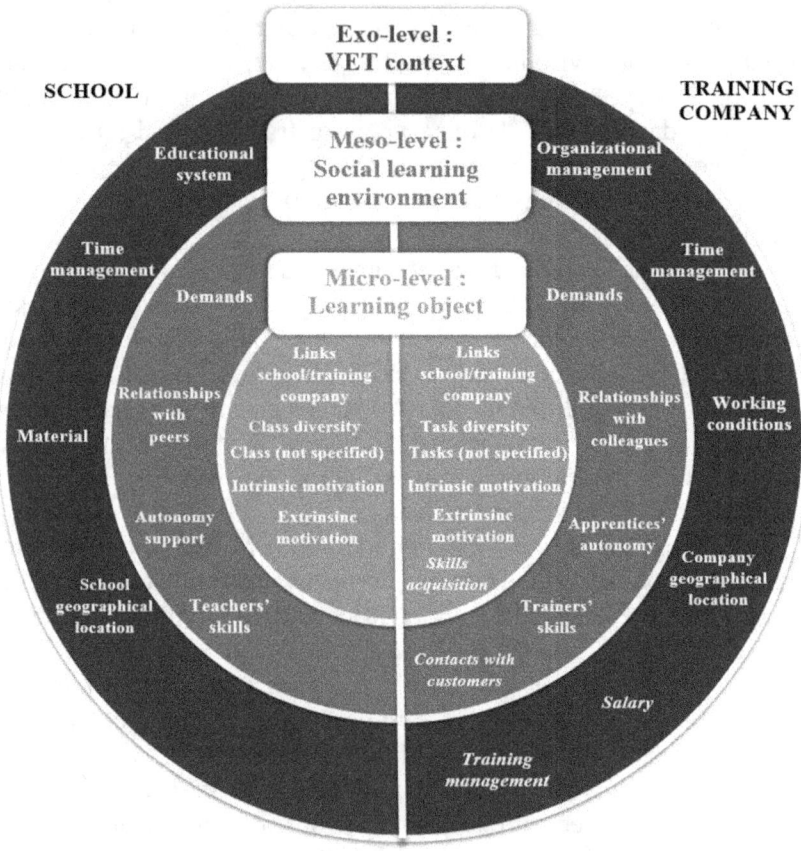

Fig. 1. Elements of quality at school and at the training company according to apprentices.

Teachers' and trainers'skills are composed by the codes "Pedagogical skills," "Trade-specific skills," "Social skills and intrinsic motivation of teachers and trainers," and "Teachers (not specified)."

Tab. 2. Aspects related to high and low quality at school and at the training company according to apprentices' perceptions.

School				Training company			
Code	Example	%	Level	Code	Example	%	Level
Aspects related to high quality							
Intrinsically motivating classes	"The lessons are enjoyable and I like them"	14.3	Micro	Relationships with colleagues	"A very good ambiance with my colleagues"	18.6	Meso
Relationships with peers	"To exchange with classmates and to make new contacts"	12.9	Meso	Pedagogical skills of trainers	"Very well supported by the trainer"	12	Meso
Links between school and training company	"The vocational knowledge classes allow us to better understand what we experience at work"	9.0	Micro	Diversity of the tasks	"The varied work, we do not do the same task all the time"	8.8	Micro
Time management	"The school gives me a break from work"	8.3	Exo	Links between school and training company	"We can practice directly what we learn at school"	7.6	Micro
Class (non specified)	"French, German, Economy classes"	8.0	Micro	Contacts with customers	"To speak with the customers"	6.7	Meso

(*Continued*)

Tab. 2: Continued

School				Training company			
Code	Example	%	Level	Code	Example	%	Level
Aspects related to low quality							
Demands, pressures and sanctions	"Less tests the same day"	14.7	Micro	Pedagogical skills of trainers	"To be supported every day and to receive feedbacks about my improvement"	17.4	Meso
School geographical location	"The school is far for some students"	11.9	Exo	Time management (hours, vacations, leaves)	"The hours: we have to be at work very early, and we finish very late"	14.5	Exo
Educational system	"The number of students in a class is too big"	11.7	Exo	Organizational management and distribution of tasks	"The communication between the shop and the direction"	13.8	Exo
Time management	"The classes finish too late"	10.2	Exo	Training management	"The training company should give more time to do the homework"	10.0	Exo
Pedagogical skills of teachers	"Some teachers should change their teaching methods"	7.2	Meso	-	-	-	

Overall, the most frequently mentioned aspects reflecting high quality referred to the learning object (micro-level) and the social learning environment (meso-level), whereas the codes associated with low quality referred mostly to the IVET context (exo-level). Results concerning the social learning environment echoed the literature relating to the need for relatedness and belonging (Baumeister & Leary, 1995; Ryan & Deci, 2017): Social interactions—in the present case with peers and teachers at school and with colleagues, customers, and trainers at the training company—played a key role in how apprentices experience IVET; notably, such interactions had strong effects on emotions and cognition.

4.2. A focus on the connections between school and training company

Previous studies revealed that the connections between learning sites contributed significantly to the quality of IVET (Ebbinghaus et al., 2010; Mulder et al., 2015; Stalder & Carigiet, 2014). In the current study, apprentices described these connections mainly through their perception of the contents learned at school or at the training company and the perceived links between theory and practice (e.g., "The mix between theory and practice," "Practical courses in adequacy with the company tasks"). In fact, 74 % of the 156 coding units referring to the links between school and training company were positive for the school; 90 % of the 120 coding units were positive for the training company. In other words, for both the school and training company, the statements related more frequently to positive aspects than to aspects to improve.[4] School-related statements about aspects to improve referred mostly to a perceived gap between what is learned at school in relation to what is considered useful for the training company (e.g., "It is not possible to apply at the workplace the knowledge learned at school"). Generally, the apprentices asked for more practice at school (e.g., "To have more practice in the theoretical courses"); in contrast, they rarely

---

4   It should be noted that of the three questions answered by the apprentices, two out of three referred to positive aspects, and one to negative aspects (see Methods section).

asked for more theory or complained about the training at the company. Moreover, the double logic in apprentices' perceptions of connections between the school and training company, as previously observed by Alves et al. (2010) and Gurtner et al. (2012), appeared to be confirmed. The school was seen as responsible for such links and was criticized for lacking connections with the training company. Furthermore, the training company was not questioned in terms of its links with school learning.

Data from the current study revealed that apprentices perceived learning across multiple learning sites as complementary: the school transmitted basic knowledge and skills that would be transferred and applied at the training company (Sappa & Aprea, 2014). Learning at school and at the training company were seen as targeting a common objective, though some discrepancies occurred. A core idea was the apprentices' perceptions of school-taught knowledge being ready for application at their current company: for example, "To increase the number of useful courses (electronics, mathematics, etc.) and to reduce the subjects that are not specific and applicable to the occupation (materials, gym)," "To practice more the theory learned [at school]." Anything else they had to learn, such as general knowledge, was considered of little relevance. Such statements revealed, according to the concept of utility value (the conformity of a task with the future objectives of an individual; Eccles, 2005), a superficial and utilitarian conception of knowledge acquisition. Thus, the focus on what was considered useful for the present and the disregard for potentially useful distant or future knowledge suggested that the apprentices' future time perspective (how far ahead one's thoughts are projected) was rather short. The degree of high utility value attributed by the apprentices is strongly tied to the effort exerted and to their learning strategies (Lens, Simons, & Dewitte, 2001). However, a limited part of the sample highlighted a number of beliefs about what was learned at school: namely, (a) it could not be learned at the training company ("To learn and to look at specific things that could not be seen in the training company"); (b) it differed from what was learned at the training company ("It allows to understand the trade outside of the training company"); (c) it could be useful in private life ("The school allows me to learn things that could be very useful in my professional life but also in my private life"); or (d) it could be useful for the future ("The courses are quite comprehensive, so that we will be able to deal with our future professional life"; utility value).

4.3. Differences between occupational fields

Regarding the third research question, the differences between the occupational fields concerning the education at school were tested using a χ^2 test. The results revealed that aspects such as the *links between theory and practice* ($\chi^2_{(1)} = 12.69$, $p < .01$) and the *material* ($\chi^2_{(1)} = 24.96$, $p < .01$) were more prominent in the perceptions of quality in the technical than in the retail field. For the latter, *contacts with peers* ($\chi^2_{(1)} = 5.75$, $p < .05$) were seen as more important. Concerning the training at the workplace, it was found that the *diversity of the tasks* ($\chi^2_{(1)} = 8.75$, $p < .01$) and the *working conditions* ($\chi^2_{(1)} = 6.83$, $p < .01$) were more important for the technical field, whereas *contact with customers* ($\chi^2_{(1)} = 71.86$, $p < .01$) and *time management* ($\chi^2_{(1)} = 5.30$, $p < .05$) were more central for retail.

The results revealed that there were differences in the apprentices' perceptions of IVET quality according to the occupational field. On the one hand, for technical occupation apprentices, quality was more strongly tied to the tasks, the materials, or the working conditions. The links between theory and practice appeared more relevant to them: compared to retail apprentices, technical apprentices mentioned connections between theory and practice as part of quality twice as frequently in their answers to the school and three times more frequently in their answers to the training company. Similar results were found by Ebbinghaus et al. (2010) with an analogous population: apprentices in IT evaluated the cooperation between learning sites as a negative element to the quality of their IVET. On the other hand, for retail apprentices, quality was more strongly associated to the social aspect, especially in terms of relationships with peers, colleagues, and customers.

These results have been interpreted in light of certain specificities of the apprenticeships and occupations. Technical occupation apprenticeships focus mainly on physical materials. The learning is largely based on manual tasks and technical gestures, which are not easily learned using a handbook. Retail apprentices, compared to technical occupations, have fewer hours of practical class and are more likely to directly educate themselves on the job. This could explain why they report perceiving a lower importance of receiving theoretical and practical connections in their education and training. Furthermore, a key skill in retail is the ability to handle people, as it constitutes the main target of this trade. Previous studies in the field of retail suggested that social relationships could help counterbalance the difficult working conditions, such as irregular working hours and stand-up work (Duemmler, Caprani, & Felder, 2018). Hence, it is not surprising that social interactions take a prominent role in the perception of quality for retail apprentices.

5. Conclusion

While the quality of IVET is a major concern at the political level, little is known concerning what constitutes quality according to its main recipients: the apprentices. This study shed light on the perceptions of IVET quality for technical and retail apprentices. In this regard, some points can be highlighted.

First, high quality, both at school and at the training company, was above all related to the learning object and the social learning environment. Social relationships with classmates, teachers, trainers or colleagues, as well as the perceived skills of teachers and trainers were the main elements that influenced the quality of IVET according to the present study.

Secondly, low quality, was often linked with certain aspects of the IVET context, such as the educational system in force or the organizational management of the training company. It was a matter of external macro factors that were beyond the control of apprentices.

Third, similar elements of quality were indicated between the school and training company; however, their relevance differed according to the learning site. As stated in previous studies (Gurtner et al.,

2012), this result indicates that apprentices experience their training at the vocational school or at the training company differently.

Fourth, differences were observed between the two occupational fields considered: technical occupations and retail. While apprentices from technical occupations appeared to link quality to aspects related to tasks or materials, for retail apprentices, quality was more influenced by social aspects. These differences can probably be explained by the peculiarities of these occupations and the respective apprenticeship.

Given the context of the dual IVET, a focus was put on the links between the vocational school and training company in terms of alignment of theory and practice and the adequacy of contents. These links were associated with the quality of IVET, especially for technical apprentices. What is highlighted is especially the lack of these connections, and the school is usually considered as the main responsible.

In conclusion, the results of the study mirror the complexity and the heterogeneity of the Swiss IVET and the difficulty in defining quality in education found in the literature. Both learning sites and occupational fields play a role in apprentices' perception of what constitutes "good" training, and they should, therefore, be taken into consideration in reflections pertaining to IVET quality. The conclusions of this study constitute a first step in identifying what IVET quality is from the viewpoints of apprentices. The next step will consider other occupational fields and actors to enlarge our understanding of the topic. Moreover, the aspects composing the quality of IVET could be shared with policymakers and potential improvements discussed.

A limitation of the current study lies in the type of data collected and its interpretation: the answers to the open-ended questions were sometimes short and vague, reflecting the difficulty of apprentices in expressing their perceptions in a written format.

Nevertheless, this analysis allowed highlighting the complexity and relatively lack of unanimity on quality in IVET. That is why it is essential "to settle for as explicit and accurate stipulations as possible, since no universal definition is to be had." (Wittek & Kvernbekk, 2011, p.683)

Appendix: Coding scheme of quality aspects

A. Learning site: Vocational school

A.1. Micro-level: Learning
A.1.1. Extrinsically motivating classes
A.1.2. Intrinsically motivating classes
A.1.3. Class diversity
A.1.4. Class (not specified)
A.1.5. Links between school and training company

A.2. Meso-level: Social learning environments
A.2.1. Teacher general pedagogical skills
A.2.2. Teacher structure skills
A.2.3. Teacher occupation-specific skills
A.2.4. Teacher social skills and intrinsic motivation
A.2.5. Autonomy-supportive teaching
A.2.6. Teachers (not specified)
A.2.7. Demands (i.e., expectations, tests, exams)
A.2.8. Relationships with peers and climate

A.3. Exo-level: VET context
A.3.1. Time management
A.3.2. Educational system
A.3.3. School geographical location
A.3.4. Material

B. Learning site: Training company

B.1. Micro-level: Learning
B.1.1. Extrinsically motivating tasks
B.1.2. Intrinsically motivating tasks
B.1.3. Skill acquisition
B.1.4. Tasks diversity
B.1.5. Tasks (not specified)
B.1.6. Links between school and training company

B.2. Meso-level: Social learning environments
B.2.1. Trainer pedagogical skills
B.2.2. Trainer occupation-specific and social skills
B.2.3. Demands
B.2.4. Apprentice's autonomy
B.2.5. Relationships with colleagues and climate
B.2.6. Contact with customers

B.3. Exo-level: VET context
B.3.1. Organizational management
B.3.2. Training management
B.3.3. Time management
B.3.4. Working conditions
B.3.5. Company geographical location
B.3.6. Salary

Biographical note

Florinda Sauli is a junior researcher at Swiss Federal Institute for Vocational Education and Training (SFIVET). Her research interests are perceptions of the training quality by institutional and field actors in the context of Swiss vocational education and training.

Matilde Wenger is a junior researcher at SFIVET. Her research interests are teachers' gender identities; apprentices', teachers', and trainers' perception of training quality; and apprentices' commitment to vocational education and training.

Jean-Louis Berger is a professor at University of Fribourg. His research interests include the perception of training quality and apprentices', teachers', and trainers' beliefs, motivation, and self-regulated learning in the context of vocational education and training.

References

Alves, S., Gosse, B., & Sprimont, P. A. (2010). Les apprentis de l'enseignement supérieur : de la satisfaction à l'engagement ? [Apprentices in higher education: From satisfaction to commitment?] *Management Avenir*, (3), 35–51.

Baumeister, R. F., & Leary, M. R. (1995). The need to belong: Desire for interpersonal attachments as a fundamental human motivation. *Psychological Bulletin, 117*(3), 497.

Behrens, M. (2007). Introduction. In M. Behrens (Ed.), *La Qualité en éducation. Pour réfléchir à la formation de demain. [Quality in education. To think about tomorrow's training.]* (pp. 3–19). Québec : Presses de l'Université du Québec.

Bouchard, C., & Plante, J. (2002). La qualité: mieux la définir pour mieux la mesurer. [Quality: Better define it to better measure it.] *Les Cahiers du Service de pédagogie expérimentale, 11, 12*, 219–236.

Bronfenbrenner, U. (1977). Toward an experimental ecology of human development. *American Psychologist*, *32*(7), 513–531.

Duemmler, K., & Caprani, I. (2017). Identity strategies in light of a low-prestige occupation: The case of retail apprentices. *Journal of Education and Work*, *30*(4), 339–352.

Duemmler, K., Felder, A., & Caprani, I. (2018). Ambivalent occupational identities under modern workplace demands: The case of Swiss retail apprentices. *Journal of Vocational Education & Training*, *70*(2), 278–296.

Ebbinghaus, M., Krewerth, A., Bönisch, I., Beicht, U., Flemming, S., Eberhard, V., Granato, M., ... & Gei, J. (2010). BIBB-Forschungsverbund zur Ausbildungsqualität in Deutschland. *Bonn*. Retrieved from https://www2. bibb. de/bibbtools/tools/dapro/data/documents/pdf/eb_22202. pdf.

European Quality Assurance in Vocational Education and Training (= EQAVET; 2019). Retrieved from: https:// www.eqavet.eu/ .

Federal Act on Vocational and Professional Education and Training of 13 December 2002 (= VPETA; CC 412.10). Retrieved from https://www.admin.ch/opc/en/classified-compilation/20001860/201901010000/412.10.pdf

Gates Foundation. (2013). *Have we identified effective teachers? Validating measures of effective teaching using random assignment MET Project: Research Paper*. Seattle, WA: Bill and Melinda Gates Foundation.

Gonon, P. (2017). Quality doubts as a driver for Vocational Education and Training (VET) reforms – Switzerland's way to a highly regarded apprenticeship system. In M. Pilz (Ed.), *Vocational education and training in times of economic crisis* (pp. 341–354). New York: Springer.

Griffin, T. (2017). *Are we all speaking the same language? Understanding 'quality' in the VET sector*. Adelaide: National Centre for Vocational Education Research. Retrieved from https://files.eric.ed.gov/fulltext/ED579516.pdf

Gurtner, J.-L., Furlan, N., & Cattaneo, A. (2018). L'articulation des connaissances n'est pas la tâche des seul·e·s apprenti·e·s. [The articulation of knowledge is not the task of apprentices only] In L. Bonoli,

J.-L. Berger, & N. Lamamra (Eds.), *Enjeux de la formation professionnelle. Le « modèle » suisse sous la loupe* [*Vocational training issues. The Swiss "model" under the microscope*] (pp. 253–266). Zürich : Seismo (Collection Recherche en formation professionnelle).

Gurtner, J.-L., Gulfi, A., Genoud, P. A., de Rocha Trindade, B., & Schumacher, J. (2012). Learning in multiple contexts: Are there intra-, cross- and transcontextual effects on the learner's motivation and help seeking? *European Journal of Psychology of Education, 27*(2), 213–225.

Krapp, A., & Lewalter, D. (2001). Development of interests and interest-based motivational orientations: A longitudinal study in vocational school and workplace settings. In S. Volet & S. Järvelä (Eds.), *Motivation in learning contexts: Theoretical advances and methodological implications* (pp. 209–232). Amsterdam: Pergamon.

Lens, W., Simons, J., & Dewitte, S. (2001). Student motivation and self-regulation as a function of future time perspective and perceived instrumentality. In S. Volet & S. Järvelä (Eds.), *Advances in learning and instruction series. Motivation in learning contexts: Theoretical advances and methodological implications* (pp. 233–248). Oxford: Pergamon Press.

Moreland, N., & Clark, M. (1998). Quality and ISO 9000 in educational organizations. *Total Quality Management, 9*(2/3), 311–320.

Mulder, R. H., Messmann, G., & Koenig, C. (2015). Vocational education and training: Researching the relationship between school and work. *European Journal of Education, 50*(4), 497–512.

Prenzel, M., & Drechsel, B. (1996). Ein Jahr kaufmännische Erstausbildung: Veränderungen in Lernmotivation und Interesse [One year of initial commercial training: Changes in learning motivation and interest]. *Unterrichtswissenschaft, 24*, 217–234.

Ryan, R. M., & Deci, E. L. (2017). *Self-determination theory: Basic psychological needs in motivation, development, and wellness.* New York: Guilford Press.

Saldaña, J. (2013). *The coding manual for qualitative researchers.* Thousand Oaks, CA: Sage.

Sappa, V., & Aprea, C. (2014). Conceptions of connectivity: How Swiss teachers, trainers and apprentices perceive vocational learning and teaching across different learning sites. *Vocation and Learning*, *7*(3), 263–287. http://dx.doi.org/10.1007/s12186-014-9115-y

Sappa, V., Aprea, C., & Vogt, B. (2018). Success factors for fostering the connection between learning in school and at the workplace: The voice of Swiss VET actors. In S. Choy, G. B. Wärvik, & V. Lindberg (Eds.), *Integration of vocational education and training experiences. Purposes, practices and principles* (pp. 303–325). Singapore: Springer.

SERI. (n.d.). *Mission statement for vocational and professional education and training 2030*. Retrieved from https://formationprofessionnelle2030.ch/images/_pdf_de_en/vision2030e.pdf

Stake, R. E., & Schwandt, T. A. (2006). On discerning quality in evaluation. *The Sage handbook of evaluation* (pp. 404–418).

Stalder, B. E., & Carigiet, T. (2014). Ausbildungsqualität aus Sicht von Lernenden und Betrieben in der Schweiz. [Quality of training from the point of view of learners and companies in Switzerland.] *Qualität in der Berufsbildung. Anspruch und Wirklichkeit. Bericht zur beruflichen Bildung*, 97–118.

Swiss Federal Statistical Office. (2017). *Choix de formation au degré secondaire II*. [Choice of education at secondary level II.] Retrieved from https://www.bfs.admin.ch/bfs/fr/home/statistiques/catalogues-banques-donnees/graphiques.assetdetail.8906542.html

Tesch, R. (1992). The mechanics of interpretational qualitative analysis. In *Qualitative research analysis types and software tools*. Basingstoke: The Falmer Press.

Tremblay, P. (2012). L'évaluation de la qualité de dispositifs scolaires: développement d'une approche multidimensionnelle et bidirectionnelle. [Assessing the quality of school systems: Developing a multidimensional and bidirectional approach.] *Mesure et évaluation en éducation*, *35*(2), 39–68.

Tynjälä, P. (2008). Perspectives into learning at the workplace. *Educational Research Review*, *3*, 130–154.

Velten, S., & Schnitzler, A. (2012). Inventar zur betrieblichen Ausbildungsqualität (IBAQ). [Inventory for in-company training quality] *Zeitschrift für Berufs-und Wirtschaftspädagogik, 108*(4), 511–527.

Wettstein, E., Schmid, E., & Gonon, P. (2018). *La formation professionnelle en Suisse: formes, structures, protagonistes. [Vocational education and training in Switzerland: Forms, structures, protagonists.]* Le Mont-sur-Lausanne : Éditions Loisirs et Pédagogie SA.

Wittek, L., & Kvernbekk, T. (2011). On the problems of asking for a definition of quality in education. *Scandinavian Journal of Educational Research, 55*(6), 671–684.

STEFAN KESSLER & PHILIPP GONON

The disruptive potential of digitalization and the current Swiss VET landscape[1]

Abstract: Digitalization is regarded as having an extensive impact on the world of work and hence, affects vocational education and training (VET). This exploratory paper seeks to discuss the disruptive potential of digitalization in the current Swiss VET context on three levels: debates and concerns, politics and practices. Firstly, topical concerns regarding the future of work and the performance of VET as a training model are discussed. Secondly, the paper argues that the level of educational practice is a promising field of study in assessing the disruptive potential of digitalization, especially in dual training systems. The examples provided in this paper show that VET providers (both schools and firms) take different courses of action with respect to digitalization. They also demonstrate that the outcomes of digitalization for educational practice vary according to training needs and occupational requirements. Thirdly, digitalization emerges to a focal point in the present political agenda. Besides the promises and premises of a fundamentally changing VET landscape, digitalization primarily takes place as a gradual process of change.

Keywords: digitalization, disruption, innovation, gradual change, Swiss vocational education and training

1 Introduction

Technological changes have always shaped educational realities and learning cultures (Messerschmidt & Grebe, 2005). Over the last few decades, digital technologies have been used for information and

---

[1] This is a revised and extended version of a paper that has been published in an earlier version in the proceedings of the 3rd Crossing Boundaries in VET conference (cf. Gonon & Kessler, 2019).

communication purposes, as well as designated tools for developing skills across all educational levels (ibid.). We can state retrospectively, that this did not often mean a fundamental redefinition of existing—or 'traditional'—forms of teaching and learning, or of the relevant educational environments: On the one hand, new educational technologies had to be integrated into existing educational contexts (e.g., as 'tools'). Their potential had to be tested and evaluated in the various fields of educational practice. On the other hand, such technologies have always emerged in circumstances not necessarily related to education and training. Therefore, in the first instance, they were often not designed for educational purposes and were instead subject to other rationalities.

Since the first personal computers hit the classrooms in the 1980s and 1990s, advocates of the implementation of digital technologies in education and training refer to the economic and social changes, resulting from the dissemination of technical innovations in the world of work and the widespread use of digital technologies in everyday life. In this view, educational providers, together with educational policy stakeholders, are expected to reflect upon these changes and perhaps modify the current state of educational practice. The prospects of innovating educational practice by means of digital technology (e.g., Euler, Seufert, & Wilbers, 2006) have, furthermore, led to continued efforts to seek new ways of providing more effective, efficient and relevant education and training. While the general body of arguments has not changed much over the years (Cuban, 2001; Hawkridge, 1990), digital technologies have gained acceptance for practical and organizational use in an educational context—even if there have been iterations of trial and rejection.

In recent years, the topic of 'digitalization' has been at the forefront of increased discussion regarding aspects of usage and overarching economic and social developments that could reverberate within the education system. Competing scenarios each offer compelling interpretations of how digitalization might affect work and education in the (near) future, thus leaving educational policy with the problem of anticipating change (Lassnigg & Bock Schappelwein, 2019). While the notion of digitalization hints at the fact that our daily lives, our work and the field of education are under permanent and increased intensity of digital data use and data-based connectivity, this still leaves much room for interpretation and thus for debate. The seemingly rapid change and the socio-economic upheaval associated with the digitalization of the world of work, encourage a great sense of urgency in the public debate regarding this issue. Digitalization is often characterized as having 'disruptive' effects on the labor market. As much as the potentiality of such occurrences is given, the direct nexus to digitalization is complicated, if we think of digitalization not as a single technology but as a multitude of technologies (Degryse, 2016) or—from a sociological perspective—as technologies 'under the surface' that are only revealed to us as black boxes (Nassehi, 2019). Yet we encounter a common view that digitalization, to a certain extent, has an impact on the labor market and thus may pose fundamental questions for a *vocational* education and training (VET) system, such as that in Switzerland. The question of how digitalization will affect the economy and society is thus linked to the question of whether the underlying qualification model, and in this case VET, remains a valid concept.

In Switzerland, the debate focuses on dual VET, due to its systemic link to the labor market, its clear acceptance among Swiss companies and because VET is the pathway chosen most often in the education system at upper-secondary level. Although digitalization is not seen as an immediate threat to the 'dual system' of VET (Aepli et al., 2017; Arvanitis, Grote, Spescha, Wäfler & Wörter, 2017), questions arise concerning the performance of this particular training model in the digital age. Taking this as a starting point, the aim of this paper is to discuss the disruptive potential of digitalization in the Swiss VET context on three different levels: How far does digitalization potentially disrupt VET as a *training model*, as well as *practices* related to vocational education? And how do VET *stakeholders* see the future of VET in the light of digitalization? We adapt the term 'disruption' from economic theory, understood broadly as a process, in which established concepts, structures and practices are being replaced by others which are either new or perform in a different way. However, with regard to 'disruptive potential,' we do not argue that digitalization is changing the economic, cultural or political preconditions *per se*. Neither do we intend to gather evidence for presenting digitalization as a disruptive technology in support of the above. Rather, we think of 'disruption' not only as an eventuality regarding the functionality of a vocationally oriented training model but also in respect of bottom-up activities from VET providers, adapting to digitalization and further developing their training model to accommodate their needs. By drawing on the concept of 'disruption,' we therefore, focus on the dynamics of digitalization that challenge the aspect of 'vocational' in dual VET and potentially transform educational practices.

Having established our argument conceptually, we will first outline current discussions regarding the impact of digitalization on VET, asking in which way the concept of dual VET is potentially challenged (Section 2). Then, we will shift our focus to the practical level, asking how providers of VET react to digitalization (Section 3). We will discuss a few examples that demonstrate different viewpoints and outcomes of the digitalization of educational practices. We will complement these two perspectives on 'disruption' with a discussion of how Swiss VET stakeholders see the future of VET in the light of digitalization (Section 4). Finally, we will discuss the potential for digitalization to disrupt VET (Section 5).

2 Topical concerns: How disruptive is digitalization for VET?

Fundamental changes regarding digitalization are often discussed in the current debate. With regard to the economy, as well as society in general, it is sometimes argued that these changes are disruptive. However, the meaning of 'disruption' in this particular debate often remains implicit and vague, as does the extent to which digitalization could change our work and social life or—regarding our subject—vocational education and training.

2.1. Disruption revisited: A conceptual approach

Topically, we can identify three perspectives regarding disruption: a classical economic approach, a technological view and a third, more utopian/dystopian outlook for the future. In Schumpeter's theory of economic development, the entrepreneur as an innovator and proactive individual, who creates a new product, plays an important role regarding change (Schumpeter, 2006). Economic development is seen as a continuous process of destruction and creation, as economic actors (i.e., the entrepreneur) actively seek to establish themselves and/or maintain their position in the market, while constantly facing the dilemma between breaking new ground and sticking to the tried and tested (Böhme, 2017). Hence, 'disruption' is seen as a natural and necessary accompaniment to any kind of economic progress.

This perspective has also been transferred to and expanded with regard to new technologies. Within the economic theories of technological innovation (e.g., Bower & Christensen, 1995; Christensen, 1997; Foster, 1986), 'disruption' marks a moment of discontinuity within a given economic or social process. For example, if in a given market, the dominant technology abruptly changes due to the entry of a new technology in that market, both the expertise and the scale that companies have built up in relation to that dominant technology, may quickly become obsolete (Fox, 2014). That is to say, established firms can rapidly lose their competitive advantage due to newcomers entering a market which make use of technological innovations or pursue new business models. Here, Bower and Christensen (1995, p. 45) distinguish between *disruptive* technologies and *sustaining* technologies. The latter are technologies used by firms that aim to improve the performance of an existing technology incrementally, in order to meet a growing market demand. Disruptive technologies, by contrast, introduce a *new quality* to the performance of a given product or process which, historically, was highly valued. The two have different performance trajectories, meaning that disruptive technologies might perform far worse in one or two important dimensions at first. Innovations are often faced with quality concerns at an early stage of their development. However, they eventually prevail and outperform existing technologies by offering distinctive alternatives and subsequently, a better performance below the line (Christensen, Raynor, & McDonald, 2015).[2]

---

2 The mass-dissemination of mobile Internet is such an example. Mobile Internet, at first, had very slow connection speeds, was expensive and was restricted to

The dynamics underlying the introduction of a potential disruptive technology into a social system implies, that the innovative nature of this technology might be the single most important factor for successful adaption and likewise, an incentive for actors to compete and succeed in this field. However, the historical context and the existing economic, political and cultural relations play an equally important role in determining whether a new technological concept succeeds in the long run.

A third viewpoint, on which we will not elaborate further here, goes beyond the economy and the advantages of new technologies for competitive capacity. The 'spirit of digital capitalism' (Nachtwey & Seidl, 2017) favors a takeover of human creative power by machines and algorithms and thus leads to a 'solutionist' society, which in the view of the adherents of this perspective, also includes a 'better world.' Herein lies the disruptive moment of digitalization that transcends societies and mankind (ibid.).

Transferring the concept of disruption to the context of education and training is interesting for two reasons: Firstly, as it leads us to consider qualitative changes or a change *in kind*, regarding an established concept or form of education. Secondly, 'disruption' encourages us to question more specifically the motives of actors that strive for a digital future and, therefore, adopt a social perspective on digitalization rather than a perspective of technological determinism. Here lies the potential to broaden our understanding of 'digitalization' from a merely technological subject to a general process of social transformation, that includes the renegotiation of present concepts and practices. We therefore understand 'disruption' not solely as 'made by technology,' but more broadly as a change in the quality of a given concept, process or practice. Thus, when considering the disruptive potential of digitalization in the field of dual VET in Switzerland, the following questions could be examined: Which developments in the world of work could potentially challenge the concept of VET given its current performance? Which actors bring new ideas to teaching and learning that have the potential to 'disrupt' present practices? And in which way is this reflected from the perspective of education policy stakeholders?

---

certain applications (recall: WAP). Today, 40 % of all Internet websites in Switzerland are accessed via mobile devices (Statista, 2019).

2.2. The Swiss dual apprenticeship model and digitalization

At present, exponents of the international debate claim that the impact of digitalization on the world of work '[...] has arguably been more disruptive than anything seen in the past' (Frey & Osborne, 2015, p. 7). In a recent publication, Frey (2019) argues, not surprisingly, that besides simply focusing on short-term effects, having a good education is a valuable asset alongside technological changes. Other authors, like Shoshana Zuboff (2018) or Paul Mason (2019) address broader issues, such as how the potential and increasingly used surveillance of individual workers and citizens can be restricted, or how being human can continue to be possible with the development of smarter machines—issues that extend beyond our focus in this paper.

Nevertheless, digitalization is generally regarded as permanently altering economic structures, as well as social and cultural relations. This image is supported by stories of 'big-bang disruptions' (Downes & Nunes, 2013) that potentially change conditions in the labor market, along with the demand for specific qualifications. A distinct feature of this *digitalization as disruption* narrative is its rather short-term horizon, that expresses a sense of urgency—also in evidence in the field of education and training. Thus, reflecting on our initial considerations, this prompts questions regarding the performance and legitimacy of any VET system. The following key functional attributes to be considered are (1) establishing a highly skilled and flexible workforce which thrives in the digital economy, (2) equipping apprentices with the 'right' skills for jobs which are in demand and hence (3) mastering the transition from 'old' to 'new' skills by providing relevant learning opportunities.

How far VET is affected, is of primary interest, since in Switzerland, VET is regarded as a key driver of the economy and is strongly influenced by associations, firms and state actors. Digitalization might not only affect the content or methods of training but might also encourage a redefinition of what is conceived as the vocational (Avis, 2018). For a dual VET system that is essentially defined by its occupations as an institutionalized form of entry into the labor market (similar to Germany and Austria, e.g., Schlögl, 2019), this may impose fundamental challenges.

At first glance, the term disruption does not play a role in the Swiss case. The economy has been thriving until now and thus, the prospects of digitalization in discussion today, seem to be more promising than alarming. The labor market is quite stable, or even growing with respect to overall employment (Degen & Jud Huwiler, 2018) and the share of unqualified work seems to be declining in importance (Oesch, 2016). On the other hand, a steady change in the digitalization of the Swiss economy is continuing, as stated in a discussion paper of Avenir Suisse (see Adler & Salvi, 2017), a liberal think tank focused on Switzerland's economic and societal future.

Moreover, the dual training model has been proven to be a remarkably stable, yet flexible concept in upholding an equilibrium of skills between the output of the education system and the demands of the labor market (Kraus, 2009). Besides the growing importance of higher education, VET qualifications are still high in demand in many occupational sectors, therefore, firms keep investing in apprenticeships. This might be, because vocational qualifications essentially represent the achievement of a level of skill, not only for application in a particular work context but also in a variety of work situations (Gonon, 2002). Traditionally, dual VET in Switzerland is orientated towards employment at a medium qualification level and is structured around particular occupations. In the development of new occupational profiles, professional associations play a key role. While bigger associations are active participants in current debates about the digitalization of VET (e.g., in the industrial, commercial and health sector), smaller associations have much fewer resources and a limited sphere of operation, often supporting the interests of just one or a few occupations. Concerns in terms of quality with regard to this functioning of VET have long been present and have repeatedly led to changes in perceptions of vocational education and training (Gonon, 2017). Interestingly, this has not yet led to fragmentation but rather to a consolidation of the general idea of 'vocational' as a major reference point for VET.

It is clear, however, that due to its close links with the world of work (i.e. its labor market orientation), the concept of VET is susceptible to change in the occupational landscape. This is evident in the shift towards a service and knowledge economy which encourages work that has an ICT focus. The industrial sector is also undergoing changes that promote shifts in its occupational structure (Zenhäusern & Vaterlaus, 2017). While job automation and the computerization of work tasks have become a reality in many occupational fields, these trends have recently led to up-skilling rather than a reduction of the number of jobs in the middle sector of the employment market (Oesch, 2016). Thus, quantitative shifts of the workforce, based on job automation, global competition and technological innovation are certainly important, but this does not mean that VET becomes immediately less important. However, it is important to note that the conclusions drawn from such developments cannot be applied to an entire training system, but must take sectoral, occupational and even regional differences and characteristics into account, as Buch, Dengler and Matthes (2016) have, for example, shown in the case of Germany.

Perhaps more foreseeable are the qualitative changes *within* occupations that lead to a convergence of competencies. The importance of general and academic skills, such as communicative, interactive, analytical and technology-complimentary non-routine skills is increasing across various occupational sectors (e.g., Aepliet et al., 2017; Schweri & Iten, 2018). Therefore, the concept of the 'vocational' (i.e., the occupational structure of apprenticeships) that historically has divided, yet simultaneously consolidated the occupational landscape in Switzerland, is becoming more even across occupations. The occupations are possibly confined to particular areas, where the skills are linked to specialist knowledge and to the practical use of information and technology. However, the inclination that VET programs gradually become more knowledge-intensive or share similar sets of academic skills, does not automatically encourage a trend of fewer training programs. Over the last decade, the number of VET programs at the upper-secondary level has remained constant, at approximately 230. A recent analysis of VET ordinances shows further differentiation within the programs through specialization (Trede & Lüthi 2018). Nevertheless, this further differentiation once again raises the question of fragmentation versus consolidation in the future. The question therefore remains whether the change will be disruptive, for example in such a way that occupations will fall into specialized study fields or develop into 'core occupations,' or rather will result in regular updating of teaching and learning objectives.

3 How Swiss VET providers react to digitalization: Selected examples

A focal point in current discussions is the question of the 'right' form of training. Historically, paradigmatic disputes about learning and instruction have not led to clear solutions regarding how best to prepare learners for their later working lives (Messerschmidt & Grebe, 2005). Neither has VET been particularly open to incorporating more general skills, due to its firm-oriented way of implementation (even though this might not be the case for larger training companies and training associations that often regard VET as a long-term investment in qualified and flexible workers).

Changing the perspective to a bottom up approach, we can observe that VET providers take different actions when dealing with digitalization. These range from technology-enhanced in-house and classroom training to distance learning models, through to the reorganization of teaching and learning—showing a plurality of forms and extending the attributes of the classic 'dual model.' Thus, one can ask, to what extent does digitalization disrupt VET from a practical, educational perspective. We will now discuss a number of cases to illustrate how innovations occur in the dual VET system. By selecting these cases we have tried to capture a range of different movements at a practical level. The selection is based on the identification of the key motives behind the outlook of VET providers with regard to digitalization, that address a broad array of issues on a continuum between the workplace and vocational learning. Therefore, we have not made an in-depth presentation of the cases but understand them as patterns, to discuss how digitalization, both intentionally and as a side effect, acts as a driver for change in educational practice. Each case indicates a change in the previous state of practice. The first three cases (Sections 3.1, 3.2, and 3.3) come from different sectors and were chosen as a result of identification of a potential 'disruptive' practice using digital technologies; the other two cases (Sections 3.4 and 3.5) are examples, in which digitalization attempts to strengthen the existing concept of VET, but could give rise to unexpected and probably disruptive consequences.

The methodology of this approach is both explorative and descriptive with regard to analysis of documents such as policy papers, statements and reports about practices, focusing on how the wording and content relating to digitalization is used and discussed.

3.1. Industry: Extending the classroom-space across national borders

An internationally renowned firm, operating worldwide and based in the Eastern part of Switzerland has developed a key partnership with the local VET school. Teachers and apprentices are willing and able to combine learning in school with that of the workplace. Since some apprentices travel to the US or China for short-term study periods, the idea of a 'flipped' classroom emerged. The learners meet for lessons, which include videoconferences with overseas colleagues. The content is discussed in parallel and extended further as a result of questions by the teacher or other students. The key motive is the integration of digital technologies as a means of promoting greater interaction and reflection in an otherwise more restricted educational space.

These close links established between classroom and firm promotes collaboration between learning practices in the workplace and those in school. Time management is key and requires organization and coordination in different time zones. Thus, the objectives and lesson content and the discussion topics in interactive sessions, must be clearly defined, also encompassing the experiences of the apprentices overseas. The role of the teacher in organizing such learning settings is also a new challenge. This means adapting learning tasks to specific time slots, when all participants are either virtually available or are present in the local classroom. This form of collaboration is also different from everyday classroom communication, including teacher feedback.

3.2. Informatics: Computer and information specialists to drive digitalization in industry and services

In informatics, teaching and learning the concept of more flexibility is a popular focus. This also applies to the training concept in a Bernese

VET school. Apprentices are encouraged to work on their study modules at school, when these coincide with their current tasks in the company. Presence in the classroom is also reduced and training programs are offered as distant learning modules, following an initial assessment phase of each module. Many tasks are aimed at meeting growing market demands. The multiplicity of tasks, new problems to solve and the personalization of learning enable students to find quick answers and solutions to practical problems, the aim being to make them more employable. One of the key motives is to develop the potential of digitalization for learning and work (Fleischmann, 2017).

This new arrangement of the curriculum allows the apprentices more space for self-organized learning. However, the apprentices are given more responsibility to cover all relevant aspects themselves, to extend their own knowledge and skills. Thus, the instructor and teacher must gain more detailed knowledge about the learners' abilities, as well as potential errors they may make. Their role as supervisors of the learning process becomes more important.

3.3. Banking: Digital and analogue practices in a paperless learning environment

The use of a tablet as a mobile consultation tool reflects the transformation of the contemporary workplace in Swiss banks. Cross-company training courses have been made paperless, designed to adapt the learning and communication of the learners. Learners should become acquainted with the new technology and discover the learning opportunities of the mobile device. The key motive behind this changeover is the anticipated need for new qualifications in the field of learning, communication and organization at work.

The primary role of a tablet in this learning environment is to enable the apprentices to transfer specific branch knowledge and digital skills to another context and vice versa. They are encouraged to use the same or similar device also in the workplace. Thus, new opportunities for individual learning are realized. On the other hand, the paperless approach changes the established practices of teaching and learning; learners especially, struggle initially to balance digital and analogue learning practices (Kessler, 2016). For example, for many students and teachers, short texts are easier to work with on a tablet, than longer explanatory papers or more complex content. Thus, not all learners wish to eliminate the use of books and paperwork, although some see the new mode of interaction with the training content as a way of expanding their learning strategies.

3.4. School and workplace: Digital tools for cooperation and transition programs

Digital infrastructures also offer new opportunities for cooperation between teachers and instructors, firms and schools. Such opportunities facilitate and establish opportunities for contact and communication. Literature has always criticized a lack of cooperation in terms of the so-called dual system, which does not systematically link learning at the different learning sites. As Navaratnarajah (2019) shows, this is because workplace learning and school-based learning have different rationalities and the actors involved do not necessarily work together for the same interests.

Thus, a project for improved cooperation has been launched in some cantons of German-speaking Switzerland, which also includes access for apprentices in some of the newer applications. However, the establishment of an online platform did not change existing practices a great deal as Peter (2014) showed in his evaluative study. Teaching and contact between branches, firms and professions, where traditionally, collaboration was less in evidence, have never been as well-established. Existing practices have simply been reinforced by this new tool. The hope, expressed in other studies, about increasing qualitative cooperation through digitalization, is thus rather dampened (for an overview see Linton, 2018).

Another area concerns the *Stellwerk* test, a kind of digital-based 'signal box,' operating in several cantons and ultimately focusing on the suitability of future learners for companies. This tool offers learners an opportunity to self-assess in certain subjects, such as language, mathematics and other disciplines. It is constructed as an adaptive test, meaning that it adapts to the individual prerequisites of the learners and they can improve their scores by taking the test several times. In some cantons, the *Stellwerk* became mandatory for all pupils at the end of the lower-secondary level. Firms are also interested in knowing the results and the level of the learners as shown in the test. They urge applicants to include the test results in their application portfolio, in order to select youngsters for apprenticeships (Goetze, Denzler, & Wissler, 2009).

However, in both selected cases, it is apparent, that the newly introduced digital infrastructure is not solving the systemic tensions between work and school. Once established, these tools remain, reinforcing existing practices and gradually adapting to new circumstances.

3.5. Daily business: Digital devices in school and workplace

One aspect already mentioned in the third example is the increasing presence of digital devices in VET, which is closely linked to the digital infrastructure. Digital devices can be relevant tools for working and learning, including handheld computers, laptops and desktop computers. They can also be regarded as part of a wider digital infrastructure that connects the various devices. Such infrastructures are not necessarily visible—or obvious—to the teachers, trainers and learners involved, unless a system stops working or breaks down. Accordingly, workplace learning may increasingly be considered as digital workplace learning (Ifenthaler, 2018), as it includes the daily problem-solving competencies in relation to the use of digital infrastructures, which are often overlooked. The introduction of new (visible) work tools or systems for learning in VET also requires learners and trainers to develop new and specific skills. For example, in the case of banking, more and more tablet computers are being introduced as consultation tools. Therefore, apprentices, as future workers, are expected to learn to work with digital data and information and to advise customers with the aid of digital devices. The apprentices need to accept that information, in the context of customer advice, is constantly changing and they must demonstrate flexibility in order to adapt to the new circumstances of a working environment, which is becoming more and more digitalized (Kessler, 2020).

The disruptive potential of digitalization

Within firms but also in VET schools, workers and apprentices have access to the Internet and to web-based information and platforms, often through their own devices. Today, nearly all apprentices are owners of a smartphone or even several devices, including tablets and laptops. In the field of VET, some new textbooks and learning materials for professional work, as well as new technological applications only exist as a digital program. Therefore, the sometimes unspoken but often clear expectation to casually rely on one's own devices has increased in the last few years. Whereas the use of mobile phones was previously regarded as disrupting classroom work, youngsters nowadays are encouraged to use their personal devices as a resource for improving the quality of their work and learning. However, teachers and trainers complain about an excessive use of these devices if social media is accessed, rather than the proposed websites and platforms (e.g., Gutmann, 2019).

During the last two years, many cantons have developed new media concepts. In the Canton of Berne, recommendations for the introduction of BYOD ('Bring your own device') in VET as well as in schools at upper-secondary level have been discussed in detail, including a roadmap for skills, upgrading of teaching methods and organizational measures together with technical support structures, which have led to the establishment of a Standing Commission (ED Berne, 2018). In Basel, a BYOD guide for learners has been developed (ED Basel, 2019). The justification for introducing BYOD or similar concepts over 'one device per learner' initiatives is clear in terms of keeping pace with new affordances, enhancing teaching and promoting the personal responsibility of learners (Sigrist & Strasser, 2018). One of the topics regularly debated is the issue of supporting the purchase of digital devices. In some schools, tablets or laptops are part of the infrastructure, in others only recommendations for suitable devices exist or suggestions for employers about how to support apprentices with their learning (BD St. Gallen, 2019). Recent developments indicate, that for most youngsters, the smartphone is an indispensable and multifunctional instrument that is 'always there with you' and often combines fun and seriousness at the same time, in the same place. Most of them view the smartphone positively, as a means of maintaining (permanent) contact with other persons, rather than contemplating the risks associated with using apps

(Heeg, Genner, Steiner, Schmid, Suter, & Süss, 2018). Schiefner-Rohs, Heinen and Kerres (2013) concede that these new projects and attitudes will affect school-development in the long run.

4 How Swiss policy-stakeholders talk about the future of VET and digitalization

As presented in Chapter 2, digitalization is a topic, which, in recent times, has evoked a range of studies and position papers in the field of social sciences and also in politics, delivered by think tanks, experts and stakeholders. The Swiss government has also recently updated its 'Digital Switzerland' strategy, following the publication of a first version in 2016 (Schweizerische Eidgenossenschaft, 2018). Education is also explicitly addressed as part of this strategy:

> *"For Switzerland to remain among the leading countries in terms of the development and use of digital technologies, it has to promote the necessary skills—in the sense of lifelong learning—at all levels and in all areas. In addition, in order to achieve the goal of equal opportunities and the participation of all inhabitants in the opportunities of digitalisation, it is important to promote basic skills in the use of the new technologies. Participants in the education system have already undertaken major developments in the context of digitalisation and are starting out from an excellent position. It will be crucial to continue along this path with no undue delay." (ibid., p. 12).*

This document highlights the strengths of a diversified Swiss education system, with its equivalent vocational and general education offerings, which is characterized as one of the most important prerequisites for this transformation. However, in order to empower people, the necessary digital and transversal competencies need to be taught more effectively (ibid. 13). These direct reflections with regard to a digital future are part of a discourse, which is also in evidence in the field of VET. Since the initial version of the 'Digital Switzerland' strategy, the Swiss Federal Council has provided two reports on the framework conditions for a digital economy and on the impact of digitalization on employment

The disruptive potential of digitalization 121

and working conditions (Schweizerischer Bundesrat, 2017a, 2017b). Another report was commissioned to the Swiss State Secretariat for Education, Research and Innovation (SERI) to further elaborate on the challenges of digitalization for education (SBFI, 2017). Some of these reports have been criticized as they all start with the premise of an already well-prepared education system (e.g., Ragni, 2018).

The cantons, traditionally responsible for education matters, also launched a common digitalization strategy (EDK, 2018). In order to provide pupils and apprentices with the necessary skills for dealing with digitalization, schools with VET should be equipped with digital infrastructures and with teachers, well trained in this domain (ibid.). In recent years, the Swiss Confederation and the cantons have formulated common educational policy goals and intend to achieve them in a coordinated manner. A new goal has just been set, which places the education system in a position of anticipation, as regards the new challenges of the digitalized world of work and its impact on society in general (WBF & EDK, 2019).

Individual cantons, such as St. Gallen, have also launched digitalization programs for the entire cantonal education system, including VET. An education package costing 75 million Swiss Francs, aimed at fostering digitalization was approved by the electorate in the form of a special loan in 2019. Such initiatives also take place at community level. In the city of Berne, an investment credit of 12 million Swiss Francs for the purchase of tablets for nearly 8000 pupils was granted in 2018. An additional 12 million was granted for follow-up operational costs (City of Berne, 2018). Some cantons complain, however, that the authorities are too slow and that especially in the field of VET, federal authorities do not have a clear idea about the direction in which to proceed. On the other hand, the SERI has also approved a total of 213 million Swiss Francs mainly for investment in VET during the period 2019–2020, exceeding the original budget of 150 million. Another viewpoint is that each canton is formulating its own policy, therefore any coordination is difficult. To achieve 'digital maturity,' advocated by the President of the Technical University, EPFL Lausanne, with reference to the classical pedagogue Johann Heinrich Pestalozzi, educational policy should not only foster computer science courses and MOOCs at universities but also programs for further adult education and VET. It is the duty of the state and of schools to deliver the digital competencies for the fourth industrial revolution (Vetterli, 2017). In line with such arguments and referring to the documents of the federal authorities, Imboden (2017), together with a group of experts, explores the strategic options and actions required in VET and in the upper-secondary level schools in the cantons over the coming years, with a specific focus on ICT infrastructures, applications and administration.

The Swiss teaching unions are also involved in this debate. They criticize the exclusive economic approach and the implicit expectation that teachers, primarily, are responsible for this transformation (Gruber, 2018). On the other hand, in 'Folio,' the journal of the umbrella association of Swiss VET teachers, opportunities for digitalization in teaching are fostered, for example, in developing research competencies for the learners (Müller, 2019) as well as encouraging an emotional enrichment of learning processes (Thomann, 2019).

At a strategic level, a group of prominent stakeholders has been debating the future of VET, under the umbrella 'VPET 2030' (Vocational and Professional Education and Training 2030) for a number of years. However, the mission statement of the social partners (including employers and unions) avoids the use of the term 'digitalization' under the headings of the ten strategic guidelines. Nevertheless, the concepts of digitalization and globalization are perceived as megatrends, which urge the partners to reform the VET system. The ten guidelines of this mission statement are based on a SWOT-analysis (Schweizerische Eidgenossenschaft, 2017). One report that has been commissioned as part of a series of working papers refers to the topic of digitalization and its potential to disrupt the dual model of VET. The author, who was commissioned to write the paper, considered modularization a viable option in reforming the VET system (Seufert, 2018).

It is evident from the aforementioned, that Swiss stakeholders in VET have initiated a continuous cycle of deliberations, including several aspects which consider the future of VET in the context of digitalization. In summary, the current debate is primarily an indicator of future expectations of how VET and further adult education might be transformed in subsequent years. Nowadays the technical and instrumental aspects seem to be in the foreground but in the future the aspect of 'digital culture' could become more important (Sgier, Haberzeth, & Schüepp, 2019; Stalder, 2016).

5 Conclusion: Swiss VET and digitalization as gradual change

The five cases and the deliberation presented, all highlight a particular element of digitalization: a subject-based connectivity, which relies on an extended learning arrangement (3.1), a curriculum-based reduction of learning presence in school (3.2) and a media-based interplay in a common learning space (3.3), furthermore an enlargement of platforms for the coordination of different learning sites and a support for transition processes (3.4) and finally, a move towards more digitized communication and work-related cooperation in schools (and the workplace).

All examples represent practices, which were developed but did not fundamentally change apprenticeships in industry, informatics and banking. In other areas, especially in schools, learners are still present, use textbooks and work with their hands. As in most fields of education, the introduction of a new technology does not automatically change everything. Learning cultures vary over time which, however, does not mean that previous types and forms of education are superseded (Messerschmidt & Grebe 2005). The partially, newly-established practices, often based on the initiatives of innovative firms, teachers or schools, seem to confirm that the dual model of VET is still working and is not subject to a fundamental change. Nevertheless, a shift towards a more 'digitized' VET can be observed. As discussed above, this is reflected, for example, in the rising importance of knowledge work and academic skills in many occupational fields, which raises the question of whether and how training programs, methods and contents develop in relation to their orientation towards specific *vocational* qualifications. While certain tendencies can be observed in the light of digitalization which point to a fragmentation of the 'dual model' of VET, from a historical perspective one can remain optimistic about its consolidating quality.

With regard to our main focus of whether digitalization is disruptive for Swiss VET, we have identified 3 levels: politics, practices and concerns of the relevant actors in the field of VET. Most policy papers regard digitalization as a long-term opportunity rather than a threat to the world of work and hence, (vocational) education and training. Certainly, the importance of some tasks and mainly low-skilled competences may become less important, however, the demand for a high skill level seems to be increasing currently.

As regards the application of digital technologies, practices developing from grassroots level are promoting new ways of learning and teaching, which has implications for VET. At different learning sites and especially in schools, a more intensive use of digital devices to enhance connectivity and network building is taking place, mainly based on individual (i.e., schools' or firms') initiatives. However, at a third level, VET and more general educational stakeholders are engaged in a discourse that is aiming to develop a strategy of improving and engaging in digitalization, in order to equip learners with the necessary skills for a future digital society.

The discourse around digitalization in Switzerland tackles the issue of whether education and more specifically, the prospects for VET today are so different from former times beset by technological challenges. The range of opportunities for instruction, teaching and learning has certainly increased. Forms of blended learning are gaining ground even in traditional settings. As previously stated, the digital infrastructures in schools and workplaces provide the material background for digitalization (Sgier et al., 2019, p. 98). However, the big changes are largely discussed in papers predicting future developments but are not so evident in the workplace, education and life in general today. The changes and prospects are, therefore, more gradual than disruptive and are oriented towards sustaining trusted concepts, as stated by the stakeholders in the 'VPET 2030' agenda, that is, that school and workplace instruction are still important and digitalization is not the only, but nevertheless an important point of reference for the development of VET. Meanwhile, the expectation for learners to cope and find their individual fit in a digital environment has increased. Technology is not an imperative, but more an incentive to modify established ways of teaching and learning. With respect to new practices evolving in the light of digitalization, we can identify a new form of 'experimentalism' (Böhme, 2017, p. 26) as the main mode of action. This produces fragile experiences and uncertainties on the one hand, but on the other hand, paves the way for more explorative learning and reflection on the part of the apprentices. In this regard, the new wave of technology has already modified teaching, learning and our lives.

Biographical note

Stefan Kessler is a team member in the Swiss National Science Foundation funded project 'Bildung in Zahlen' (education by numbers) at the Chair of Historical Research in Education and Governance of the Education System at the University of Zurich, Switzerland. Previously, he was a research and teaching assistant at the Chair of Vocational Education and Training at the same University. His current research interests concern the digitalization of vocational education (VET) and the development of VET in a historical perspective.

Philipp Gonon, Dr. phil., is a professor of Vocational Education and Training at the University of Zurich, Switzerland. Previously, he served as a Full University Professor of Education at the University of Trier in Germany in the field of adult education. He published several books and numerous articles on the history and theory of vocational pedagogy, politics of education and policy studies in an international comparative context. His topical research focus is the development and change of vocational education systems in an international perspective.

References

Adler, T., & Salvi, M. (2017). *Wenn die Roboter kommen.* Zürich: Avenir Suisse.

Aepli, M., Angst, V., Iten, R., Kaiser, H., Lüthi, I., & Schweri, J. (2017). *Die Entwicklung der Kompetenzanforderungen auf dem Arbeitsmarkt im Zuge der Digitalisierung* (SECO Publikation Arbeitsmarktpolitik No. 47). Zollikofen: Eidgenössisches Hochschulinstitut für Berufsbildung (EHB)/INFRAS.

Arvanitis, S., Grote, G., Spescha, A., Wäfler, T., & Wörter, M. (2017). *Digitalisierung in der Schweizer Wirtschaft: Ergebnisse der Umfrage 2016 – eine Teilauswertung im Auftrag des SBFI* (KOF Studien No. 93). Zürich: KOF Konjunkturforschungsstelle, ETH Zürich.

Avis, J. (2018). Socio-technical imaginary of the fourth industrial revolution and its implications for vocational education and training: A literature review. *Journal of Vocational Education & Training, 70*(3), 337–363.

BD St. Gallen (Bildungsdepartement St. Gallen) (2019). *FAQ zu digitalen Arbeitsgeräten an Berufsfachschulen*. St. Gallen: Amt für Berufsbildung. Retrieved from https://www.sg.ch/bildung-sport/berufsbildung/berufsfachschulen/schulorganisation---schulbetrieb.html [09.12.2019].

Böhme, H. (2017). Das Schumpetersche Paradox und die späte Triebtheorie Freuds. In W. Bergande (Ed.), *Kreative Zerstörung. Über Macht und Ohnmacht des Destruktiven in den Künsten* (pp. 18–56). Wien: Turia + Kant.

Bower, J. L., & Christensen, C. M. (1995). Disruptive technologies: Catching the wave. *Harvard Business Review, 73*(1), 43–53.

Buch, T., Dengler, K., & Matthes, B. (2016). Relevanz der Digitalisierung für die Bundesländer. Saarland, Thüringen und Baden-Württemberg haben den größten Anpassungsbedarf. *IAB-Kurzbericht, No. 14*. Nürnberg: Institut für Arbeitsmarkt und Berufsforschung (IAB) der Bundesagentur für Arbeit.

Christensen, C. M. (1997). *The innovator's dilemma. When new technologies cause great firms to fail.* Boston, MA: Harvard Business School Press.

Christensen, C. M., Raynor, M., & McDonald, R. (2015). What is disruptive innovation? *Harvard Business Review, 93*(12), 44–53.

City of Berne (2018). *Abstimmungen vom 25. November 2018. Neue Schulinformatik "base4kids2": Investitions- und Verpflichtungskredit.* Retrieved from https://www.bern.ch/themen/stadt-recht-und-politik/abstimmungen-und-wahlen/abstimmungen/abstimmungsresultate-seit-2000/resultate-2016-2020/abstimmungen-vom-25-november-2018 [09.12.2019].

Cuban, L. (2001). *Oversold and underused. Computers in the classroom.* Cambridge: Harvard University Press.

Degen, K., & Jud Huwiler, U. (2018). Schweizer Arbeitsmarkt gut aufgestellt. *Die Volkswirtschaft, 2018*(1–2), 11–14.

Degryse, C. (2016). *Digitalisation of the economy and its impact on labour markets.* Brussels: European Trade Union Institute (ETUI).

Downes, L., & Nunes, P. F. (2013). Big-bang disruption. *Harvard Business Review, 91*(3), 44–56.

ED Berne (Erziehungsdepartement des Kantons Bern) (2018). *Empfehlungen zur Einführung von BYOD. Schulen der Sekundarstufe II.* Bern: Erziehungsdirektion des Kantons Bern. Retrieved from https://www.erz.be.ch/erz/de/index/direktion/organisation/mittelschul-_undberufsbildungsamt/publikationen/ict-strategie-schulen-sek-ii-2017-2021.html [09.12.2019].

ED Basel (Erziehungsdepartement des Kantons Basel) (2019). *Wegleitung BYOD für Lernende. Schuljahr 2019/20.* Basel: Allgemeine Gewerbeschule. Retrieved from https://www.agsbs.ch/news/news/25ba-bring-your-own-device-byod-an-der-ags [09.12.2019].

EDK (Schweizerische Konferenz der kantonalen Erziehungsdirektoren) (2018). *Digitalisierungsstrategie. Strategie der EDK vom 21. Juni 2018 für den Umgang mit Wandel durch Digitalisierung.* Bern: Schweizerische Konferenz der kantonalen Erziehungsdirektoren. Retrieved from http://www.edk.ch/dyn/12277.php [09.12.2019].

Euler, D., Seufert, S., & Wilbers, K. (2006). eLearning in der Berufsbildung. In R. Arnold, & A. Lipsmeier (Eds.), *Handbuch der Berufsbildung* (2nd ed., pp. 432–450). Wiesbaden: VS Verlag.

Fleischmann, D. (2017). Lernen, wann und wie es richtig ist. *Panorama. Bildung Beratung Arbeitsmarkt, 2017*(2), 14–15.

Foster, R. N. (1986). *Innovation. Die technologische Offensive.* Wiesbaden: Gabler.
Fox, J. (2014, September 17). The disruption myth. *The Atlantic.* Retrieved from https://www.theatlantic.com/magazine/archive/2014/10/the-disruption-myth/379348/ [09.12.2019].
Frey, C. B. (2019). *The technology trap. Capital, labor, and power in the age of automation.* Princeton: University Press.
Frey, C. B., & Osborne, M. (2015). *Technology at work. The future of innovation and employment* (Citi GPS: Global Perspectives & Solutions). New York: Citigroup. Retrieved from https://www.oxfordmartin.ox.ac.uk/downloads/reports/Citi_GPS_Technology_Work.pdf [09.12.2019].
Goetze, W., Denzler, N., & Wissler, P. (2009). *Evaluation Stellwerk, Kurzbericht.* Thalwil: BfB Büro für Bildungsfragen. Retrieved from https://www.stellwerk-check.ch/index.aspx?PID=1.3.0.326.0.0.0.326.0.N.0.Y.0.0.0.0 [09.12.2019].
Gonon, P. (2002). Neue Technologien und Berufspädagogik – ein Spannungsverhältnis. In P. Gonon, & S. Stolz (Eds.), *Arbeit, Beruf und Bildung* (pp. 64–76). Bern: hep-Verlag.
Gonon, P. (2017). Quality doubts as a driver for vocational education and training (VET) reforms – Switzerland's way to a highly regarded apprenticeship system. In M. Pilz (Ed.), *Vocational education and training in times of economic crisis. Lessons from around the world* (pp. 341–354). Cham: Springer.
Gonon, P., & Kessler, S. (2019). The disruptive potential of digitalisation—The current Swiss VET landscape. In F. Marhuenda, & M. J. Chisvert-Tarazona (Eds.), *Pedagogical concerns and market demands in VET. Proceedings of the 3rd Crossing Boundaries in VET conference, Vocational Education and Training Network (VETNET)* (pp. 378–383). https://doi.org/10.5281/zenodo.2641689
Gruber, J. (2018). Mit digitalen Kompetenzen fit werden. *vpod bildungspolitik. Zeitschrift für Bildung, Erziehung und Wissenschaft, 205*(February 2018), 5–6.

Gutmann, M. (2019). *Berufsbildner*innen-Befragung. Ergebnisse und nächste Schritte*. Zürich: Universität Zürich – Fachgruppe berufliche Grundbildung (ppt).
Hawkridge, D. (1990). Who needs computers in schools, and why? *Computers & Education, 15*(1–3), 1–6.
Heeg, R., Genner, S., Steiner, O., Schmid, M., Suter, L., & Süss, D. (2018). *Generation smartphone. Ein partizipatives Forschungsprojekt mit Jugendlichen*. Olten: FHNW & ZHAW.
Ifenthaler, D. (2018). How we learn at the digital workplace. In D. Ifenthaler (Ed.), *Digital workplace learning. Bridging formal and informal learning with digital technologies* (pp. 3–8). Cham: Springer.
Imboden, S. (2017). *Digitaler Wandel in Schulen. Megatrends, Thesen und strategische Handlungsoptionen für die Sekundarstufe II*. Sion: HES SO.
Kessler, S. (2016). Branchen- und lernortspezifische Herausforderungen beim Einsatz von Tablets in der überbetrieblichen Ausbildung der Schweizer Banken. In J. Seifried, S. Seeber, & B. Ziegler (Eds.), *Jahrbuch der berufs- und wirtschaftspädagogischen Forschung 2016* (pp. 125–140). Opladen: Barbara Budrich.
Kessler, S. (2020). Changing requirements in the skills of bankers: The role of work tools and the role of learning. In R. Helmrich, & M. Tiemann (Eds.), *Defining work tools: Studying effects of digitalising work tools* (pp. 33–52). Bonn: Bundesinstitut für Berufsbildung.
Kraus, K. (2009). Beruf und Berufsbildung. In S. Andresen, R. Casale, T. Gabriel, R. Horlacher, S. Larcher Klee, & J. Oelkers (Eds.), *Handwörterbuch Erziehungswissenschaft* (pp. 60–75). Weinheim: Beltz.
Krummenacher, J. (2019, January 28). Digital lehrt jeder Kanton wie er will. In der Schweizer Bildungspolitik fehlt es an Koordination und Bündelung digitaler Ausbildungsprogramme. *NZZ Neue Zürcher Zeitung*, p. 9.
Lassnigg, L., & Bock-Schappelwein, J. (2019). Die Debatten um Industrie 4.0 und Bildung. Szenarien der Digitalisierung und ihr politischer Widerhall in Österreich und Deutschland. In

R. Dobischat, B. Käpplinger, G. Molzberger, & D. Münk (Eds.), *Bildung 2.1 für Arbeit 4.0?* (pp. 25–47). Wiesbaden: Springer VS.

Linton, M. (2018). *Lernorte und Lernortkooperation in der beruflichen Bildung. Auswahlbibliografie*. Bonn: Bundesinstitut für Berufsbildung.

Mason, P. (2019). *Clear bright future. A radical defence of the human being*. London: Penguin Books.

Messerschmidt, R., & Grebe, R. (2005). *Zwischen visionärer Euphorie und praktischer Ernüchterung. Informations- und Bildungstechnologien der vergangenen fünfzig Jahre* (QUEM-report. Schriften zur beruflichen Weiterbildung No. 91). Berlin: Arbeitsgemeinschaft Betriebliche Weiterbildungsforschung e.V.

Müller, S. (2019). Förderung digitaler Recherchekompetenz im ABU. *Folio, 2019*(4), 14–19.

Nachtwey, O., & Seidl, T. (2017). *Die Ethik der Solution und der Geist des digitalen Kapitalismus* (IFS Working Paper No. 11). Frankfurt am Main: Institut für Sozialforschung.

Nassehi, A. (2019). *Muster. Theorie der digitalen Gesellschaft*. München: C.H.Beck.

Navaratnarajah, T. (2019). *Lernortkooperation in der Berufsbildung. Eine Mehrperspektivenanalyse vor dem Hintergrund des Kooperationsverständnisses der Lernorte*. Unpublished bachelor thesis, University of Zurich.

Oesch, D. (2016). Wandel der Berufsstruktur in Westeuropa seit 1990: Polarisierung oder Aufwertung? In A. Franzen, B. Jann, C. Joppke, & E. Widmer (Eds.), *Essays on inequality and integration* (pp. 184–210). Zürich: Seismo.

Peter, K. (2014). *Der Einfluss von Online-Plattformen auf Lernortkooperation: Fallanalyse in zwei Kantonen anhand ausgewählter Berufe*. Zürich, University of Zurich, Faculty of Arts.

Ragni, T. (2018). Fürchtet euch nicht! Ein Kommentar zum Digitalisierungsbericht des Bundesrates. *vpod bildungspolitik. Zeitschrift für Bildung, Erziehung und Wissenschaft, 205*(February 2018), 13.

SBFI (2017). *Herausforderungen der Digitalisierung für Bildung und Forschung in der Schweiz*. Bern: Staatssekretariat für Bildung, Forschung und Innovation.

Schiefner-Rohs, M., Heinen, R. & Kerres, M. (2013). *Zeitschrift für Theorie und Praxis der Medienbildung*, 1–20.
Schlögl, P. (2019). Digitalisierung – oder: Wenn Technik nicht Probleme löst, sondern erneut eine Bestimmung beruflicher Handlungsfähigkeit herausfordert (Bildung und Arbeit). In R. Dobischat, B. Käpplinger, G. Molzberger & D. Münk (Eds.), *Bildung 2.1 für Arbeit 4.0?* (pp. 303–318). Wiesbaden: Springer VS.
Schumpeter, J. (2006). *Theorie der wirtschaftlichen Entwicklung* (Repress of the 1st edition of 1912). Berlin: Duncker & Humblot.
Schweizerische Eidgenossenschaft (2017). *Berufsbildung 2030. Vision und strategische Leitlinien. Hintergrundbericht zum Leitbild*. Bern: SBFI.
Schweizerische Eidgenossenschaft (2018). *Strategie Digitale Schweiz*. Biel: BAKOM – GDS.
Schweizerischer Bundesrat (2017a). *Auswirkungen der Digitalisierung auf Beschäftigung und Arbeitsbedingungen – Chancen und Risiken. (Bericht des Bundesrates in Erfüllung der Postulate 15.3854 Reynard vom 16.09.2015 und 17.3222 Derder vom 17.03.2017)*. Bern: Schweizerische Eidgenossenschaft.
Schweizerischer Bundesrat (2017b). *Bericht über die zentralen Rahmenbedingungen für die digitale Wirtschaft*. Bern: Schweizerische Eidgenossenschaft.
Schweri, J., & Iten, R. (2018). Berufe passen sich der Digitalisierung an. *Die Volkswirtschaft*, 2018(1–2), 20–23.
Seufert, S. (2018). *Flexibilisierung der Berufsbildung im Kontext fortschreitender Digitalisierung. Bericht im Auftrag des SBFI im Rahmen des Projekts „Berufsbildung 2030 - Vision und Strategische Leitlinien"*. Bern: Staatssekretariat für Bildung, Forschung und Innovation.
Sgier, I., Haberzeth, E., & Schüepp, P. (2019). Wie gehen Weiterbildungsinstitutionen mit der Digitalisierung um? Resultate einer empirischen Studie. In: Sgier, I., Haberzeth, E. (Eds.), *Digitalisierung und Lernen* (pp. 95–118). Bern: hep.
Sigrist, B. & Strasser, R. (2018). BYOD und Berufsbildung. *Schulblatt Thurgau*, 2/2018, 51–52.
Stalder, F. (2016). *Kultur der Digitalität*. Frankfurt am Main: Suhrkamp.

Statista (2019). Anteil mobiler Endgeräte an allen Internet-Seitenaufrufen in der Schweiz von Januar 2013 bis September 2019. Retrieved from https://de.statista.com/statistik/daten/studie/431557/umfrage/anteil-mobiler-endgeraete-an-allen-internet-seitenaufrufen-in-der-schweiz/ [09.12.2019].

Thomann, C. (2019). Lernen ist (mehr als) Arbeiten. *Folio*, 2019(4), 39–41.

Trede, I., & Lüthi, I. (2018). Wie können Bildungsverordnungen aktuell bleiben? (OBS EHB Trendbericht). In J. Schweri, I. Trede & I. Dauner (Hrsg.), *Digitalisierung und Berufsbildung. Herausforderungen und Wege in die Zukunft* (pp. 13–17). Zollikofen: Eidgenössisches Hochschulinstitut für Berufsbildung (EHB).

Vetterli, M. (2017, November 17). Digitale Mündigkeit. Pestalozzi und die digitale Revolution. *NZZ Neue Zürcher Zeitung*, p. 10.

WBF (Eidgenössisches Departement für Wirtschaft, Bildung und Forschung), & EDK (Schweizerische Konferenz der Erziehungsdirektoren) (2019). *Chancen optimal nutzen. Erklärung 2019 zu den gemeinsamen bildungspolitischen Zielen für den Bildungsraum Schweiz.* Bern: WBF/EDK.

Zenhäusern, P., & Vaterlaus, S. (2017). *Digitalisierung und Arbeitsmarktfolgen. Metastudie zum Stand der Literatur und zu den Entwicklungen in der Schweiz.* Luzern: Fondation CH2048.

Zuboff, S. (2018). *The age of surveillance capitalism. The fight for a human future at the new frontier of power.* New York: Public Affairs.

2.
Apprenticeships in dual and non-dual systems: Adaptation and opportunities to develop

ENNI PAUL & CAMILLA GÅFVELS

Apprenticeship education and school-based vocational programmes in the Swedish upper secondary school: Different tracks towards the same goal?

Abstract: Apprenticeship education is formally a part of the Swedish upper secondary school Vocational Education and Training (VET). Half of the educational time is work based, as compared to a minimum of approximately 14 percent in the school-based VET programs. However, apprenticeship education is based on the curriculum of the school-based VET programs, which seems contradictory according to a situated perspective on learning. The purpose of this small-scale ethnographic case study, is, thus, to explore differences in the vocational knowing afforded in the Swedish apprenticeship education compared to school-based education and how this shapes participation in the workplace. The results highlight how different dimensions of knowing intersect with ways of being, which sets the participation of apprenticeship students and VET-school students' in the workplace a part. This study argues that the current way of organizing the apprenticeship education seems to rest upon a failure to recognize differences in ways of knowing, such as *knowing that* and *knowing how*, or that the situated character of learning in two different practices, school and workplaces, will lead to development of different aspects of vocational knowing. This failure to recognize these differences has consequences for apprenticeship students, as their knowing is assessed on the basis of aims in the curriculum originally formulated for the school-based VET.

Keywords: vocational knowing, participation, work tasks, school tasks.

1. Introduction

Since the autumn of 2011, apprenticeship education has been part of Swedish upper secondary school's vocational education and training

(VET). An explicit purpose of the apprenticeship education is to offer an "alternative" for both students and employers to the regular school-based VET programs by providing opportunities to develop vocational knowing at workplaces (Prop. 2008/09:199). Hence, apprenticeship students spend at least half of their educational time at one or several workplaces in workplace-based learning (i.e., on-the-job-training), compared to approximately 14 percent (15 weeks) of workplace-based training in the regular VET-programs (CEDEFOP, 2019), which highlights the different possibilities in terms of student participation in workplace.

However, a potential obstacle for the apprenticeship education is that the curriculum is identical to that of the school-based VET. This means that the vocational knowing of apprenticeship students is assessed on the basis of the learning outcomes in the curriculum originally formed for the school-based VET. Even though both schools and workplaces function as sites for learning, they differ as practices (Akkerman & Bakker, 2012; Billett, 2001; Carlgren, 2015). For instance, in school, production is separated from learning or only works as a background figure, whereas it is in the forefront in workplace activities and knowing is what is used for production (Billett, 2001; Lindberg, 2003). Furthermore, school teaching is mediated by words and organized in age-based groups (Nielsen & Kvale, 2000), which is constrained and afforded by materials and resources available (Berner, 2009). In the Swedish case, VET-education aims at preparing students for future citizenship, further learning and for developing a broad general vocational knowing (Lindberg, 2003). In many workplaces mistakes can slow the amount of work completed, whereas making mistakes or being slow in performing a vocational task in school is not as problematic but can be transformed in to a lesson (Billett, 2006; Gåfvels, 2016, Lindberg, 2003). Vocational knowing in workplaces is further characterized by its tacit dimensions (Polayni, 1966/2009), often only possible to verbalize through metaphors (Fillietaz, de Saint-Georges, & Duc, 2010). Vocational knowing at school, in turn, has to be changed into a particular kind of content. This process often includes a theorization as the content is shaped to fit a school logic, which often promotes formalized and formulated knowing (cf. Carlgren, 2017; Edwards & Miller, 2008; Wärvik & Lindberg, 2018). Hence, what counts as crucial vocational knowing as well as which opportunities to develop vocational knowing are afforded differ between the systems (Aarkrog, 2005; Tangaard, 2006). Becoming and being a member of a school-VET community of practice hardly means the same as becoming and being a member of a workplace community of practice (Lave & Wenger, 1991). Still, the Swedish upper secondary apprenticeship education and the school-based VET programs follow the same curriculum, have the same learning goals and leads to the same exam. It is also possible for students to switch tracks at any time during their three-year education.[1]

In this chapter, we will therefore explore differences in the vocational knowing afforded in the Swedish apprenticeship education as compared to school-based education and how these difference shapes participation in the workplace. This research is guided by the research question: *What characterizes student (inter-)action in work and school tasks in the two tracks and how do the students in the different tracks participate in these tasks?*

2. The Swedish upper secondary VET and apprenticeship education

Swedish basic VET follows a school-based model; it is state-controlled and has a rather large number of general subjects but a weak apprenticeship tradition (Nylund, 2013; Olofsson, 2010). This is a consequence of political decisions made in the 1940s concerning VET, where a previous "labour market educational regime" was replaced by a "school regime" (Lundh Nilsson & Nilsson, 2015; Olofsson 2005). The change has had consequences for how vocational knowing has been re/shaped in to a content; that is, in the school-based model it is framed within a school logic and formed as a subject matter (Berner, 2009; Broberg, 2014; Carlgren, 2017). As a result, practical and theoretical knowing

---

[1] Switching between the apprenticeship track and school-based VET is possible as long as the particular school offers both tracks.

have become separated both in terms of content and in regards of physical space (Broberg 2014). Practical knowing involves learning content in school workshops or method rooms, whereas vocational theory is taught in ordinary classrooms as a separate content (Broberg, 2014). Learning in workplaces, which have been part of the upper secondary curriculum since the 1970s within the school-based VET, has also been subordinated to the school's regulations, curricula, time frame and assessment practices (Broberg, 2014). The work-based learning in the Swedish context most often mean that it is the students who do all or most of the boundary-crossing between school and work (cf. Akkerman & Bakker, 2012; Berglund et al., 2017).

Apprenticeship education within the framework of upper secondary VET had existed in a small scale prior to the 2011 school reform, when it was made a permanent feature of the upper secondary VET. Previous attempts to launch apprenticeship education since the 1970s had largely been unsuccessful in terms of number of students choosing apprenticeship education and in terms of little interest from the labor market (Kristmansson, 2016; Lemar & Olofsson, 2010). There seems to be a common belief in Sweden that apprenticeship education is particularly suitable for "practically minded" persons (Berglund, 2009; Berglund & Henning Loeb, 2013; cf. CEDEFOP 2017 on attitudes in Sweden to VET education), who learn by doing and not by thinking or reading—as if thinking or reading were not embedded within doings of vocational tasks (cf. Karlsson, 2006; Schön, 1983/2003). The previous apprenticeship trials, as well as apprenticeship education since 2011, have struggled with conflicting views about what the object of apprenticeship education should be: is it an education targeting youth at risk or is it a way to better foster vocational knowledge matching the demands of the labor market (Berglund & Henning Loeb, 2013)? Another contradiction is how the upper secondary VET in general since the 2011 reform is supposed to make the VET students ready to enter work directly after their exam, even though the vocational content has become more theoretical with each school reform since the 1970s (Lindberg & Wärvik, 2017; Wärvik & Lindberg, 2018). An example of this is how VET teachers in the fifth apprenticeship trial (2008–2011), especially in the Health- and Social care program and Electricity and Energy program, found it difficult to reach the curriculum goals as the vocational content was perceived as being theoretical and thus not possible to develop at the workplaces (Berglund et al., 2017).

Today, the Swedish upper secondary VET consists of 12 national vocational programs. They are aimed at different sectors, and each program have one or several different orientations. All of the programs last for three years (2500 credits), and the students study both vocational subjects (1600 credits) and general subjects (600 credits), even though there are less general subjects than before the reform (150 credits less).[2] Prior to the 2011 reform, the VET programs led to basic eligibility to university studies, today VET students have to actively choose additional general subjects to gain basic eligibility. Of the 12 national VET programs, two are explored in this chapter: the Child and recreation (CR) program as well as the Vehicle and transport (VT) program. As mentioned in the introduction, since autumn of 2011, all of the national VET programs have also been offered as apprenticeship education. In Sweden, the majority of apprenticeship students are not employed, even though since 2014, it has been possible to be employed as an apprenticeship student (SFS 2014:421).

3. Theoretical points of departure

In vocational activities, knowing is embedded in actions (Schön, 1983/2003) and in the use of material and intellectual tools (Säljö, 2005/2013; Vygotsky, 1978; Wertsch, 1998). Grounded in a social understanding of learning as situated and knowing as relational, this chapter builds upon descriptions of how vocational knowing is developed through a movement from a peripheral position as a newcomer in a community of practice—whether a workplace or a VET-class—towards a more central position. At the workplace, the newcomer is afforded restricted tasks in a specific order according to a workplace curriculum, under

---

[2] Added to this are 100 credits final project and 200 credits of individual choice where both general and vocational subjects can be chosen depending on what is offered at the particular school.

direct and indirect guidance (Billett, 2001; Lave & Wenger, 1991). As previously novel and difficult tasks gradually become more routine over time, the learner is able—in an expansive learning environment (Fuller & Unwin, 2001) and depending on the learner's own agency—to move to more demanding and significant work tasks (Billett, 2001; Lave & Wenger, 1991). During this movement, the person learns how to do things, how to act, what concepts to use, as well as what attitudes and dispositions to have (Billett, 2001; Lave & Wenger, 1991). The movement from peripheral tasks to more central ones expands and reshapes what the learner knows, that is, what he/she can experience and differentiate (cf. Carlgren, 2015). Learners will eventually, provided his/her own agency in relation to what is afforded, in a more knowledgeable and autonomous way complete work tasks, and in the process, transform their way of belonging to the community of practice (Billett, 2001; Lave & Wenger, 1991). Thus, in this chapter, different ways of being in terms of participation, are interpreted as expressions of different ways of knowing. In a parallel way, a VET student will through affordances formed through the school curriculum and through the teacher's instruction develop vocational knowing afforded in the tasks at school and in the process become a member of the school's VET-community of practice. However, as is the case of this study, the complex movement from school to the world of work ideally involves not only knowing how to do specific tasks but knowing how to participate in order to gain membership in a community of practice different from the school. Thus, it is a question of becoming and being.

A large part of vocational knowing is tacit (Polanyi, 1966/2009). It is inscribed in embodied experience, formed in the interface between sensory experience and description, and made visible as "knowing in practice" (Carlgren, 2015; Janik, 1991). This can be tied to Ryle's (1949) critique of the idea of thought precedes action (i.e. that practice is applied theory). Through Ryle's concepts of *knowing that* and *knowing how*, different yet relational aspects of knowing are possible to explore. In school, epistemic knowing that is both formal and formulated (Carlgren, 2015) is at the forefront, for example, in the area of childcare, different stages in child development are presented in oral as well as written form. In workplaces, other aspects of knowing are in the center, such as knowing what to do when and how; for instance, what kind of physical activity may be reasonable to plan for a group of children who are three years old. In workplaces, theory is embedded within actions and not separated from practice, which is the case at school (Broberg, 2014) where all knowing has to be transformed in to school content. At school, students learn how to participate in the school practice and develop vocational knowing in relation to what is afforded by the tasks given in school, whether they are school tasks, vocational tasks or simulated tasks (Carlgren, 2015; Lindberg, 2003). Traditionally, school knowledge is to a higher degree acknowledging propositional knowing (i.e., knowing that rather than knowing how) (Ryle, 1949). As a consequence, the complexities of vocational knowing developed during workplace-based learning is often reduced to propositional knowing and workplace-based learning is assessed on the basis of written school tasks (Wyszynska Johansson, 2015). In a study conducted during the 1980s, apprentices and upper secondary VET students in Sweden in the industrial sector were compared (Berner, 1989). According to the results apprentices were more skilled in doing tasks within the vocation, whereas the school VET students could better articulate what they were doing and why. Several studies on assessment during workplace-based learning for school VET programs or for apprenticeship education also point to how different aspects of vocational knowing are emphasized in workplaces and schools, as they form contradictory assessment practices (Akkerman & Bakker, 2012; Fjellström & Kristmansson, 2016; Sandal, Smith, & Wangensteen, 2014; Wyszynska Johansson, 2015). A study on Norwegian upper secondary VET show how students perceive "school knowledge" and "practical knowledge" at workplaces as unrelated, since the students' perceive both the content of the learning and learning contexts as different (Sandal, Smith, & Wangensteen, 2014). This disparity was heightened in the comments of the VET teachers in student portfolios, where the students were asked to reflect on learning in a theoretical sense related to aims in the VET curriculum. The workplace instructors, in contrast, gave feedback regarding the practical prerequisites of the actual work tasks instead of the academic and institutional requirements. Wyszynska Johansson's (2015) study of Swedish students enrolled in the Child and recreation program show similar results concerning how workplace-based learning is almost exclusively assessed through written form, which makes the students' tacit knowing in areas such as care and service invisible. Thus, the assessment practices highlight a perceived division between theory and practice.

4 Methodological framework

This is a small-scale ethnographic case study conducted over a period of six months during 2018–2019 (El Guindi, 2004; Pink, 2009). Two of the 12 national Swedish upper secondary VET programs are studied: the child and recreation (CR) program and Transport and vehicle program (VT). The apprenticeship track and the regular school-based VET track are investigated within both programs.

The data consists of participatory observation at three different schools during vocational lessons as well as participatory observation during the workplace-based part of the education. During these observations, field-notes, photographs and videos were taken. Semi-structured interviews with 11 ($N=11$) students, six ($N=6$) teachers and seven ($N=7$) supervisors were conducted. Also, written school-tasks in relation to the workplace-based learning were collected. Five ($N=5$) students were followed at the workplaces (total amount of six workplaces) for one to two days each. All of the participating students were in their second year of the three-year education and were described by their teachers as engaged students, which also seemed the case according to observations and interviews.[3] Thus, the differences in experiences between school-based and apprenticeship students should not be influenced by differing attitudes towards education. The workplace-based learning was organized in different ways in the classes studied, as shown in the figure below.

---

3   The study follow the ethical rules for research as stipulated by the Swedish research council (Vetenskapsrådet 2017).

Fig. 1: Organization of workplace-based learning in year 2 of the Child and recreation programme (CR) and Vehicle and transport programme (VT).

CR apprenticeship year 2	CR school-based year 2	VT apprenticeship year 2	VT school-based year 2
Three days at a workplace and two days at school each week during the school year	Three weeks at a workplace in the autumn Four weeks at a workplace in the spring	Two weeks at a workplace and two weeks in school the entire school-year	Two weeks at a workplace in the autumn Two weeks at a workplace in the spring
Assessment through tripartite conversations between teacher, student and supervisor, written school texts, VET-teacher observations	Written school texts, supervisors' written assessment	Assessment through tripartite conversations between teacher, student and supervisor, as well as list of work tasks done signed by a supervisor	Assessment through tripartite conversations between teacher, student and supervisor, as well as list of work tasks done signed by a supervisor
Rotation of workplaces with new workplace each year	Rotation of workplaces with new workplace each workplace-based period	Ideal of no rotation	Rotation of workplaces

The data was analyzed by the two researchers. The first phase included transcription of interviews, writing up field notes into ethnographic accounts, reading through the student assignments, viewing the films and photographs several times. Codes (Braun & Clarke, 2006) based on the identification of similarities and differences in the data material were constructed. In line with a relational view of knowing and a sociocultural understanding of learning, the tasks the students participated in and students (inter-)actions with the tasks were explored in order to describe what characterizes the knowing students are afforded and forms ways of being in terms of participation. After further exploring the dataset, the material was further sorted and organized as patterns began to emerge. Eventually, three themes were created by the researchers in relation to theoretical frame guiding the study as well as previous research in the area.

In a small-scale case study set in a specific national context (i.e. a Swedish context), it is not possible to draw broader conclusions concerning differences in vocational knowing developed in apprenticeship education and school-based VET programs. Yet in a dialog with previous research, analytical generalization is possible, as patterns concerning knowing and participation in schools and workplaces emerge and are highlighted (Larsson, 2009).

5 Findings: Distinctive ways of being

Three themes: *being a student, being responsible and being independent* were elicited from the analysis of the students' actions in school tasks and work tasks as well as from the interviews by students, teachers and supervisors. These themes convey different ways of being (i.e., participating), as well as expressions of distinctive ways of knowing.

Being a student

Being a student includes actions of a particular kind. In the Care and recreation-program these actions involved, for instance, sitting down and listening to the VET-teacher's lecture, answering questions posed by the teacher, individually writing assigned texts both at school and during the workplace-based learning part in different school genres (like log-books or academic genres such as reports), reading texts in schoolbooks (school text) or online like the pre-school curriculum (vocational text), searching on the internet, and writing dead-lines in a calendar. In Vehicle and transport-program, the actions also included parts of those mentioned above: listening to lectures, taking notes, working individually with online study material (school texts), and answering questions during lessons. But it also involved watching and discussing newscast under the guidance of the VET teachers, as a part of preparing for students' future citizenship (cf. Lindberg, 2003). For the school-based students in the VT-program, being a student also included doing defined

Apprenticeship education and school-based vocational 145

tasks in the school automobile workshop in a particular order set by the teachers, in the form of practical work with dismantled vehicle parts, which was tied to content in the curriculum. These tasks were a mix of individual and group work. In regards to the character of the VT program, the economic aspects tied to workplaces became evident in how the school was described as a safe place to train, which was in contrast to the workplace, where errors would be costly. A VT apprenticeship student explained the following:

> *I have almost never changed a cambelt [at the workplace]. It is a little terrifying because if you mess it up, you have messed up the entire engine. (VT apprenticeship student)*

Economic issues were not evident in the actions or expressions for the CR students; instead, care and communication (with children) was stressed, where differences in verbal expressions and way of acting between school and workplaces become evident:

> *Well, you aren't the same there [at the workplace] that you are in school, because you think about language a lot there [at the workplace]. At school I am a person who swears a lot and uses nasty words but it's not like I would say such things at the workplace. That's like a big no no. (CR school-based student)*

Verbal actions in both educational programs at school included using certain type of utterances, including chit-chatting with friends during lessons, swearing, as well as negotiating about deadlines or given tasks. In both the apprenticeship and school-based track of CR and VT education, being a student also involved repeatedly asking the teacher for help, being told by the teacher what to do, and following the teacher's instructions:

> *You have more responsibility during the work-based learning than in school, because at school we have always have a teacher there for us who will help us with stuff and such, but the supervisor at the workplace-based training just looks at you from a distance and observes the work you do. (CR school-based student)*

In almost all of the interviews, students stressed the contrast between expected independence at the workplace and continuous and close access to teachers at school. Also, several students highlighted that VET-teachers were good at explaining in contrast to supervisors. VT students in particular stressed the ability of VET-teachers to explain for instance mechanical or electrical processes:

> *At the workplaces, they won't go through how things work for real. It's more how you change [a car part] and why. (VT school-based student)*

Additionally, using a phone or social media on a tablet or computer, doing something else than the task at hand, or acting in ways which made the teacher intervene in order to get the student back on task were behaviors observed at school but not at the workplaces. A CR apprenticeship student explained this as follows:

> *At school, you can sit and rest and take breaks, but at the workplace you have to be in constant motion. (CR apprenticeship student)*

At school, the students explained their participation as listening to what the teacher told them to do. At the workplace, in contrast, the students were expected to act in a more independent way and "like adults," as both students and VET teachers expressed it. Thus, vocational knowing in terms of *knowing how*—for instance, having developed a vocational gaze (Gåfvels, 2016) or a vocational judgment (Lindberg, 2003), which is foundational for independence and responsible action at the workplaces—is not expected in the same way in relation to school tasks. Instead, propositional knowing is promoted in a large part of the school tasks both in school and in relation to school tasks at the workplace, especially in the CR program. A major difference between the CR and VT program is that half of the VT vocational lessons were held in a school workshop and consisted of working on practical tasks. These tasks were characterized by being designed by the teachers, involving dismantled parts of engines, and involving constant interaction between the teachers and students. For the tasks held in the VT workshop, technical aspects of doing were promoted, but these lessons were always held in connection to vocational theoretical lessons that preceded the content in the workshop. Being a student in both the studied tracks for both programs also involved actions in which participation in the school community of practice could be shaped as resistance or avoidance of doing school tasks as well as specific ways of talking, dispositions and procedures for action. This involved doing school tasks and classmate oriented-actions, characterized by belonging to a homogenous age group (17–18 year olds).

Being responsible

Being responsible was a category construed from the data on the basis of observing the workplace-based students' actions during their workplace-based learning and describing their actions in interviews. Both school-based VT students and CR students described workplace-based learning as a place where their actions involved taking responsibility and acting in a self-regulating manner in contrast to school:

> *During the worplace-based learning, it is more independent. It might sound weird but it is I who has to resolve a conflict between the children. It is not someone else. Sure, you can speak with your work colleagues but it is still I who has to do it.* (CR school-based student)

The students explained this in terms of contrasting "doing things," "being independent," "more responsibility" and "treated as adults" at the workplace with "sitting and listening," "access to teachers," "being told by teachers what to do" and "learning theory" in school. The former was portrayed as engaging whereas the latter was described as disengaging in worst cases. Experiencing and doing work tasks were explained as contributing to actual learning on the basis of being responsible, in contrast to how vocational content was presented in school and where the teacher was the one in control:

> *During the workplace-based learning you get more experience, and you learn like that. Then you have to learn by yourself kind of. If you do something wrong then, you know, alright, I'll do it in another way. You have to do a lot on your own. Here [at school] it is just the teacher telling you what to do and then you do it. (CR- school-based student)*

Personal experience, thus, forms a basis for vocational judgment. There are several ways to solve situations, and more importantly, the activities go on, whereas in school it is possible to stop and reverse. In CR, a basis for independent action was learning the routines of the elementary school and leisure time center where the workplace-based learning in the spring semester of year two was conducted. By getting a hold of the daily routines, the students then could show initiatives for action. In many ways, the school-based CR-students were treated as assistants who could relieve the regular staff by being a pair of extra hands—for instance working separately with pupil's in need of extra support, fetching computers from another room and distributing them, setting the table for snack time, or managing a small group doing a certain task while the teacher could focus on another group of pupils.

The VT school-based students also explained how they would gradually become more independent at the workplace by doing certain limited tasks and were given some responsibility. But the more complex work tasks were not made available for the school-based VT-students at their workplaces:

> *At the beginning, he [the supervisor] instructed me most of the time, but then I got to work at little bit more independently. Then he did all the computer work and I did the grunt work. But there weren't any big jobs, it was mostly service jobs, and I did them. In the beginning, they were easy jobs, like brakes and changing the oil. [...] But, of course, if you get to gearboxes or engines, then it gets hard. But that's what we learn here in school. (VT school-based student)*

At work, the students could do restricted tasks on their own, but in comparison to the VT apprenticeship student, the school-based students did not get the opportunity to work on more complex tasks, because they did not have the necessary experience. The tasks were tied to economical risks. Further, they could not keep up with the pace doing the tasks or complete entire work orders on their own. Neither could they suggest what to do next, which the apprenticeship students could. As one school-based VT student explained:

> *I checked brakes and stuff and then installed a diesel heater and that took an entire week because it was the first time I did that.*

The tasks stayed new for the school-based students because of the limited time at the workplace. One auto mechanic supervisor elaborated on the problem with the school-based students' workplace-based learning being that the students might have been to several different workplaces before, where they had done the same kind of "beginners tasks," since all newcomers in workplace-based learning according to the supervisor were given easy tasks in order to check what they can do before giving them more complicated and central tasks. Thus, the students were hindered from expanding their knowing and broadening their repertoire during the workplace-based learning.

Both CR students and the VT students stressed the situated character of knowing at the workplaces compared to the broader general knowing at school:

> *At a workshop, you become a specialist, but not here at school. (VT school-based student)*

Being independent

During the observations of the apprenticeship students, it was evident that they worked independently and acted on their own initiatives. They expressed feeling like co-workers and were also described by their supervisors as vital members of the work unit:

> *I feel like I am a part of the work team, and the children wonder a lot when I am not here on Mondays and Tuesdays when I am at my own school. (CR apprenticeship student)*

The apprenticeship students participated in significant tasks in a self-governing way. The situated character of the work tasks and work activities, as well as the personal experiences as a basis for vocational knowing, was stressed by the students:

> *I learn a lot in school too, but it is not until I am here [at the workplace] that I see what really works. (CR apprenticeship student)*

Students elaborated on how important communication with the children is, as well as how important it is to trust the child and understand what they say, think and feel. One student explained how while speaking with a child, she would kneel on the child's level so she can meet the child eye to eye. But that the most important thing is to get to know each individual child to know to understand which approach would work best. This kind of vocational gaze and vocational judgment came in to play in situations in which the CR apprenticeship students had to discern when and how to intervene in the childrens' activities. That the students were seen as a co-worker was also evident in such actions as coming up with their own ideas for lesson plans and activities for the children, making suggestion on how to redecorate the classroom, and participating in teacher conferences at the workplace sharing knowledge about particular children. Thus, the apprenticeship students appeared more like colleagues than aides, which is a sign of their more central position at the workplaces than the school-based students.

Similarly, the VT apprenticeship student completed work orders involving service on a car from start to finish independently, and only asked the supervisor to check his work before writing up the work order. The mechanical work involved several sequences and tasks building up the whole work order. In the process, the student had to make conclusions based on previous experiences as well as use general descriptions in a digital manual for the car brand and translate those to the particular car being worked on. These actions involve use of vocational judgment. Similarly, to the CR apprenticeship students the VT apprenticeship student stressed feeling as if he actually worked at the workshop, which he tied to getting to do a wide range of tasks:

> *It is not just changing breaks and tidying up. I get to do a lot and that makes you feel at home. In fact, I feel like I work here. (VT apprenticeship student)*

Being a more significant part of the community of practice was something that set the apprenticeship students apart from the school-based ones. This was for instance visible during break times, such as in the verbal actions as the VT apprenticeship student joined in on the jokes and workplace jargon.

Furthermore, the apprenticeship students in both programs showed in their actions that they understood how tasks in the workplaces were aligned instead of apprehending tasks as isolated units (cf. Billett, 2001; Lave & Wenger, 1991). A VT supervisor elaborated on the difference between apprenticeship students and school-based ones:

> *A school-based student and an apprenticeship student can actually be equally skilled, but the apprenticeship student is aware of how the entire business works in a different way and can go into production at once. A student from school has to learn the organization first and won't be as effective directly. (VT supervisor)*

Apprenticeship education and school-based vocational 151

Thus, the crucial difference does not seem to be in skills per se, but understanding how the activities at a workplace are aligned and the significance of different tasks, which, in turn, make it possible judge how to act in different situations based on previous experiences upon which the student can make generalizations in to the specific situations. Time as a factor explains why apprenticeship students can act in a more self-sufficient way, as they have the possibility to regularly participate in work tasks, making them routine tasks, thereby getting the opportunity to do more significant tasks and also develop a deeper understanding for the workplace activity (Billett, 2001; Lave & Wenger, 1991). This exemplifies how intersecting aspects such as taking initiative, responsibility, accountability, and autonomy, come into play with situated tacit knowing in the students' personal experiences. The apprenticeship students have more opportunities to encounter situations in which contextualized knowing, involving such aspects as vocational judgment and vocational gaze, is at the forefront. An apprenticeship-teacher in VT program said the following:

> *At school, we create problems [in the cars] but outside of school, the problems are of a kind you can't pre-program [...]. These are problems no one has seen or heard of in a car before; these problems are more difficult to create at school. [...] To get that external vision, you have to know how to go on digging and that is a knowing you can't get at school. [...] You can teach someone how to change brakes in a week, no problem, but you can never teach anyone how to troubleshoot. (VT apprenticeship teacher)*

Troubleshooting, as explained by the teacher, is built upon personal experience and familiarity with practice, which helps to create the capability to discern what one should do next in order to solve a problem.

6. Discussion and concluding remarks

There are similarities in the two educational tracks. Both apprenticeship students and school-based VET students participate in school tasks and work tasks, and are, thus, provided opportunities to develop knowing afforded in respective community of practice (Lave & Wenger, 1991). But differences in the amount of time spent at the workplaces as well as how learning is framed within workplace(s) vs. school, shapes differences in the vocational knowing afforded in each track and in the end forms distinctive ways of being. The results illuminate that technical skill and practical wisdom are prioritized in workplaces, while more general and formal dimensions of knowing are prioritized at school—especially in the CR program (cf. Carlgren, 2015).

The apprenticeship students in both educational programs in year 2 were viewed as more significant members of the workplace community, as they gained access to more significant work tasks and performed these autonomously, whereas the school VET students' participation during workplace-based learning remained more peripheral, as the supervisors regularly instructed them about which tasks they were to do next. Further, the tasks they were given were more peripheral and delimited. This result evokes Rintala & Nokelainen's (2019) study on the learning experiences of Finnish apprentices compared to school-based VET-students during workplace-based learning. The apprentices gained full membership compared to the school-based VET students, whose participation remained peripheral. Even though the school VET students, in this study, did show initiatives and were given some responsibility, the work tasks had not become routine tasks (Billett, 2001); thus, real autonomy was neither possible nor expected. The apprenticeship students, in contrast, exhibited independence during a majority of the work they did and were described as co-workers by their supervisors. As the school-based students only had been a couple of weeks of training at the specific workplaces compared to the apprenticeship students, who had been at their workplaces three days a week for the CR program and two weeks in a row every other week for the VT programs during their second year, this difference was hardly surprising. Hence, time is essential to the development of both technical skills as well as vocational judgment; the latter which is foundational for being able to take initiative and act independently, as the learner needs to be able to "see" (i.e. vocational gaze) and draw on previous experiences while working.

In contrast to the workplaces the object of school tasks was, to a large degree, to develop a basic theoretical comprehension as a ground for practice, regardless of whether this was for practical work is in the school workshop or for workplace-based learning. This means that vocational theory is seen as foreshadowing vocational practice, which is perceived as applied theory (Carlgren, 2015, 2017; Schön, 1983/2003). This was especially the case in the CR program, where school tasks mainly focused on propositional knowing, emulating the academic tradition of the program (Wyszynska Johansson, 2015). Thus, there is a theorization of the content, whereas tacit dimensions, such as practical wisdom and technical skills, remain hidden. In the VT school-based program practical work was done in a school workshop, which promoted development of basic skills, but the VET teachers' interviews illuminated how lessons on vocational theory were seen as predicting practical work. The tasks in the school workshop were divided up in to distinct units, which are different to work tasks, where no-one knows beforehand what the problem is.

As previously stated, one rudimentary difference between the two tracks is that apprenticeship students are supposed to develop vocational knowing primarily at one or several workplaces, whereas school-based students are to develop most of their vocational knowing in school. This study confirms previous research illuminating how workplace communities of practice and school as a community of practice emphasize different aspects of vocational knowing which is tied to different ways of being (cf. Akkerman & Bakker, 2012; Rintala & Nokelainen, 2019; Sandal, Smith, & Wangensteen, 2014). In this study, three categories—being a student, being responsible and being independent—emerged as illustrations of differing participation in work tasks as a school-based student and work-tasks for apprenticeship students. Apprenticeship students spend half of their educational time at a workplace; thus, approximately 80 percent of their time in the vocational subjects are conducted at workplaces (Berglund et al., 2017). Based on the results of this study, apprenticeship students get access to situated and contextualized vocational knowing. Thus, it is contradictory for the apprenticeship students to be assessed based on factors belonging to the school-based VET curriculum, which means that vocational knowing in school practice is to a large degree re/shaped into propositional form. This tension became evident, for instance, when the apprenticeship teachers tried to fit the apprenticeship students' experiences in the workplaces within learning outcomes in the curriculum that did not match how work tasks were done at workplaces. Therefore, the organization of the apprenticeship education in Swedish upper secondary VET seems to build upon the idea that *reading about* content during school lessons, as during most CR lessons or during VT vocational theoretical lessons, leads to the development of the same vocational knowing as *learning-in-practice*. There is a failure to recognize different dimensions of knowing, such as *knowing that* and *knowing how* (Ryle, 1949), as well as a failure to recognize how activities at school and workplaces form different communities of practice that have differing objects (cf. Lave & Wenger, 1991). At the end of the day, Swedish apprenticeship education is still a school-based education as it adheres to a school logic (cf. Berglund & Lindberg, 2012; Berglund et al., 2017), in which apprenticeship teachers have to adapt to a curriculum with learning goals that does not readily fit with complex situations students participate in at work.

References

Aarkrog, V. (2005). Learning in the workplace and the significance of school-based education: A study of learning in a Danish vocational education and training programme. *International Journal of Lifelong Education, 24*(2), 137–147.

Akkerman, S. F., & Bakker, A. (2012). Crossing boundaries between school and work during apprenticeships. *Vocations and Learning, 5*(2), 153–173.

Berglund, I. (2009). *Byggarbetsplatsen som skola – eller skolan som byggarbetsplats? En studie av byggnadsarbetares yrkesutbildning.* [The construction-site as school – or school as construction-site? A study of the vocational education of construction workers. In Swedish.] (Doctoral dissertation). Stockholm: Stockholm university.

Berglund, I., & Henning Loeb, I. (2013). Renaissance or a backward step? Disparities or tensions in to new Swedish pathways in VET. *International Journal of Training and Research*, 11(2), 135–149.

Berglund, I., Höjlund, G., Kristmansson, P., & Paul, E. (2017). *Gymnasial lärlingsutbildning ur ett pedagogiskt och didaktiskt perspektiv med utgångpunkt i försöksverksamheten 2008–2014.* [Upper Secondary apprenticeship education from a pedagogical and didactical perspective in the pilot project during 2008–2017. In Swedish.] University of Gothenburg. RIPS, Reports from the Department of Education and Special Education.

Berner, B. (1989). *Kunskapens vägar. Teknik och lärande i skola och arbetsliv* [The ways of knowledge. Technology and learning in school and working life]. Lund: Arkiv.

Berner, B. (2009). Learning control. Sense making, CNC-machines and change in vocational training for industrial work. *Vocations and Learning, 2*(3), 177–194.

Billett, S. (2001). *Learning in the Workplace: Strategies for Effective Practice.* Crows Nest: Allen & Unwin.

Billett, S. (2006). Constituting the workplace curriculum. *Journal of Curriculum Studies, 38*(1), 31–48.

Braun, V., & Clarke, V. (2006). Using thematic analysis in psychology. *Qualitative Research in Psychology, 3*(2), 77–101.

Broberg, Å (2014) *Utbildning på gränsen mellan skola och arbete. Pedagogisk förändring i svensk yrkesutbildning 1918–1971.* [Education on the border between school and work. Educational change in Swedish vocational education and training 1918–1971. In Swedish] (Doctoral dissertation). Stockholm university: Department of education.

Carlgren, I. (2015). *Kunskapskulturer och undervisningspraktiker.* [Cultures of knowledge and teaching practices]. Göteborg: Daidalos.

Carlgren, I. (2017). Yrkesdidaktiska vägval. In A. Fejes, V. Lindberg, & G. B. Wärvik (Eds.), *Yrkesdidaktiken mångfald.* [Diversity of vocational didactics] (pp. 255–268). Stockholm: Lärarförlaget.

CEDEFOP (2017). *Cedefop European public opinion survey on vocational education and training.* Luxembourg: Publications Office of the European Union.

CEDEFOP (2019). *Flash thematic country review on apprenticeships Sweden.* Luxemburg: Publications Office. Thematic country reviews.

Edwards, R., & Miller, K. (2008). Academic drift in vocational qualifications? Explorations through the lens of literacy. *Journal of Vocational Education and Training, 60*(2), 123–131.

El Guindi, F. (2004). *Visual Anthropology: Essential Method and Theory*. Oxford: Altamira Press.

Filliettaz, L., de Saint-Georges, I., & Duc, B. (2010). Skiing, Cheese Fondue and Swiss Watches: Analogical discourse in vocational training interactions. *Vocations and Learning, 3*(2), 117–140.

Fjellström, M., & Kristmansson, P. (2016). Learning as an apprentice in Sweden: A comparative study on affordances for vocational learning in school and work life apprentice education. *Education + Training, 58*(6), 629–642.

Fuller, A., & Unwin, L. (2003). Learning as apprentices in the contemporary UK workplace: Creating and managing expansive and restrictive participation. *Journal of Education and Work, 16*(4), 407–426.

Gåfvles, C. (2016). *Skolad blick på blommor: Formandet av yrkeskunnande i floristutbildning*. [Educated Gaze on Flowers: The Formation of Vocational Knowing in Floristry Education. In Swedish]. (Doctoral dissertation). Stockholm University: Department of Education.

Janik, A. (1996). *Kunskapsbegreppet i praktisk filosofi*. Eslöv: B. Östlings bokförlag. Symposion.

Karlsson, A.-M. (2006). *En arbetsdag i skriftsamhället: ett etnografiskt perspektiv på skrift-användning i vanliga yrken*. [A workday in the literacy society: an ethnographic perspective on literacies in common vocations. In Swedish]. Stockholm: Nordstedts akademiska förlag.

Kristmansson, P. (2016). *Gymnasial lärlingsutbildning på Handels- och administrationsprogrammet: en studie av lärlingsutbildningens förutsättningar och utvecklingen av yrkeskunnande*. [Upper Secondary Apprenticeship Education in the Business and Administration Programme. A study of preconditions of upper secondary apprenticeship education and development of professional skills. In Swedish] (Doctoral dissertation). Umeå: Umeå university.

Larsson, S. (2009). A pluralist view of generalization in qualitative research. *International Journal of Research & Method in Education*, *31*(1), 25–38.

Lave, J., & Wenger, E. (1991). *Situated Learning: Legitimate Peripheral Participation*. Cambridge: Cambridge University Press.

Lemar, S., & Olofsson, J. (2010). Bilaga 4. Om lärlingsrådens funktioner. [Appendix 4. On the function of apprenticeship councils]. In Nationella lärlingskommitén (Ed.). *Gymnasial lärlingsutbildning – utbildning för jobb. Erfarenheter efter två års försök med lärlingsutbildning*. SOU 2010:75 (pp. 283–324). Stockholm: Fritzes.

Lindberg, V. (2003) Vocational knowing and the content in vocational education. *International Journal of Training Research*, *1*(2), 40–61.

Lindberg, V., & Wärvik, G.-B. (2017). Vad är ett yrkesämne? [What is a vocational subject?]. In A. Fejes, V. Lindberg, & G.-B. Wärvik (Eds.), *Yrkesdidaktikens mångfald*. [Diversity of vocational didactics] (pp. 23–58). Stockholm: Lärarförlaget.

Lundh Nilsson, F., & Nilsson, A. (2015). Challenging the 'School Model' in vocational education: Role of companies in initial vocational education in Sweden 1910–2014. In A. Heikkinen & L. Lassnigg (Eds.) *Myths and Brands in Vocational Education*. Newcastle: Cambridge Scholars Publishing.

Nielsen, K., & Kvale, S. (2000). Mästarlära som lärandeform idag. [Apprenticeship as a current form of learning]. In K. Nielsen & S. Kvale (Eds.), *Mästarlära: Lärande som social praxis* [Apprenticeship: learning as a social practice] (pp. 27–48). Lund: Studentlitteratur.

Nylund, M. (2013). *Yrkesutbildning, klass och kunskap. En studie om sociala och politiska implikationer av innehållets organisering i yrkesorienterad utbildning med* fokus på 2011 års gymnasiereform. [Vocational Education, Class and Knowledge. A Study of Social and Political Implications of Content Organization in Vocational Education, Focusing on the Upper-Secondary School Reform of 2011. In Swedish] (Doctoral dissertation). Örebro: Örebro Universitet.

Olofsson, J. (2005). *Svensk yrkesutbildning – vägval i internationell belysning*. [Swedish vocational education – approaches in an international light. In Swedish.] Stockholm: SNS.

Olofsson, J. (2010). *Krisen i skolan – utbildning i politiken och i praktiken*. [The crisis at school – education in policy and practice. In Swedish.] Umeå: Borea.

Panican, A., & Paul, E. (2019). *Svensk gymnasial yrkesutbildning – en framgångsfaktor för en effektiv övergång från skola till arbetsliv eller kejsarens nya kläder?* [Swedish apprenticeship education – success factor for effective transition from school to work or the emperor's new clothes± In Swedish.] Lund: Forte & Svenska ESF-rådet.

Paul, E. (2017). *Skriftbruk som yrkeskunnande i gymnasial lärlingsutbildning. Vård- och omsorgselevers möte med det arbetsplatsförlagda lärandets skriftpraktiker.* [Literacies as Vocational Knowing in Upper Secondary Apprenticeship Education: Apprentice students participation in literacy practices during workplace based learning in health care and social work. In Swedish] (Doctoral dissertation). Stockholm: Stockholms Universitet.

Pink, S. (2009). *Doing Sensory Ethnography*. Los Angeles: Sage.

Polayni, M. (1966/2009). *The Tacit Dimension*. Chicago: Chicago University Press.

Prop. [Government Bill] (2008/09:199). *Högre krav och kvalitet i den nya gymnasieskolan.* [Higher demands and quality in the new upper secondary school. In Swedish]. Stockholm: Fritzes.

Rintala, H., & Nokelainen, P. (2019). Vocational education and learners' experienced workplace curriculum. *Vocations and Learning*. https://doi.org/10.1007/s12186-019-09229-w.

Ryle, G. (1949/2002). *The Concept of Mind*. Chicago: Chicago University Press.

Säljö, R. (2005/2013). *Lärande och kulturella redskap: om lärprocesser och det kollektiva minnet* [Learning and cultural tools: On processes of learning and collective memory. In Swedish]. Lund: Studentlitteratur.

Sandal, A. K., Smith, K., & Wangensteen, R. (2014). Vocational students experiences with assessment in workplace learning, *Vocations and Learning*, *7*(2), 241–261.
Schön, D. (1983/2003). *The Reflective Practitioner: How Professionals Think in Action*. Aldershot: Ashgat.
SFS (2014:421). [Education Act]. *Lag (2014:421) om gymnasial lärlingsanställning*. [Law about apprenticeship employment]. Stockholm: Utbildningsdepartement.
Tangaard, L. (2006). Situating gendered learning in the workplace. *Journal of Workplace Learning*, *18*(4), 220–234.
Vetenskapsrådet (2017). *God forskningssed* [Good research practice]. Stockholm: Vetenskapsrådet.
Vygotsky, L. (1978). *Mind in Society. The Development of Higher Psychological Processes*. Cambridge, MA: Harvard University Press.
Wärvik, G. B., & Lindberg, V. (2018). Integration between school and work: Changes and challenges in the Swedish VET 1970–2011. In S. Choy, G. B. Wärvik, & V. Lindberg (Eds.), *Integration of Vocational Education and Training Experiences* (pp. 279–298). Technical and vocational education and training: Issues, concerns and prospects, Vol 29. Singapore: Singer.
Wertsch, J. V. (1998). *Mind as Action*. New York: Oxford University Press.
Wyszynska Johansson, M. (2015). *Gymnasieungdomars erfarenheter av hur yrkeslärande bedöms*. [Students' experiences and perception of the assessment of vocational knowing. In Swedish.] (Doctoral dissertation). University of Gothenburg: Department of Education and Special Education.

DIETMAR FROMMBERGER, MATTHIAS PILZ, MICHAEL GESSLER

International cooperation in the field of vocational education and training: Concepts, approaches, and empirical findings from a German perspective

Abstract: From a German perspective, international cooperation in the field of vocational education and training is often aimed at the development of dual structures of vocational education and training systems in partner countries. In part 1 of this contribution, conceptual approaches and empirical findings on the transferability and replication of the dual system abroad are presented. In part 2, we focus on international cooperation in vocational education and training, and in part 3, we discuss prerequisites and possibilities for the development of German 'core principles' of a dual system in partner countries. This contribution concludes with an overall reflection.

1. Transferability: Conceptual approaches and empirical findings

Among others, Euler (2013) and Gonon (2012, 2014) addressed the possible transferability of the dual training system abroad (Li & Pilz, 2021). Both authors explore the question on a theoretical-conceptual level without specifically addressing a recipient country. A complete transfer of the dual system abroad is excluded. The transfer of certain elements of the dual vocational training system, however, is certainly possible. Euler (2013) divided the dual VET system into 11 constitutive elements that can be selected, adapted, and transferred by the recipient country according to its framework conditions. Gonon (2012) distinguished between dual systems and dual models, the latter of which are certainly transferable. Thus, the 'spirit of duality' (p. 184) could be transferred as 'sector-specific solutions or partial elements of an education system' (p. 171), but not entire systems. Against this background, Gonon (2012) identified seven criteria necessary for the exportability of dual models (see also Bliem et al., 2014).

Companies' willingness to provide training is an elementary component of a dual model. Euler (2013) also made it clear that the company or 'business setting is essential for learning since it is the only place where learning can occur under real-life conditions' (Euler, 2013, p. 30). In this respect, companies represent a core element of dual training structures regardless of how a possible transfer is oriented towards the model of the donor country. It is only when appropriate framework conditions—such as job descriptions and training regulations geared to the needs of companies, simple administrative structures, and efficient support mechanisms—are in place that companies will find training worthwhile (Bliem et al., 2014, p. 10). In addition, Gonon (2012) referred to the great importance of vocational schools. Here too, companies are an important component. Even if the school-based portion of a specific curriculum is available as part of the transfer, companies must still be prepared to use this potential for cooperation and combine it with their own training activities (Gonon, 2012, p. 172 f). According to the author, further framework conditions are essential: a legal framework that makes it possible to recognise qualifications and integrate them into the entire education and employment system; the inclusion of scientific knowledge in addition to experience-based knowledge; the joint organisation of vocational education and training by state, industry, and social partners; orientation towards a holistic occupational profile; and the recognition of vocational education and training as a career-relevant measure.

Wolf (2009) also focused on transferability at the theoretical-conceptual level. His concept of the work-cultural background of vocational qualification provides an analytical instrument for examining the complex context in which vocational training elements are embedded. His work-cultural concept should contribute to a better assessment of the chances of success of an educational transfer. The author referred to the influence exerted by a country's production of goods and services on its specific VET system, breaking it down into six dimensions. The needs and perspectives of other interest groups (e.g., companies, young people, public officials, representatives of the education systems, representatives of trade unions), which are determined by the regional framework conditions, must also be included. To this end, Pilz (2016a, 2016b) proposed a systematic country analysis based on a typology and provided a corresponding multi-perspective approach. Building on this, he derived six characteristics to be considered in every transfer project: the concrete needs, the provision of necessary resources, experienced training personnel, the avoidance of the risk of fluctuation of trained skilled workers (poaching), evaluation and certification mechanisms with permeability in the education system, and adequate employment conditions for skilled workers (Pilz, 2017).

In addition to these theoretical-conceptual debates, there are extensive empirical, more application-oriented (Langthaler, 2017) approaches in the field of vocational training cooperation. Schippers (2009) examined the Mubarak-Kohl Initiative in Egypt, which has been designed to strengthen the Egyptian economy by training young people since 1996. In view of an impact-oriented analysis model, the results show that a cooperative vocational training system is generally possible in Egypt. However, Schippers (2009, p. 366) concluded that partially opaque organisational structures, such as an unclear, contradictory distribution of tasks within an organisation, create major challenges for implementation. Furthermore, sustainability and self-financing power must be viewed critically: After the withdrawal of German consultancy services, the quality deteriorated (Schippers, 2009, p. 368).

Stockmann and Silvestrini (2013) carried out a meta-evaluation of a total of 25 vocational training projects of the former Gesellschaft für Technische Zusammenarbeit, the German Development Service, in order to assess the effectiveness and sustainability of its approaches to support the developments in the field of vocational education and training in several countries. The authors noted that most of the projects were limited to a small pilot framework and did not spread either geographically or over time. Stockmann (2019) used these findings to develop an extended model of the key variables for sustainable transfer activities. This model includes four factors: flexible control, ownership, personnel, and system compatibility. The study concluded, among other things, that projects with a limited demand profile achieve higher sustainability than those with a multi-level approach that aims to have a broad impact. Also, the adjustment between the projects' objectives and the needs of the economy was insufficient. Due to the concentration on formal vocational training, the informal employment sector was not considered (Stockmann & Silvestrini, 2013). The German Fraunhofer-Zentrum für Mittel- und Osteuropa (MOEZ) also referred to the great significance of the respective framework conditions in a global analysis of government-funded vocational training export projects. The research group identified differences in education systems, social acceptance, and responsibility for vocational education and training as substantial obstacles to the export of vocational education and training measures (MOEZ, 2012).

While German comparative VET research has primarily looked at transfer activities at the systemic level, some studies have been devoted to individual companies as relevant influencing factors; here, the studies by Aring (2014), Gessler (2017), Gessler and Peters (2017), Holle (2019), Li (2019), Peters (2019), Pilz (2016a, 2016b), Pilz and Li (2014), and Wiemann and Pilz (2017) are to be cited. These scholars followed the question of the extent to which German enterprises practice dual training in their subsidiaries abroad and reflected on the findings considering the transferability of German vocational training. The results also demonstrated the great influence of local framework conditions, in particular, the (vocational) education and training and employment system (Pilz, 2016a; Pilz & Li, 2014). Aring (2014), however, determined a German influence in the North American subsidiaries of Volkswagen, BMW, and Siemens as part of a case study conducted by the ILO. Nevertheless, a strong adaptation to the local context took place. Gessler (2017) identified successful transfer activities in a study on the training behaviour of Mercedes-Benz in Alabama. The local context, however, led to significant deviations in the company's implementation. Therefore, one could speak of a transformation rather than a transfer.

A research group at the University of Cologne (Wiemann, 2020; Wiemann et al., 2019) analysed the extent to which German training standards are transferred abroad and how they interact with the respective national and regional players in the field of vocational education and training on the basis of a study carried out in 2015 and 2016 in German companies at their production sites in India, China, and Mexico. Legal and social framework conditions also play an important role here. Although the three countries surveyed are very different, they have in common that hotspots of direct investment have emerged in their conurbations and that there is therefore high demand for skilled workers. Specifically, the focus was on the cities of Bangalore and Pune in India, the Shanghai metropolitan area in China, and the Mexican highlands. More than 30 expert interviews with company representatives and seven other interviews with experts from the (vocational) education sector in the respective countries were conducted based on theory-based key questions to obtain data. These interviews were then evaluated using text analysis of the transcripts and compacted into findings. The results of the surveys were rounded off by visits to production and training facilities. The macro, meso, and micro levels were examined. At the macro level, the focus was especially on companies' willingness to invest in training. Furthermore, their integration into the educational system and labour market was analysed. At the meso level, training activities were considered at the overall operational level. The allocation and significance of certificates, as well as the qualification of teaching staff, were examined. At the micro level, the focus was on concrete teaching/learning activities. The findings of the study can only be partially reported. For example, a clear connection to the local context is recognisable. This finding could largely be generated identically for all countries. For a small number of technical specialties, the influence of the German model can be ascertained in all three countries. The ability to connect to formal vocational school systems has proven to be an important influencing factor. However, companies complain about the low practical orientation as well as the often-outdated curricula and poor technical equipment in these institutions (which, however, does not apply to China). For specialist positions, particularly in Mexico and India, qualification is often carried out outside the formal national programmes. Such activities, however, have so far not been nationwide measures but rather lighthouse projects in the examined regions.

In addition to the link to the existing vocational training system, the production regimes also represent an inhibiting factor in the transfer of the dual model. Since production processes are often less automated than in Germany and contain more manual and less complex activity profiles, many of the companies surveyed saw no need for comprehensive training according to the dual model. The labour market in the three regions surveyed also proved to be an inhibiting factor. Due to the danger of emigration, many companies have shied away from cost-intensive and protracted investments in large parts of the workforce.

2. International cooperation in the field of vocational education and training[1]

German international cooperation in the field of vocational education and training is several decades old and is aimed at supporting the further development of vocational education and training in partner countries, mostly, but not exclusively, in developing and emerging countries. As 'vocational training assistance,' it has long been practised primarily in connection with German development cooperation, in particular by the Ministry for Economic Cooperation and Development and its predecessor institutions. Next to this, the iMOVE initiative (founded in 2001), based at the Federal Institute for Vocational Education and Training (BIBB), and the funding by the Federal Ministry of Education and Research (BMBF) of projects aimed at opening international markets to German training and further training service providers are examples of vocational training cooperation as a business model. There is also evidence of a growing interdependence between development policy–driven vocational training cooperation and German industry, for example through the Agency for Business and Economic Development (AWE), which was founded in 2016, and a number of funding programmes (including Vocational Training Partnerships [BBP], the SkillsExperts Programme, the ExperTS Programme, EZ-Scouts, and the develoPPP.de Programme) aimed at industry-related players, such as chambers of industry and commerce, chambers of skilled trades,

---

1   This section is based on Frommberger and Baumann (2019).

business associations, and companies. At the same time, specialists and managers from companies are to be recruited as experts for vocational training cooperation (e.g., the Senior Expert Service programme). Therefore, it is also an important objective from the German perspective to support the foreign trade activities of German companies by focusing on the development of skilled workers in the target countries.

Also, vocational training cooperation is organised by the German side on the supranational level, for example within the EU and the Donor Committee for dual Vocational Education and Training (DC dVET, founded in 2016), which represents the German-speaking part of Europe. For some time now, efforts have been made within Germany, given the large number of players in the field of vocational training cooperation, to ensure a coordinated approach (i.e., 'international vocational training cooperation from a single source'). The federal government's strategy paper of 2013 created new institutional structures, formulated strategic goals, defined the responsibilities of the actors, and currently forms a central and interdepartmental orientation for German VET cooperation (see BMBF, 2013). Five 'core principles' for international cooperation in the field of vocational education and training were formulated in this strategy paper: (a) cooperation between social partners, economic organisations, and the state; (b) learning in the context of work; (c) acceptance of national regulations and standards (curricula); (d) training of vocational teachers and trainers; and (e) research on vocational education and training. This strategy is also in response to a steady stream of enquiries from abroad to support the development of dual vocational training approaches. In international vocational education and training cooperation, experience has shown that actors in partner countries have a very strong interest in the development of dual vocational education and training structures (BMBF, 2013).

The question arises as to whether and to what extent it has been and could be possible to develop dual vocational training structures further in a significant and sustainable way in areas where they did not and do not exist. Against this background, the German Federal Ministry of Education and Research launched larger programme lines in 2017 and 2018 to promote further development and research in the field of international vocational training cooperation. One component of this funding is the investigation of reform developments in the field of vocational education and training in the partner countries. In this context, the implementation of a 'German' approach is not being discussed anymore. Rather, 'elements' or 'core principles' of German vocational education and training are analysed that could offer orientation in a partner country, considering its economic, political, and social institutions as well as its history. In the following, experiences from international vocational training cooperation are described (see also Baumann et al., 2020; DLR, 2018).

3. Prerequisites and possibilities for developing the 'Core Principles' of vocational education and training in partner countries

The implementation of the above-mentioned first core principle of 'cooperation between social partners, economic organisations, and the state' depends to a large extent on the institutional constitution of the interests of these actors. This even applies to rich OECD countries such as Australia, Ireland, or Great Britain (Vossiek, 2018). Company and trade union employee interest groups in many countries are very fragmented, are not involved in political decision-making, or take on tasks that are not conducive to vocational education and training as a strategically important topic. Regarding company qualification strategies, trade unions frequently argue against the dual vocational training model, especially when the development of young talent represents competition for existing skilled workers or serves to attract 'cheap labour.' Other economic organisations, such as sectoral or employer umbrella organisations, are not always organised on a nationwide basis, either. Often, they are not accepted by the individual companies, especially not with a view to strategies in the field of human resource development. In addition, the responsibilities of (often different) ministries tend to focus on very different approaches to dual vocational training provision or vary greatly from region to region due to federalism. Also, dual approaches to vocational education and training are usually rejected, especially in ministries of education, as school-based vocational training programmes are preferred. In many countries, institutions are being set up to initiate cooperation between these various interests for the purpose of developing dual vocational training provision ('National Training Authorities' or 'TVET Authorities').

From the German perspective, the core principle of 'learning in the context of work' is primarily directed towards vocational training at the workplace as a place of learning and towards the didactic design and securing of learning opportunities. In most countries, however, the number of companies providing in-company vocational training is very low. Therefore, this principle is often implemented through in-company internships as part of school-based vocational education, through learning phases in laboratories, in learning offices and workshops, or through other approaches to simulating working practices. In this respect, a dualisation of vocational education and training is often achieved by linking school-based vocational education and training with in-company experience. In many countries, systematic learning opportunities close to the area of work are more common in in-company continuous training. In other words, employees who have already worked at a company for several years are offered the opportunity to acquire partial vocational qualifications based on their professional experience. Dual vocational training approaches are therefore very common in continuing vocational training in enterprises ('adult apprenticeships'). From an international perspective, the greatest challenge lies in the systematic integration of in-company learning into a form of vocational education and training that is standardised under public law.

The reasons for the internationally widespread marginalisation of in-company vocational training as part of a standardised and regulated system of vocational education and training and for the implementation of this form of vocational training in only a few countries are manifold (Frommberger, 2017). The further development of greater participation by companies is often only possible through specific pay-as-you-go financing models with which companies can refinance their participation costs, especially if it is not possible to guarantee that the person undergoing training will remain in the company after the training has been completed.

The core principle of 'acceptance of national regulations and standards (curricula)' also meets very different requirements in international cooperation. From the German point of view, this principle refers to statutory regulations and legally derived ordinances, for example, training ordinances. These sets of regulations aim to set minimum quality standards for vocational education and training. Such curricular frameworks are quite common and widespread internationally for forms of schooling that are the responsibility of the state, but the regulation of company training activities based on state-certified standards is often comparatively underdeveloped. The acceptance of such standards is often lacking here. This lack of acceptance of the targeted competences, training content, training periods, final examinations, etc. is usually more pronounced the less the company's interest groups are involved in the development of these standards. It is also of great importance how comprehensive these standards are for in-company training and to what extent they cover the direct training requirements. Very comprehensive and broadly based training occupations that, in some cases, go far beyond the immediate training requirements prove to be particularly difficult. The introduction of training occupations based on the German model is usually unlikely to be successful and is not implemented due to the relatively high level of regulation. More successful as a rule are qualification modules and certificates that are tailored more closely to needs and can be completed step by step and with greater flexibility. In contrast to what is often understood on the German side, these modularisation approaches can directly serve the standardisation of training practices, especially where these standardisation approaches have not existed until now. However, there are also very different international experiences of the role and function of legal and quasi-legal regulatory means.

Another core principle of German international vocational training cooperation is 'training of vocational teachers and trainers.' The qualification prerequisites for teachers and trainers vary greatly from country to country, and the standards are rather low, especially for in-company training activities. The attractiveness of working as a teacher or trainer is often low (e.g., due to remuneration and/or in view of the lack of opportunities for further development and promotion within the framework of this activity). Approaches aimed at qualifying the teachers and trainers concerned usually focus on subject-specific content (deepening or studying an academic discipline) as well as pedagogical-didactic competences and experience. However, due to the low importance and recognition of in-company training activities and the very heterogeneous composition of the vocational teaching staff, the implementation of unified standards poses a major challenge.

Another core principle of German vocational education and training cooperation is research on vocational education and training. Generally, scientific knowledge on vocational education and training is regarded as an important prerequisite for further development and quality assurance in relevant fields but is often only rudimentarily available. This status description is true almost worldwide, since vocational education and training is a relatively small subject area for scientific activities in many countries. VET research can be found in very different scientific disciplines and is not institutionalised to a great extent. There is also a lack of acceptance of this research area.

However, despite the many challenges outlined above, vocational education and training and international cooperation therein are (again) increasingly gaining importance. A long breath is required to develop and implement the existing approaches and desired changes further. Greater consideration must be given to the approaches to vocational education and training that predominate in partner countries as a principle of international cooperation in VET. In this respect, the further development of VET in partner countries is more likely. The core principles of German dual vocational education and training can only be understood as impulses that meet very different prerequisites and must be shaped and supplemented to very different degrees.

Conclusions

The previous remarks have attempted to reflect past and present discussions on the international transfer of vocational education and training from a German perspective. There are at least two striking aspects that are reflected in the discussion:

On the one hand, it is noticeable that the discussion about VET transfer and development has been intensively conducted in Germany for many years, at both the political and the academic level. At the same time, however, it should also be noted that the topic, in some cases, has disappeared from the discourse for years, only to reappear suddenly with high priority (Li & Pilz, 2021).

On the other hand, the debate on international VET transfer and development from a German perspective is only structured to a limited extent and is not defined in a unified way. The vague educational policy and scientific discourse are often marked by assumptions, presumptions, and, in some cases, misjudgements. At the same time, they are surrounded by myths which manifest themselves in fears and anxieties as well as wishes and expectations. An example is the vocational education and training policy. German vocational education and training, and in particular dual training, have been propagated both as an instrument of development cooperation and as a vehicle of economic and foreign policy. Under slogans such as 'training quality made in Germany' and 'export bestseller: German dual system,' the German approach has repeatedly been offered to other countries.

This approach, in turn, incorporates two different stakeholder perspectives. The first is that of the German provider side. Here, a normative change can be observed over past decades, ranging from the 'export of vocational training' (in the sense of a full transfer of the German dual system) via a moderate transfer approach to 'vocational training cooperation.' The other perspective is that of the recipient and partner countries. These are attracted by advertising and ask for large amounts of support in the implementation of dual structures, which cannot always be provided in full by the German side for reasons of capacity.

A further perspective of the partner countries is relevant here. In these countries, the slogans cited above often arouse expectations and hopes which, given the country-specific circumstances and the complexity of the education and training system, cannot always be fulfilled in the short term. Consequently, disappointments and failures are inevitable. In consequence, the political discourse often 'rows back.' This situation has also led to the hefty 'ups and downs' that the topic of vocational education and training transfer has experienced in the German debate in recent years.

In a final observation, as research actors, we refer to the research. Here, aspects such as normative foundation or definitory classification have so far not been very concrete. In addition, it is obvious that conceptual approaches or pragmatic individual cases dominate empirical findings in the research landscape. It is also surprising that research findings from various scientific disciplines have rarely been integrated or received. Also, it is not uncommon for generalisations to be made about completely different approaches in the context of development cooperation in contrast to private-sector activities. Here too, no clearly defined perspective can be established.

Biographical note

Prof. Dr. Dietmar Frommberger is Full Professor in Vocational Education and Training at the University of Osnabrück. He coordinates the series on International Research on Vocational Education and Training in Springer VS ad well as the Handbook on International Vocational Education in Barbara Budrich Verlag.

Prof. Dr. Matthias Pilz is Chair of Economics and Business Education at the University of Köln, where he directs G.R.E.A.T. (German Research Center for Comparative Vocational Education and Training). He is Editor in Chief of the International Journal of Training and Development and coordinates the series on International Research on Vocational Education and Training in Springer VS.

Prof. Dr. Dr. h.c. Michael Gessler is Full Professor in Vocational Education at the Institut Technik und Bildung at the University of Bremen. He is Editor-in-Chief of the Open Access Journal "International Journal for Research in Vocational Education and Training (IJRVET)". He coordinates the series on International Research on Vocational Education and Training in Springer VS.

References

Aring, M. (2014). *Innovations in Quality Apprenticeships for High-Skilled Manufacturing Jobs in the United States at BMW, Siemens, Volkswagen.* Geneva: ILO.

Baumann, F.-A., Frommberger, D., Gessler, M., Holle, L., Krichewsky-Wegener, L., Peters, S., & Vossiek, J. (2020). *Berufliche Bildung in Lateinamerika und Subsahara-Afrika: Entwicklungsstand und Herausforderungen dualer Strukturansätze.* Wiesbaden: Springer.

Bliem, W., Schmid, K., & Petanovitsch, A. (2014). *Erfolgsfaktoren der dualen Ausbildung: Transfermöglichkeiten.* Vienna: Institut für Bildungsforschung der Wirtschaft.

BMBF Bundesministerium für Bildung und Forschung/Federal Ministry of Education and Research (2013). *Strategiepapier der Bundesregierung zur internationalen Berufsbildungszusammenarbeit aus einer Hand.* Unterrichtung durch die Bundesregierung. Drucksache/Deutscher Bundestag. 17/14352 v. 05.07.2013.

DLR Projektträger (ed.). (2018). *Berufsbildung International. Berufsbildung im Fokus: Afrika und Lateinamerika.* Bonn: DLR Deutsches Zentrum für Luft- und Raumfahrt.

Euler, D. (2013). *Germany's Dual Vocational Training System: A Model for Other Countries?* Gütersloh: Bertelsmann-Stiftung.

Frommberger, D. (2017). Der Betrieb als Lernort in der beruflichen Bildung – internationale Entwicklungen im Vergleich. *bwp@ Berufs- und Wirtschaftspädagogik – online, 32*, 1–20.

Frommberger, D., & Baumann, F.-A. (2019). Internationalisierung der Berufsbildung. In: Arnold, R., Lipsmeier, A., & Rohs, M. (eds.), *Handbuch Berufsbildung.* Wiesbaden: Springer (https://doi.org/10.1007/978-3-658-19372-0_54-1).

Gessler, M. (2017). Educational transfer as transformation: A case study about the emergence and implementation of dual apprenticeship structures in a German automotive transplant in the United States. *Vocations and Learning, 10*(1), 71–99.

Gessler, M., & Peters, S. (2017). Implementation of dual training programmes through the development of boundary objects. A case study. *Educar*, *53*(2), 309–331.
GIZ Deutsche Gesellschaft für internationale Zusammenarbeit, & KfW Kreditanstalt für Wiederaufbau (eds.) (in print). *Governance und Finanzierung kooperativer Berufsbildung. Die Rolle von privaten Akteuren und Verbänden stärken*. Eschborn und Frankfurt.
Gonon, P. (1998). *Das internationale Argument in der Bildungsreform. Die Rolle internationaler Bezüge in den bildungspolitischen Debatten zur schweizerischen Berufsbildung und zur englischen Reform der Sekundarstufe II*. Bern: Peter Lang.
Gonon, P. (2012). Entwicklungszusammenarbeit in der Berufs- und Erwachsenenbildung. Das deutsche Modell der Berufsbildung als globales Vorbild? In: Gieseke, W. (ed.), *Reflexionen zur Selbstbildung* (pp. 169–186). Bielefeld: Bertelsmann.
Gonon, P. (2014). Development cooperation in the field of vocational education and training: The dual system as a global role model? In: Maurer, M., & Gonon, P. (eds.), *The Challenges of Policy Transfer in Vocational Skill Development* (pp. 241–259). Bern: Peter Lang.
Holle, L. (2019). *Personalstrategische Maßnahmen von deutschen Unternehmen in China: Eine Fallstudie am Beispiel mittelständischer Unternehmen*. Wiesbaden: Springer.
Langthaler, M. (2017). *Policy Transfer im Bildungswesen mit einem Fokus auf den Transfer des dualen Lehrlingssystems im Rahmen der Entwicklungszusammenarbeit*. 15. Briefing Paper Österreichische Forschungsstiftung für Internationale Entwicklung. Vienna: ÖFSE.
Li, J. (2019). Vom Transfer lernen: Potenzial des Policy-Transfers für die Weiterentwicklung der Policy im Geberland am Beispiel des Peer-Review-Verfahrens. In: Gessler, M., Fuchs, M., & Pilz, M. (eds.), *Konzepte und Wirkungen des Transfers Dualer Berufsausbildung* (pp. 601–630). Wiesbaden: Springer.
Li, J. & Pilz, M. (2021). International transfer of vocational education and training: a literature review. *Journal of Vocational Education and Training*, online first.

MOEZ Fraunhofer-Zentrum für Mittel- und Osteuropa (2012). *Treibende und hemmende Faktoren im Berufsbildungsexport aus Sicht deutscher Anbieter*. Leipzig: MOEZ.
Peters, S. (2019). *Bildungstransfer im Unternehmenskontext*. Wiesbaden: Springer.
Pilz, M. (2009). Initial vocational training from a company perspective: A comparison of British and German in-house training cultures. *Vocations and Learning*, 2(1), 57–74.
Pilz, M. (2012). International comparative research into vocational training: Methods and approaches. In: Pilz, M. (ed.), *The Future of Vocational Education and Training in a Changing World* (pp. 561–588). Wiesbaden: Springer.
Pilz, M. (2016a). Training patterns of German companies in India, China, Japan and the USA: What really works? *International Journal for Research in Vocational Education and Training*, 3(2), 66–87.
Pilz, M. (2016b). Training like at home or like the domestic competitors? A study of German and Indian Companies in India. In: Yasin, A., & Shivagunde, R. B. (eds.), *Emerging Trends in Technical and Vocational Education and Training (TVET)* (pp. 2–14). New Delhi: Lenin Media.
Pilz, M., & Li, J. (2014). Tracing Teutonic footprints in VET around the world? The skills development strategies of German companies in the USA, China and India. *European Journal of Training and Development*, 38(8), 745–763.
Pilz, M., & Wiemann, K. (2017). 'You train them, you teach them, and then they leave you!' Ein Vergleich der betrieblichen Bildungsaktivitäten deutscher und indischer Unternehmen in Indien. *BWP@ Berufs- und Wirtschaftspädagogik – online*, 32, 1–21.
Schippers, S. (2009). *Systemberatung zwischen Anspruch und Wirklichkeit: eine wirkungsorientierte Analyse der "Mubarak-Kohl-Initiative" in Ägypten*. Marburg: Tectum.
Stockmann, R. (2019). Ziele, Wirkungen und Erfolgsfaktoren der deutschen Berufsbildungszusammenarbeit. In: Gessler, M., Fuchs, M., & Pilz, M. (eds.), *Konzepte und Wirkungen des Transfers Dualer Berufsausbildung* (pp. 121–162). Wiesbaden: Springer.

Stockmann, R., & Silvestrini, S. (2013). *Metaevaluierung Berufsbildung.* Münster u.a.: Waxmann.
Vossiek, J. (2018). *Collective Skill Formation in Liberal Market Economies? The Politics of Training Reforms in Australia, Ireland and the United Kingdom.* Bern: Peter Lang.
Wiemann, J. (2020). *Qualifizierungspraxis deutscher Produktionsunternehmen in China, Indien und Mexiko: Eine Analyse der Übertragbarkeit dualer Ausbildungsansätze.* Wiesbaden: Springer.
Wiemann, K., & Pilz, M. (2017). Berufliche Ausbildung durch mexikanische und deutsche Unternehmen in Mexiko: Ein Home-International-Vergleich. *Tertium Comparationis, 23*(2), 217–245.
Wiemann, J., Wiemann, K., Pilz, M., & Fuchs, M. (2019). Duale Ausbildung im Ausland: Ein 'Heimspiel'? Zur Qualifizierung von Produktionsbeschäftigten in deutschen Unternehmen in China, Indien und Mexiko. In: Gessler, M., Fuchs, M., & Pilz, M. (eds.), *Konzepte und Wirkungen des Transfers Dualer Berufsausbildung* (pp. 359–392). Wiesbaden: Springer.
Wolf, S. (2009). *Berufsbildung und Kultur: Ein Beitrag zur Theorie der Berufsbildung in der Entwicklungszusammenarbeit.* Tönning: Der andere Verlag.
Wordelmann, P. (2010). Internationale Kompetenzen in der Berufsbildung. Stand der Wissenschaft und praktische Anforderungen. In: Wordelmann, P. (ed.), *Internationale Kompetenzen in der Berufsbildung. Stand der Wissenschaft und praktische Anforderungen* (pp. 7–31). Bielefeld: Bertelsmann.

M'HAMED DIF

Apprenticeship in France: Institutional patterns, organisation, methods and performance

Abstract: Apprenticeship constitutes institutionally an important component of the French initial vocational education and training (IVET) system. It integrates within the overarching framework of a dominantly company-based apprenticeship model. It is initiated via an employment contract signed between the company and an apprentice and implemented through an alteration between mostly on-the-job (60–75 % of the time) and in-house training for the remaining time. Its major aim is to facilitate transition from school to work by allowing young people aged from 16 to 30 years (and even over) to develop their work-based skills and competences and have access to all related types and levels of formal vocational qualifications referenced within the NQF Directory of vocational qualifications. This paper is an analytical exploration into the historical background developments, institutional governance patterns, funding arrangements, organisation and methods of training and the inclusive performance of apprenticeship. The adopted investigation method is primarily based on scientific desk research and available data, documentation and performance evaluation studies and reports published by the ministries of education and labour, completed by a set of semi-structured interviews conducted with the representatives of the involved stakeholders. One of the main outcomes of this research confirms that apprenticeship is the most inclusive IVET component within the labour market.

Keywords: company-based apprenticeship, work-based alternating training, vocational qualifications, inclusive performance,

Introduction

Apprenticeship is the pioneering form of work-based learning in France constituting institutionally at present an important component of the initial vocational educational (IVET) system. It integrates within the framework of a dominantly company-based apprenticeship model (CEDEFOP, 2016, 2018, 2019; European Commission, 2012; Gessler, 2019; ILO-IBRD, 2013). Accordingly, apprenticeship is primarily initiated via a work contract signed between the apprentice and a company, which is implemented through an alteration between dominantly (60–75 %) on-the-job and in-house training for the remaining apprenticeship time. Its main aim is to allow young people aged from 16 to 30 years (and even over for handicapped people and creators or undertakers of activities requiring specific qualifications) to have access to all types and levels of national vocational qualifications (from EQF level 3–7) validated and referenced within the NQF Directory of vocational qualifications (*RNCP – Répertoire National des Certifications Professionnelles*) (MT, 2019b). Apprenticeship is observed to be the most inclusive IVET component within the labour market as in February 2018, 72 % of apprentices on average find jobs (56 % on permanent employment contracts) within a seven-month-period following their graduation in 2017, compared to only 51 % of the school-based IVET graduates (Marchal, 2019a, 2019b).

This paper on apprenticeship in France is the outcome of an exploratory research conducted through three main interrelated sections. The first main section dealing with the institutional patterns gives an overview concerning the historical and legal background developments of the apprenticeship system and the current setting of institutions and stakeholders involved in its governance and funding arrangements. The second section on the processes of training organisation and methods provides an insight into the current practices of training organisation within and between apprenticeship training centres (CFA) and on-the-job training companies, the adopted training pedagogy and methods and the accompanying assessment and quality assurance mechanisms. The last section deals with the inclusive performance in terms of statistically observed apprentices' access to both company-based apprenticeship contracts and employment within the labour market after the completion of their apprenticeship programmes. This research exploration over three main sections is is primarily and dominantly based on desk research and the use of available statistical data, documentation and related inclusion performance evaluation studies and reports published by the research bodies connected with the ministries of education and labour, namely: (a) – the evaluation, forecasting and performance department (DEPP – Direction de l'évaluation, de la prospective et de la performance) of the ministry of education which contributes to the evaluation of policies conducted in the fields of education and training, (b) – the department of the ministry of labour in charge of research, studies and statistics (DARES – Direction de l'animation de la recherche, des études et des statistiques) in fields related to the themes of work, employment, vocational training and social dialogue. This basic research exploration is completed (basically in its second main section) by conducting, within some directly involved stakeholders (namely with trainers within apprenticeship training centres and companies) a set of exploratory semi-directive qualitative interviews basically focused on questions connected with the adopted apprenticeship training organisation and methods.

1 Institutional patterns

This first main section of the paper provides an insight into the background historical, legal and institutional developments of the French apprenticeship system, the current institutional setting of involved governance institutions and stakeholders and the adopted contractual and funding arrangements.

1.1. Background developments

The French apprenticeship system is historically rooted back into the medieval guilds with their strict hierarchy, journeymen and master craftsmen until their suppression by the French revolution in 1791. Then came the first apprentice Law (1851 Act of the 22nd of February) to regulate the contracts binding apprentices to their masters. This was completed in 1919 by the Astier Act of July the 25th which gave the local authorities the responsibility of organising vocational training within the industrial sector for young people aged from 14 to 17 years old. Following the introduction of the apprenticeship tax and the creation of the chambers of trades and crafts in 1925, the formally written apprenticeship contract with a company was effectively introduced in 1928. In 1937, Wallter-Paulin's Act of the 10th March allowed the chambers of trades and crafts to have the fundamental role of organising apprenticeship and creating related guidance offices. In 1961, the first apprenticeship training centres (*CFA – Centre de Formation d'Apprentis*) were created following the related inter-professional agreement of the 16th May. Apprenticeship became legally an important component of the initial vocational education and training (IVET) system via Guichard's Act of the 16th July 1971 on apprenticeship. The Decentralisation Act of the 17th January 1983 extended the regions role in connection with apprenticeship organisation and funding managements. One year after the extension of apprenticeship access age limit to 26 years old (Order of 16th July 1986), the range of qualifications acquired through apprenticeship was widened from EQF level 3–7 via Séguin's Act of the 23rd July 1987. Then, in terms of 1997 Act of the 16th October, apprenticeship was formally established within the non-industrial and non-commercial public sector. The Social Modernisation Act of the 17th January 2002 provided apprentices with new guarantees mainly connected with their working duration, security and wage remuneration. Access to apprenticeship was further reinforced through the 2014 Act of March the 5th on "vocational training, employment and social democracy" (Abriac, Rathelot, & Sanchez, 2009; Cedefop, 1999; Guès, 2009; Sanchez & Zamora, 2007; Terrot, 1997).

Due to the existence of some structural and dis-functioning weaknesses hindering further future development of apprenticeship, the implementation of a set of related major reform measures undertaken within the framework of the VET Reform Act n° 2018–771 of the 5th September 2018 concerning "the freedom to choose one's professional future," was effectively launched at the beginning of 2019. It is an overall restructuring reform of apprenticeship institutional setting and mode of governance and funding. These major reform measures concentrated basically on: (a) – liberalising apprenticeship provision market and transferring its regional governance to the concerned professional activity branches, (b) – creating *"France compétences"* as a unique national governance institution and (c) – promoting the attractiveness and accessibility to apprenticeship (CARIF-OREF, 2019; Dif, 2019; DM, 2019a, 2019b, 2019c; MT, MEN, & MESRI, 2018; MT, 2019a).

1.2 Institutional setting

This sub-section provides an overview of the main settings and roles of institutions and stakeholders currently involved in the effective functioning and funding of the apprenticeships system.

1.2.1. Involved institutions and stakeholders

There is a variety of stakeholders directly and indirectly involved through a networking of cooperation and partnerships. They can be grouped into two main categories: alternating training providers and other involved stakeholders (Dif, 2013; DM, 2019a, 2019b, 2019c; MT, 2019a; MT, MEN & MESRI, 2018).

The first category concerns the alternating providers (i.e. apprenticeship training providers) which constitute the basic stakeholders directly involved in alternating training provision. It includes companies and the usual in-house training providers:

- **Companies:** they are responsible for on-the-job work-based training (for 60–75 % of the whole contractual training time), including the payment of the trainee's salary. They can also take in charge the remaining off-the-job training in cases where they possess their own in-house training centres.
- ***Apprenticeship training centres* (CFA – *Centres de Formation d'Apprentis*)**: they provide in-house (off-the-job) polyvalent and specialised theoretical and practical alternating training to apprentices aged from 16 to 30 years old (and even over for some cases) in all vocational and technological domains leading to obtaining formal national qualifications validated and registered within the national qualification framework (NQF) directory on both levels:

- the upper secondary level starting from the EQF level 3 such as the CAP (Professional Aptitude Certificate) to EQF level 4 such as the Bac.Pro. (Professional Baccalaureate) and the BP (Professional Diploma),
- the higher education level from EQF level 5 such as the High Technician Diploma (BTS) and the University Diploma in Technology (DUT) to EQF level 6 professional Bachelors and EQF level 7 professional Masters and the engineers' diplomas.

With the transfer of apprenticeship governance from regions to sectoral activity branches and the liberation of apprenticeship provision market through the reform Act of the 5th September 2018, all training organisations (including companies) can, starting from January 2019, create their own apprenticeship training centres (CFA) after obtaining prior formal quality assurance certification (DM, 2019c).

The second category of stakeholders concerns all those who are directly or indirectly involved in the qualification design processes, governance, implementation and follow up of apprenticeship contracts and their financing arrangements, including quality assurance, inclusive coaching and guidance provision services. These governance and intermediary stakeholders are mainly the following:

- *National institutions:* they include in addition to the State institutions such as the usually involved ministries of education, Labour & VET, agriculture, economy, healthcare, culture youth and sports the following national governance bodies, namely:
  - *"France compétences"*: it is a quadripartite national institution representing the State, the regions and the social partners called *"France compétences"* under the responsibility of the Minister in charge of VET within the Ministry of Labour. It was created on the 1st of January through the implementation of the VET Reform Act of the 5 September 2018 to replace and absorb the activities and roles of the previous national governance institutions such as the National Commission for Vocational Qualification (*CNCP – Commission Nationale de la Certification Professionnelle*), the National Council for Employment, Training and Vocational Guidance (*CNEFOP – Conseil National de l'Emploi, de la formation et de l'Orientation Professionnelles*) and the

Parity Fund for Securing Career Pathways (*FPSP – Fonds Paritaire de Sécurisation des Parcours) Professionnels*). Its main missions are mainly (DM, 2019; MT, 2019a): (a) taking in charge the regulation and control of the quality of vocational training programmes and qualifications via its newly created vocational qualification commission (*CCP – Commission de la Certification Professionnelle*) in charge of assessing and validating newly created qualifications and the updating and management of the NQF Directory for vocational qualifications (*RNCP – Répertoire National des Certifications Professionnelles*) and the Specific Directory (*RS – Répertoire Spécifique*) for complementary vocational qualifications (Decree n°2018–1172 of 18th December 2018); (b) playing an important financial role by ensuring, via its newly created operators of competences (*OPCO – Opérateurs de Compétences*) the reallocation of the funds collected from employers by "the Union for Recovering Social Security Contributions and family Allowances (*URSSAF – Unions de Recouvrement des cotisations de Sécurité Sociale et d'Allocations Familiales*)" or the Agricultural Social Mutuality (*MSA – Mutualité Sociale Agricole*); (c) promoting the development of an expertise networking and contributing to the public debate on the efficiency of policies connected with training and accessing to employment.

- <u>The operator of competences (*OPCO-Opérateurs de compétences*)</u>: they are also created within the framework of VET Reform Act of the 5 September 2018 (by the Decree n°2018–1209 of 21st December 2018) to replace effectively starting from 2019/2020 both the organisations collecting apprenticeship tax (*OCTA – Organismes colleteurs de la Taxe d'Apprentissage*) from the enterprise (representing 0.68 % of the enterprises' gross wage bill) and the accredited vocational training funds collectors and managers (*OPCA – Organismes Paritaires Collecteurs Agréés*) and also to take in charge the management of skill formation and support provision to small and medium companies.

- **Social partners:** In cooperation and partnerships with all the other involved stakeholders, they play an important consultative and decision making role in vocational qualification formation processes and their implementation on national, sectoral and regional levels through basically the following advisory bodies (Dif, 2013; DM, 2019b; MT, MEN & MESRI, 2018):
  - <u>Vocational Consultative Commissions (CPC – Commissions Professionnelles Consultatives)</u>: they are attached to different ministries awarding national qualifications through VET (including apprenticeship) in the upper secondary vocational certifications (such as the EQF level 3 "CAP" and both the EQF level 4 "BT" and the Professional baccalaureate) including EQF level 5 "BTS" (High Technician Diploma). There are now 11 sectoral, inter-sectoral and multi-sectoral CPC's taking in charge the design and updating of qualifications and their related occupational and certification/qualification referential standards.
  - <u>The National Pedagogical Commission (CPN – Commission Pédagogique Nationale)</u>: it is in charge of the establishment and updating of qualifications and referential standards in 25 specialities specific to the vocational two-year-university-diploma in technology (*DUT – Diplôme Universitaire de Technologie*) at EQF level 5.
  - <u>The Commission for Engineers' Grades (CTI – Commission des Titres d'Ingénieurs)</u>: it is an independent body, mandated by French law since 1934 to accredit all engineers' qualifications (including those obtained through apprenticeship), to develop the quality of training and to promote the engineer's grade and profession in France and abroad.
  - <u>National Council for Higher Education and Research (CNESER – Conseil National de l'Enseignement Supérieur et de la recherche)</u>: it is responsible for all higher education qualifications and certifications.
  - <u>Other higher education monitoring and follow-up bodies</u> such as: (a) the Bachelors, Masters and Doctorates monitoring committee (*CSLMD – Comité de suivi des cycles licence, master*

et doctorat) established within the ministry of higher education (Order of the 3rd March 2017), and (b) the committee for monitoring vocational training and qualifications in management (*CEFDG – Commission d'Évaluation des Formations et Diplômes de Gestion*) within higher education schools/institutes of management and commerce (Decree n° 2001–295 of 4th April 2001).

- **Chambers**: the chambers of commerce and industry (*CCI – chambres de commerce et de l'industrie*), the chambers of trades and crafts (*CMA – chambres de métiers et de l'artisanat*) and the chambers of Agriculture (*chambres de l'agriculture*) are highly involved in apprenticeship promotion and provision. They play an important role connected with guidance provision on regional level concerning access to training, qualifications, employment, etc. They also intervene as mediators in resolving disputes between employers and apprentices or their families. They are also expected, in cooperation with the operators of competences (OPCO) of "France compétences," to support companies in preparing their upcoming apprenticeship contracts (DM, 2019a).
- **Regions**: with the transfer of apprenticeship governance to the sectoral activity branches in accordance with implementation of the VET reform Act of the 5th September 2018 starting from January 2019, the regions conserve their role in promoting the attractiveness of apprenticeship through guidance provision in cooperation with the information and guidance centres (*CIO –Centres d'Information et d'Orientation*) and the national career guidance organisation (*ONISEP – Office National d'Information sur les Enseignements et les Professions*). They also conserve some roles in apprenticeship funding. In addition to the possibility of subsidising the investments of apprenticeship centres, they can complete this funding via their financial contribution to the current costs of apprenticeship contracts in accordance with their regional criteria for spatial and regional development. This regional complementary funding can be obtained via agreements by objectives and means concluded with the operators of competences (OPCO) (DM, 2019a).

1.2.2 Contractual and funding arrangements

Accessibility to apprenticeship within the framework of a company-based model is conditioned by the nature of its objectives and the accompanying contractual access and funding arrangements.

1.2.2.1 Objectives and access conditions

As a dual work-based alternating training, the French apprenticeship system integrates within the framework of a dominantly company-based apprenticeship model (CEDEFOP, 2016, 2018, 2019; European Commission, 2012; Gessler, 2019; ILO-IBRD, 2013). Its major aim is to facilitate transition from school to work of young people aged from 16 to 30 years old (and over for handicapped people and creators or undertakers of activities requiring specific qualifications) by allowing them to have access to certification-based professional qualifications (from EQF level 3–7) through an alternation between dominantly on-the-job work place training within the enterprises (from 60 % to 75 % of apprenticeship time) and off-the-job training within accredited apprenticeship training centres called CFA (*Centres de Formation d'Apprentis*). Undertaking apprenticeship is initially subject to signing an employment work contract between the apprentice and the employer. The duration of this contract is usually equivalent to the required period for obtaining the targeted qualification. Since the launch in January 2019 of the implementation of the reform Act of the 5th September 2018, the hiring schedule of apprentices is loosened by allowing accessibility to apprenticeship contracts through the whole year without the usual constraint of the hiring season imposed by the apprenticeship centres (CFA). This was accompanied by introducing more flexibility in apprenticeship contract signed with a company, as it will no longer be mandatory to go through labour courts to break a contract after the trial period of 45 days (as, for instance, the employer may terminate the contract for a serious professional malpractice). (Dif, 2013, 2019; MT, 2019b; MT, MEN, & MESRI, 2018; ONISEP, 2019).

1.2.2.1 Funding arrangements

As a company-based system, apprenticeship funding is taken in charge by the enterprises themselves through the payment of apprentices' wages and apprenticeship tax.

Funding arrangements for the apprentices

For the whole duration of their apprenticeship contracts, the apprentices are subject to the same rules and regulations within the employing enterprises like the rest of the employees. They have the right to a minimum apprenticeship salary paid by the employer as a percentage of the French minimum guaranteed wage (*SMIC – Salaire minimum interprofessionnel de croissance*) of €1521.22 in 2019 or the minimum wage for the occupation guaranteed by a collective agreement (*SMC – salaire minimum conventionnel de l'emploi occupé*), which increases with the apprentice's age and progression level in apprenticeship as described in the exemplary Tab. 1 below (MT, 2019b).

Tab. 1: Minimum monthly wage rates for apprentices since January 2019

Apprenticeship year	Under 18 years old	18–20 years old	21–25 years old	26 years old and over
First year	27 %	43 %	53 %	100 %
Second year	39 %	51 %	61 %	100 %
Third year	53 %	65 %	78 %	100 %

The apprentice's salary is exempted from the income tax within the limit of the annual minimum guaranteed wage. It is also exempted from the mandatory payment of the generalised social contribution (*CSG – contribution sociale généralisée*) and the contribution to the repayment of the social debt (*CRDS – contribution au remboursement de la dette sociale*).

Funding arrangements for the CFA

Apprenticeship is financed, within the framework of the implementation of the reform Act of the 5th September 2018, through a new unique mandatory funding contribution to vocational training and apprenticeship (*CUFPA – contribution unique à la formation professionnelle et à l'alternance*) by both, the enterprises with 11 and more employees and those with less (DM, 2019a):

- 1,68 % (1,44 % in Alsace-Moselle) of the annual gross wage bill of companies with more than 10 employees where 1 % for vocational training contribution and 0.68 % as an apprenticeship tax (with 0.44 % in Alsace-Moselle).
- 1.23 % (0.99 % in Alsace-Moselle) of the annual gross wage bill of companies having at most 10 employees with a contribution to vocational training of 0,55 % and an apprenticeship tax of 0,68 % (with only 0.44 % in Alsace-Moselle).

Moreover, companies with at least 250 employees where apprentices represent less than and 5 % of apprentices of their workforce must additionally pay a supplementary contribution to apprenticeship (*CSA – Contribution supplémentaire à l'apprentissage*) of 0.05–0.60 % of the gross wage bill depending on the percentage (from 4 % to 5 %) of employed apprentices.

This unique contribution of employers to CVT and apprenticeship funding (including CSA) will be collected by "the Union for Recovering Social Security Contributions and family Allowances (URSSAF – *Unions de Recouvrement des cotisations de Sécurité Sociale et d'Allocations Familiales*)" or the Agricultural Social Mutuality (*MSA – Mutualité Sociale Agricole*). Then it will be transferred to "*France compétences*" national agency, which takes in charge the funding re-allocation via its operators of competences (*OPCO – Opérateurs de compétences*) (Dif, 2019; DM, 2019a).

In this connection 87 % of the collected funding will be reallocated to the apprenticeship centres (CFA) on the basis of the real number of individual apprenticeship contracts concluded with the recruiting companies. Companies possessing their own apprenticeship centres (CFA) can deduct the related share of apprenticeship provision expenditure. The remaining part of 13 % of the apprenticeship tax is intended for the employer-paid out-of-pocket expenses. These expenses are incurred to promote the development of initial technological and vocational training (payments to certain institutions or schools) and subsidies paid to the apprenticeship training centres (CFA) in the form of equipment and materials that meet the needs of training provided. The supplementary apprenticeship (CSA) can also be deducted for companies possessing their own apprenticeships centres (CFA) from this part of apprenticeship tax (DM, 2019a).

In addition to the possibility of subsidising the investments of apprenticeship training centres, the regions can complete this funding via their financial contribution to the current costs of apprenticeship contracts in accordance with their regional criteria for spatial and regional development. This regional complementary funding can be obtained via agreements by objectives and means concluded with the operators of competences (OPCO) (Dif, 2019; DM, 2019a).

2 Organisation and methods

This second main section of the paper is an exploration of the French apprenticeship training organisation and methods, including related assessment and quality assurance mechanisms.

2.1 Training organisation and methods

As a dual company-based system, apprenticeship is organised through an alternation between on-the-job-workplace training and off-the-job in-house training. On-the-job training within a company is dominant and represents from 60 % to 75 % of the overall training time and off-the-job training within an apprenticeship training centre represents 25–40 % of the whole training programme. About two thirds of the undertaken in-house training time is devoted to general, technical and vocational subjects, whereas the remaining third is dedicated to professional and practical training as a usual complement to workplace training (CEDFOP, 2018; Dif, 2013, 2019; European Commission, 2012).

In contrast with the practice in the school-based training system, the apprenticeship training centres (CFA) are committed to respect the following basic principles connected with the concept of "alternating pedagogy" specific to apprenticeship training provision (CDEFOP, 2010; Dif, 2013):

- focussing on work-based training where teachers and trainers use workplace experience in the development of their teaching and training programmes and methods,
- distributing learning and training activities between on and off the job training according to specifically adapted schedules,
- guaranteeing a complementary role of the in-house training provision to on-the-job training by completing observed insufficiencies in the workplace training programme within the enterprise,
- securing the management and continuing communication between the apprenticeship training centre, the company and the apprentice via well-established coordination, control and follow-up intermediary tutors and instruments.

Although the off-the-job training providers (including their educational and training staff) have a large autonomy in choosing their own in-house training methods and supporting instruments at all NQF levels, the degree of their autonomy in curricular design and implementation is dependent on whether they are upper secondary or higher education training providers. The upper secondary alternating training providers are generally committed to implement the learning outcome and competence-based training programmes (including the assessment) in accordance with the established qualifications' related occupational and qualification/certification referential standards. But within higher education, the alternating training providers, especially apprenticeship centres are more autonomous in designing and implementing their own educational and training programmes. The training programmes for all alternating providers are composed of learning outcome and competence-based educational and professional training units. The educational units are exclusively taken in charge by off-the-job training providers. As for the practical knowledge, skills and competences connected with the professional training units, they are basically acquired on-the-job within the enterprise. However, there are cases where these professional units are jointly taken in charge by both the enterprises and the training providers through a complementarity-based alternating training programmes (as it is observed through conducted interviews within certain alternating training providers within the construction and machinery sectors), given that the depth and the width of acquired practical knowledge and skills in the field of the targeted qualifications are not sufficient, due to the limited size and/or activities of the involved enterprises. Moreover, the in-house training provision is based on the use of the "inductive and active learner-centred teaching method" (CEDEFOP, 2010; Dif, 2013). The practice of this training method goes from specific to general, as it is based on starting from concrete specific case studies or experiments in training provisions by building-up progressively on the learner's individual experiences, knowledge, capacities, expectations and constraints. Consequently, the theoretical and vocational knowledge which complete practical training can be effectively acquired within the training providers' classrooms and workshops by using updated supporting instruments and tools. As for the vocational practical knowledge, skills and competences, they are acquired basically on-the-job training within the enterprise through the programmed competence-based professional units (CEDFOP, 2010; Dif, 2013).

Within the framework of the implementation of these alternating training pedagogy concepts and methods, there are usually two basic types of follow-up and coordination tutors: the apprenticeship master and the pedagogical tutor

- _The workplace apprenticeship master:_ He/she may be the head of the company or a qualified employee. The appointed supervising master/tutor has to meet the following qualifying requirements: a)- holding a qualification at least equivalent to that targeted by the apprentice and having additionally three years at least of occupational experience in the workplace training field; b)- possessing in the field of training two years of supervisory experience with pedagogical and tutoring skills and competences in case the master does not possess the required qualification.

  The in-house training pedagogical tutor of the apprentice: He/she is appointed by the person in charge of the pedagogy and training programme in which the apprentice is enrolled within the CFA. The tutor takes in charge the responsibility of the follow-up of the apprentice's training and progress within the CFA and the enterprises through the coordination and follow-up documents and instruments.

Moreover, a smooth functioning of the apprenticeship alternating training between the CFA and the company requires a continuous coordination between the apprentice, the company and the CFA. In this connection, three follow-up and coordination instruments are also used: the apprenticeship liaison booklet, the liaison document and the company-CFA link sheet (CFA-MENDE, 2019; Dif, 2013; Lapprenti, 2019).

- *Apprenticeship liaison booklet (livret d'apprentissage)*: This mandatory coordination document between the on-the-job training company and the in-house training centre (CFA) enables them to determine the objectives to be achieved by the apprentice and effective follow-up. It contains the basic information concerning the apprentice, the training time-table, planned presence within the enterprise, and detailed training programme units and their contents, summary of the targeted qualification referential standards (including implementation follow-up sheets) within both the apprenticeship training centre and the enterprises. It constitutes an extremely useful coordination and follow-up instrument.
- *Liaison document (document de liaison)*: Usually drawn-up by the regional educational directorate, it specifies the competences and skills to be acquired by the apprentice and allows the apprenticeship master to carry out regular assessment of the apprentice's real progress in acquiring the targeted vocational knowledge, skills and competences;
- *The company-CFA link sheet (Fiche navette entreprise – CFA)*: It is designed and used to establish dialogue and regular feed-back connections between the CFA, the enterprise and the apprentice.

2.2 Assessment and quality assurance mechanisms

The quality of obtained targeted qualifications, skills and competences by the apprentices through their apprenticeship programmes is ensured

Apprenticeship in France: Institutional patterns 195

via the existence of well-established assessment and quality assurance mechanisms within the system.

2.2.1 Assessment of progression and access to qualifications

The apprenticeship follow-up instruments presented above such as the apprenticeship booklet, the liaison document or the enterprise-CFA link sheet are simply formative assessment tools enabling carrying out the assessment of the progress and the level of achievement made by the apprentices in the course of their training activity. However, these tools cannot provide material for credit units leading to certification and obtaining formally the targeted qualifications. In order to obtain formally the targeted qualification through apprenticeship, the apprentices have to take the required examination for the diplomas, or the titles/grades laid down in their apprenticeship contracts, given that the undertaken tests and examinations constitute the purpose and the end of their contracts. In this connection there are, during the cycles of the apprenticeship duration, two types of assessment methods in use: continuing assessment during the course of undertaken training called CCF (*contrôle en cours de formation*), introduced at the beginning of the 1990s, and the usual traditional punctual assessment method (*CP- contrôle ponctuel*). However, the use of one or the other or both is dependent on whether the in-house training provider is an upper secondary or a higher education institution. Within the upper secondary VET providers, only accredited alternating training centres (by the rector) can use CCF for the assessment of professional units connected with acquired skills and competences within the enterprise and the CP for the assessment of general and technical units connected with the courses provided within the in-house alternating training provision centres. The non-accredited alternating training providers are limited exclusively to the use of the punctual assessment method (CP) for all training units (professional and general/technical). In higher education, the assessment practice is based on the use of both CCF and CP during each semester of the academic year. The units, connected with the acquisition of academic knowledge, are exclusively assessed within the alternating training provision centres (such as apprenticeship centres). As for the professional units (including the end-of-the-programme professional project) connected with the operational vocational knowledge, skills and competences are assessed and validated by the alternating training providers in a joint collaboration with the enterprise (basically with its appointed training tutor) and professionals in the field (Billet, Cahuzac, & Perrin, 2002; Dif, 2013).

2.2.2 Quality assurance

Concerning the quality assurance, apprenticeship (as it is the case within the whole educational and training system) is basically subject to following overarching quality assurance evaluation mechanisms (CEDEFOP, 2009; Dif, 2013; DM, 2019b; Lombardi, 2010; MT, 2019a):

- Evaluation and quality accreditation/certification of training providers and trainers,
- the evaluation of the educational and training system (including apprenticeship) and its teaching methods by various inspection and evaluation organisations and bodies,
- quality assurance via the learning outcomes certification process (assessment, validation, recognition and certification awarding) implemented within the framework of a mixed approach of regulation combining both prescriptive and cooperative characters,
- the existence of referential framework of standards combining occupational and qualification/certification standards for all awarded vocational qualification which are also, evaluated, validated, updated, referenced and registered within the NQF repertory (RNCP) by the vocational qualification commission (*CCP – Commission de la Certification Professionnelle*) of "*France competences*" national agency.

3 Performance

The performance of apprenticeship is analysed in terms of effectively achieved access to both company-based apprenticeship contract and to the labour market after the completion of apprenticeship programmes.

3.1 Access to apprenticeship

448,127 apprentices were following their apprenticeship at all levels of the French five-level-NQF by the end of 2018 representing 1.6 % of the occupied work force (INSEE, 2019; Lombard & Demongeot, 2019). As detailed in Table 2 below, they were dominantly enrolled (at 59.9 %) within the upper secondary apprenticeship training centres (CFA), where 36.8 % at the NQF Level 5 (EQF level 3) and 23.1 % at NQF level 4 (EQF level 4). With 40.1 % apprentices in higher education, 19.8 % of them targeted NQF level 3 (EQF level 5) qualifications which included dominantly the "high technician certificate (BTS)" with 16.2 % and the "university diploma in technology (DUT)" (1.7 %), followed by the EQF level 7 (Master's degree level) and EQF level 6 (Bachelor's degree level) vocational qualifications with 13.3 % and 7 % respectively.

Tab. 2: Distribution and evolution of the number of enrolled apprentices at the end of 2018 by level of targeted qualifications

Qualification levels/diplomas	Apprentices in 2018		Evolution (%) 2017–2018
	Number	%	
NQF level 5 (EQF level 3):	164 874	36.8	1,4
where: – *CAP (Professional aptitude certificate)*	*152 268*	*34.0*	*1.4*
NQF level 4 (EQF level 4):	103 453	23.1	2.5
where: – *Bac pro (Professional Baccalaureate)*	*51 859*	*11.6*	*2.0*
- BP (Professional diploma)	*39 107*	*8.7*	*0.0*
Upper secondary	**268 327**	**59.9**	**1.8**
NQF level 3 (EQF level 5):	88 551	19.8	7.7
where: – *BTS (Professional aptitude certificate)*	*72 608*	*16.2*	*7.7*
- DUT (University diploma in technology)	*7 669*	*1.7*	*11.1*
NQF level 2 (EQF level 6): – Bachelor's degree level	31 582	7.0	6.2
NQF level 1 (EQF level 7): – Master's degree level	59 667	13.3	9.8
Higher education	**179 800**	**40.1**	**8.1**
All qualification levels	**448 127**	**100.0**	**4.2**

Source: DEPP: Note information, n° 19.30 (Juillet 2019).

In terms of the annual inflow, 317,315 new apprenticeship contracts were signed between the apprentices and private and public employers in 2018 (PLF-2020, 2019). Out of the 302,128 newly signed contracts in 2018 within the dominant private sector with 95.2 % of all new contracts, 81.2 % were taken in charge by small and medium enterprises with less than 250 employees, leaving only 18.8 % to the larger ones. 58.9 % of these new apprenticeship contracts were signed within the service sector companies. The remaining 41.1 % of the apprenticeship contracts were taken in charge by the enterprises of the production sectors, namely the industry (21.4 %), the construction (16.2 %) and the agriculture (3.5 %)). About two thirds (69.9 %) of the new apprentices in 2018 within the private sector were initially holders of vocational qualifications (where 28 % at EQF level 4, 21.6 % at EQF level 5 and over and 20.4 % at EQF level 3) (PLF-2020, 2019). The weight of newly participating apprentices with the lowest initial NQF level (EQF level 3) or without any qualification went down from 94.8 % in 1992 to 50.5 % in 2018. This decrease touched more specifically those without any initial formal qualifications as the share of their participation in the new apprenticeship contracts decreased from 60.5 % in 1992 to 30.1 % in 2018 (DARES, 2018; PLF-2020, 2019). Moreover, most of the new beneficiaries of apprenticeship contracts in 2018 (85.7 %) came from the initial educational tracks, where 58.5 % from initial school-based system and 27.2 % from apprenticeship and 6.9 % were already employed. As for those who were unemployed or job seekers represented only 5.1 % of the beneficiaries in 2018 (PLF-2020, 2019).

3.2 Access to labour market

As a dominantly company-based system working through an alternation between on-the-job and in-house work-based training, apprenticeship offers a better access to the labour market than the school-based component of the VET system. 72 % of all the apprentices, who completed their apprenticeship up to EQF level 5 in 2017, had an effective access to employment (56 % on permanent employment contracts) within the following seven months as compared to only 51 % (35 % on open-ended work contracts) for those completing their school-based

VET programmes at the same EQF levels. About half of the apprenticeship graduates at all NQF levels in 2017 are kept by the enterprises within which they completed their on-the-job training (Marchal, 2019a, 2019b).

The access rate is even higher for the holders than for the non-holders of vocational qualifications. In apprenticeship, 76 % of graduates holding vocational qualifications up to EQF level 5 have access to a job within the first seven months following their graduation (57 % of them on permanent employment contracts), compared to only 59 % of graduates non-holders of vocational qualifications (52 % on open-ended work contracts). By contrast, this access rate is far lower for the holders of the same vocational qualifications up the EQF level 5 within the school-based system as only 53 % of them (35 % on open-ended contract) have access to a job seven after the graduation (Marchal, 2019a, 2019b).

Moreover, the access rate to the labour market is generally observed to be increasing with the increased level of obtained vocational qualifications through apprenticeship, as it goes up from 67 % for EQF level 3 up to 82 % for EQF level 6 and 7. However, some of the well-established intermediary vocational qualifications obtained via apprenticeship remain characterised by allowing their holders to have even a higher access rate, such as the EQF level 5 BTS (High Technician Certificate) and the EQF level 4 PB (professional certificate) at access rate of 83 % and 84 % respectively within seven months after the graduation in 2017 (Marchal, 2019a, 2019b).

Conclusion

Apprenticeship remains the best performing component of the French IVET in terms of accessibility to both work-based training and employment contracts. As work-based training and employment contracts, their inflow number has increased from 129,616 in 1992 to 317,315 new apprenticeship contracts that is, 144.8 % with an annual average increase of 5.6 %. This was basically obtained within the dominant private sector despite its relatively decreased weight from 100 % in 1992 to 95.2 % of the overall accessibility inflow in 2018. The highest increase during this period was achieved in higher eduction apprenticeship, as the weight of the annual inflow of new apprentices preparing higher education vocational qualifications via apprenticeship within the overall annual inflow of new apprenticeship contracts has gone up from only 2.2 % in 1992 to 38.8 % in 2018 (DARES, 2018; PLF-2020, 2019). Concerning the effective accessibility to the labour market after graduation, over two thirds on average of the apprentices completing their apprenticeship programmes, have a direct access to the labour market, dominantly via permanent work contracts. Moreover, about four out of five on average of the holders of vocational qualifications through apprenticeship find jobs within a period of seven month after the completion of their apprenticeship (DEPP, 2019a; Marchal, 2019).

However, despite this observed positive inclusive performance, apprenticeship further development still hindered by some remaining structural institutional and functioning weaknesses (Cart & Toutin-Trelcat, 2010; Dif, 2013, 2019), namely: (a) – the complexity of proliferated networks of institutions and stockholders involved in apprenticeship governance and funding mechanisms; (b) – the persisting existence of a traditionally held poor image and perception of work-based vocational training including apprenticeship as route leading to excellence in comparison with the general education; (c) – the existence of relatively high risk of apprentices' defection especially during the first year of the apprenticeship contractual period where about a third of apprentices abandon apprenticeship within the trial period. But, this defection risk is also observed to be decreasing with the apprentices' increased age and level of initial and targeted vocational qualifications. In connection with all these structural issues, the implementation of a set of related major reform measures integrating within the framework of the VET reform of the 5th September 2018, was launched at the beginning of 2019. The undertaken measures are mainly focussed on simplifying the institutional governance setting and funding mechanisms and promoting the attractiveness and accessibility to apprenticeship.

M'Hamed DIF (Dr.) is a senior associate researcher within BETA-Céreq Alsace at the University of Strasbourg (France), working in the following research areas: Lifelong learning and qualification systems, inclusion and VET-labour market relationships, competence assessment and validation of experiential learning, work identities and HRD, innovation and learning organisations and regions. He is also a "VET-NET" board member and a reviewer to the ECER (EERA) and IJRVET.

References

Abriac, D., Rathelot, R., & Sanchez, R. (2009). *L'apprentissage, entre formation et insertion professionnelles.* INSEE, Formations et emploi, édition 2009. Retrieved from http://www.insee.fr/fr/ffc/docs_ffc/ref/formemp09e.PDF.

Billet, J.-C., Cahuzac, R., & Perrin, J. (2002). *Le contrôle en cours de formation: 10 propositions pour 2002.* Rapport à Monsieur le Ministre de l'Éducation Nationale et Monsieur le Ministre délégué à l'enseignement professionnel. Paris: CNRAA. Retrieved from http://media.education.gouv.fr/file/04/4/6044.pdf.

CARIF-OREF (2019). *Reforme de la formation professionnelle – France compétences.* Centre d'animation de ressources et d'information sur la formation Observatoire régional emploi formation (CARIF-OREF), Juin 2019. Retrieved from http://www.c2rp.fr/publications/reforme-de-la-formation-professionnelle-france-competences.

Cart, B., Toutin-Trelcat, M.-H., & Henguelle, V. (2010). Apprenticeship contracts: why they are breached? *Training & Employment*, n° 89, October-November, Céreq, Marseille. Retrieved from http://pmb.cereq.fr/doc_num.php?explnum_id=5020.

CEDEFOP (1999). *Apprenticeship in France: 1999.* Training village – ETV library.

CEDEFOP (2009). *Relationship between quality assurance and VET certification in EU Member States.* Office des publications

officielles des Communautés européennes, Luxembourg, 2009. Retrieved from https://www.cedefop.europa.eu/files/5196_en.pdf.
CEDEFOP (2010). *Learning outcomes approaches in VET Curricula: a comparative analysis of nine European countries.* Publication Office of the European Union, Luxembourg, 2010. Retrieved from https://www.cedefop.europa.eu/files/5506_en.pdf.
CEDEFOP (2016). *Governance and financing of apprenticeships.* Luxembourg: Publications Office of the European Union, 2016. Retrieved from https://www.cedefop.europa.eu/files/5553_en.pdf.
CEDEFOP (2018). Apprenticeship in European countries: acrossnation overview, Luxembourg: Publications Office of the European Union, 2018. https://www.cedefop.europa.eu/files/4166_en.pdf.
CEDEFOP (2019). *Cedefop's analytical framework for apprenticeships.* CEDEFOP, July 2019. Retrieved from https://www.cedefop.europa.eu/files/8130_en.pdf.
CFA-MENDE (2019). *Suivi de formation.* Le Centre de Formation par l'Alternance Interprofessionnel. Henry GIRAL de MENDE (CF-Mende). 2019. Retrieved from http://cfa-mende.fr/suivi-formation/.
DARES (2018). *Les caractéristiques des contrats d'apprentissage de 1992 à 2017.* Ministère du Travail, DARES 2018. Retrieved from https://dares.travail-emploi.gouv.fr/dares-etudes-et-statistiques/statistiques-de-a-a-z/article/le-contrat-d-apprentissage.
DEPP (2019a). *l'éducation nationale en chiffres: 2019.* Direction de L'Évaluation, de la Prospective et de la Performance (DEPP), Ministère de l'Éducation Nationale (MEN), Nov. 2018. Retrieved from https://www.education.gouv.fr/cid57111/l-education-nationale-en-chiffres.html.
DEPP (2019b). R*epères et références statistiques sur les enseignements, la formation et la recherche 2019.* Direction de l'Évaluation, de la Prospective et de la Performance (DEPP), Édition 2018, France. Retrieved from https://www.education.gouv.fr/cid57096/reperes-et-references-statistiques.html.
Dif, M. (2013). Country case studies: France. In E. Smith & R. Brennan Kemmis (Eds.). *Towards a Model Apprenticeship Framework: A Comparative Analysis of National Apprenticeship Systems.* International Labour Organisation (ILO) and World Bank (IIBRD)

Publication, Geneva, Dec. 2013 (pp. 81–91). Retrieved from https://www.ilo.org/wcmsp5/groups/public/---asia/---ro-bangkok/---sro-new_delhi/documents/publication/wcms_234728.pdf.

Dif, M. (2019). On the inclusive performance of apprenticeship within the French VET system and the current reform of its governance and related institutional setting. In B. E. Stalder & C. Nägele (Eds.). *Trends in Vocational Education and Training Research. Vol. II. Proceedings of the European Conference on Educational Research (ECER), Vocational Education and Training Network (VETNET)* (pp. 106–115). Bern, Switzerland, September 2019. https://doi.org/10.5281/zenodo.3371452.

DM (2019a). *Apprentissage: système de financement et gouvernance*, Dossier novembre 2019, in Défi Métier (DM). Retrieved from https://www.defi-metiers.fr/dossiers/apprentissage-systeme-de-financement-et-gouvernance.

DM (2019b). *Le système français de la certification professionnelle: points de repère.* Dossier novembre 2019, in Défi Métier (DM). Retrieved from https://www.defi-metiers.fr/dossiers/le-systeme-francais-de-la-certification-professionnelle-points-de-repere.

DM (2019c). *Les nouvelles règles applicables aux CFA et aux formations en apprentissage.* Dossier octobre 2019, in Défi Métier (DM). Retrieved from https://www.defi-metiers.fr/dossiers/les-nouvelles-regles-applicables-aux-cfa-et-aux-formations-en-apprentissage.

European Commission (2012). *Apprenticeship supply in the member states of the European Union. Final report.* Publications Office of the European Union, Luxembourg. Retrieved from https://op.europa.eu/en/publication-detail/-/publication/3b34aeca-d9bb-4ac1-a3dc-d106e43bc2bf.

Gessler, M. (2019). Concepts of apprenticeship: strengths, weaknesses and pitfalls? In S. McGrath et al. (Eds.). *Handbook of Vocational Education and Training: Developments in the Changing World of Work.* Springer Nature Switzerland AG, 2019 (pp. 1–34). Retrieved from https://doi.org/10.1007/978-3-319-49789-1_94-2.

Gues, P. (2009). *Repère sur l'alternance.* Le Lien des Responsables: Le journal des maisons familiales rurales d'éducation et d'orientation,

UNMFREO, n° 207, décembre 2009. Retrieved from http://www.unaf.fr/IMG/pdf/LR_decembre_2009_2_.pdf.

ILO-IBRD (2013). *Towards a Model Apprenticeship Framework: A Comparative Analysis of National Apprenticeship Systems*. International Labour Organisation (ILO) & World Bank (IBRD) Publication, Geneva, Dec.2013. Retrieved from https://www.ilo.org/wcmsp5/groups/public/---asia/---ro-bangkok/---sro-new_delhi/documents/publication/wcms_234728.pdf.

INSEE (2019). *Tableaux de l'économie française*. INSEE, Édition 2019. Retrieved from https://www.insee.fr/fr/statistiques/3696937.

Lapprenti (2019). *Les outils de liaison du CFA*, Association L'Apprenti (Lapprenti.com): Centrale d'information sur l'alternance. Retrieved from https://www.lapprenti.com/html/cfa/outils.asp.

Lombardi, L. (2010). *Structures des systèmes d'enseignement et de formation en Europe -France, version 2009–2010*. EACEA, European Commission.

Lombard, F., & Demongeot, A. (2019). *L'apprentissage au 31 décembre 2018*. Note d'information, n°19.30-juillet 2019, Direction de l'évaluation, de la prospective et de la performance (DEPP A1). Retrieved from https://cache.media.education.gouv.fr/file/2019/94/2/depp-ni-2019-19-30_1156942.pdf.

Marchal, N. (2019a). *Le diplôme et la conjoncture économique demeurent déterminant dans l'insertion des apprentis*. Note d'information n°19.11, DEPP-A1, avril 2019, France. Retrieved from http://www.c2rp.fr/sites/default/files/atoms/files/c2rp-depp-ni-2019-19-11-le-diplome-et-la-conjoncture-economique-demeurent-determinants-dans-insertion-des-apprentis_1106645_2.pdf.

Marchal, N. (2019b). *Le diplôme et la conjoncture économique demeurent déterminant dans l'insertion des lycéens professionnels*. Note d'information n°19.10, DEPP-A1, avril 2019. Retrieved from http://cio.ac-amiens.fr/IMG/pdf/depp-ni-2019-19-10-le-diplome-et-la-conjoncture-economique-restent-determinants-dans-insertion-des-lyceens-professionnels_1106643.pdf.

MT (2019a). *France compétences*. Ministère du Travail (MT), janvier-mars, 2019. Retrieved from https://travail-emploi.gouv.fr/ministere-agences-et-operateurs/article/france-competences.

MT (2019b). *Contrat d'apprentissage*. Ministère du Travail (MT), octobre 2019. Retrieved from https://travail-emploi.gouv.fr/formation-professionnelle/formation-en-alternance-10751/apprentissage/contrat-apprentissage.

MT, MEN, & MESRI (2018). *Transformation de l'apprentissage: L'apprentissage fait sa révolution copernicienne.* Ministère du Travail (MT), Ministère de l'Éducation Nationale (MEN) & Ministère de l'Enseignement Supérieur, de la Recherche et de l'Innovation (MESRI), 9 février 2018, France. Retrieved from http://cache.media.education.gouv.fr/file/Fevrier/65/7/DP_apprentissage_Web_Bdef_895657.pdf.

ONISEP (2019). *le contrat d'apprentissage.* ONISEP 8 Octobre 2019. Retrieved from http://www.onisep.fr/Cap-vers-l-emploi/Alternance/Le-contrat-d-apprentissage-le-contrat-de-professionnalisation/Le-contrat-d-apprentissage.

PLF-2020 (2019). *Annexe au projet de loi de finance pour 2020: formation professionnelle.* Ministère des finances et des comptes publiques. Novembre 2015. Retrieved from https://www.performance-publique.budget.gouv.fr/sites/performance_publique/files/farandole/ressources/2020/pap/pdf/jaunes/Jaune2020_formation_professionnelle.pdf.

Sánchez, R., & Zamora, P. H. (2007). Retour sur quelques jalons de l'histoire de la formation professionnelle en alternance. In: DARES: *Éducation & formations* n° 75, octobre 2007 (pp. 109–116). Retrieved from http://cache.media.education.gouv.fr/file/79/8/20798.pdf.

Terrot, N. (1997). *Histoire de l'éducation des adultes en France.* L'Harmattan, 1997.

3.
Dual VET and education-business cooperation in Spain

REINA FERRÁNDEZ-BERRUECO, LUCÍA SÁNCHEZ-TARAZAGA & STEPHAN HUMPL

The interest of companies in participating in higher education

Abstract: This chapter focuses on the interests of companies in participating in Higher Education as a way to improve the relationship between university and labour market. For that purpose, we offer in the first place a literary review about the impact of university-business cooperation and after that we contextualise the theoretical findings into an empirical research study that help might us frame these benefits within the Spanish context. Results from the Principal Components Analysis summarise the benefits reported by companies collaborating in external placements into five factors: Innovation, Economy, Social Image, CSR and Strategic Planning. Nevertheless, the survey should be considered as an initial approach to the issue. For more consistent results, it would be needed a bigger sample from different educational levels and companies collaborating in different ways, not only in external placements. Finally, new research should also take into account the international scope that helps clarify whether companies' expectations remain the same unchanging wherever the collaboration takes place.

1. Introduction

Partnerships between companies and education improve students' opportunities to acquire competences (OEDC, 2012). Moreover, the learning processes rooted in the working environment offered by institutions and companies help professional education providers to interpret and respond pedagogically to increasingly uncertain and complex social, economic and demographic challenges (Barnett & Coate, 2005; Devins et al., 2015).

However, analysis of the current situation in Europe, and in particular western and southern European countries, suggests that Higher Education systems (especially universities) are not responding quickly enough to these changes in society, and are failing to adapt programmes to the needs of the economy and the labour market. Higher Education Institutions (HEI) do not always understand what companies expect from such collaborations and forget that they are motivated by some form of financial compensation or other. Conversely, companies are not always aware of the potential benefits and impact of this collaboration (Ferrández-Berrueco et al., 2016a, 2016b).

Whatever the case, collaboration is increasingly necessary. To be meaningful and sustainable, vocational training systems need to be aware of how to encourage such partnerships and maximise their potential.

As for HE, previous works (Ferrández-Berrueco & Sánchez-Tarazaga, 2019, pp.86) have reported different ways of collaboration between the labour market and universities:

1. **On-demand training**. This is the case when a big company wants to update a sector of its employees. The company contacts a HEI to plan and design a customised programme. Here the gain is two-fold: the employees obtain a HE qualification and company uses their knowledge and expertise. The main disadvantage is that the company may control the entire programme, and the HEI will provide only the teachers.
2. **SMEs' confederation**. When a group of companies in the same sector identify a need to ensure the availability of appropriately skilled recruits, they may work as a cooperative. They have their own training centre (a private HEI institution), which is another company within the confederation. The training centre and the companies work as one body; this appears to be the perfect relationship.
3. **SMEs as curriculum planners**. Some regulations at institutional or even national level require HEIs to contact SMEs to develop a programme. Their involvement may vary from a simple administrative role to cover legal requirements to a real partnership. In the event of partnership, SMEs also take part in programme delivery and student assessment.
4. **SMEs as placements**. In this case, the programme requires students to undertake a placement. Usually, HEI staff in charge

of the practicum look for companies to provide placements, though students sometimes have their own contacts. If learning outcomes are not well defined, placements may provide only general work experience.
5. **SMEs go to a HEI**. A way to bring work experience into classrooms. Apart from individual initiatives from some academic staff, this is an alternative when placements for students are insufficient. The advantage is that workload and difficulty level are the same for all students, whereas the main disadvantage is loss of authenticity.

1.1. Workplace training in universities in Spain

Of all the ways of collaboration outlined above, the one most often used by Spanish universities is that of workplace placements (Aneas & Vilà, 2018).

For that reason, we can find numerous research studies on this issue. We have grouped these studies according to Latorre and Blanco's (2011) synthesis in the following areas:

- Formative sense and usefulness: Álvarez, Iglesias, and García (2008), Egido (2017), Latorre (2007), Ryan, Toohey, and Hughes (1996), Sarceda-Gorgoso and Rodicio-García (2018), Serrano (2013) and Valle and Manso (2011).
- Effectiveness of the programme: Villa and Poblete (2004).
- Expectations, perceptions and assessments of the academic agents involved (students and tutors): Verde (2001) and Whittington and Ferrández-Berrueco (2007).
- Integration of new technologies: Cebrián and Monedero (2009).
- Employability opportunities: Marhuenda, Bernad and Navas (2010).
- Organisation, general structure: Zabalza (2008, 2011).

Mention is also made on a normative level of the relevance of curricular practices as a privileged space for the development of the profession's competencies. Thus, Royal Decree 592/2014, of 11 July, regulates the external academic practices of university students and, in its initial article, indicates that they must favour the acquisition of student competences, so as to prepare them for exercising professional activities, facilitate their employability and foster their capacity for innovation and creativity.

In line with this approach, it is during the internship period that university education is brought closer to the demands of society and the professional world (Zabalza, 2008). In other words, emphasis is placed on a less academic and more practice-oriented approach to training in real situations, within a framework in which students have the opportunity to develop the skills of the profession.

Universities are aware that they alone cannot guarantee their students will graduate with the necessary skills during their initial training and have established channels of dialogue with future employers (Aneas & Vilà, 2016; Clanchy & Ballard, 1995; Mendoza & Covarrubias, 2016). However, these channels appear not to be sufficiently effective, as communication is not as fluid as it should be (Ferrández-Berrueco et al., 2016a, 2016b). With regard to this failing communication, a fresh look at the legislative frame of reference (Royal Decree 592/2014) reveals that it sets out the recognised functions of the collaborating firms, with few references to its rights and numerous obligations. The company's rights are listed below, as they are more closely linked to the object of this paper (Art.11):

(a) recognition of their collaborative activity by the university under the terms of the educational cooperation agreement;
(b) information about the regulations that regulate external practices, as well as the formative project and the conditions of its development;
(c) access to the university in order to obtain the necessary information and support for the fulfilment of the purposes of their function;
(d) other specific considerations that the university may establish.

From this declaration, we can infer that collaboration, in terms of company rights, is limited to a passive role, which we can summarise as recognition and information.

> It is therefore clear that collaboration is necessary. For this to happen in a meaningful and sustainable way, companies should have a more active role. Not only should they act as workplace providers,

they should also provide real cases or define the professional competences required by the curriculum, as seen in other European countries like Austria, Finland, Germany or the UK (Devins et al, 2015; Ferrández-Berrueco et al., 2016a). The legal framework is insufficient as it only recognises a passive role. It is therefore essential that universities improve their understanding of how to encourage and maximise the potential of this type of cooperation. To that end, the university must understand the motivations, benefits and potential impact perceived by such organisations.

With this purpose in mind, the next sections will attempt to answer the following questions as the main aim of this paper: what motivates a firm to collaborate with the university? What benefits do they expect to obtain? What is the expected and received impact of such collaboration?

Thus, Section 2 will explore the literature of the last 15 years on the university-labour market relationship. Section 3 will then contextualise the theoretical findings into an empirical research study within the Spanish context.

2. Benefits[1] of collaboration for companies. Literature review

In this section we will begin by exploring the reasons set out in the European Commission's report (Healy et al., 2014) about the impact of

---

[1] We assume that *motivations*, *benefits* and *impacts* are essentially dealing with the *effect* of the collaboration. In that sense we will consider them as synonyms along the text. Thus, when this effect is the reason for an action, it is a motivation, in this sense, motivation is an expectation, the effect of which is not yet evident but expected. Once the effect has taken place it can be positive or negative. When the effect is positive, it is a benefit (if it is negative, it may be referred to as harmful). Lastly, this benefit or harmful effect will become a positive or negative impact depending on its actual resonance in the organisation, which is usually measured over the long term. We may therefore consider that the same effect can be a motivation for action, a benefit or an impact depending on its timing in relation to the action: (a) motivation takes place before the action; (b) benefit is the direct consequence – that is, it happens at the same time as the action; and (c) impact takes place after the action and usually persists over time.

university-business cooperation. These motivations will articulate the discursive thread of this section and will be complemented by other sources.

We chose this document, in which 41 cases from a total of 16 countries were analysed, as a starting point because of its thoroughness and international vision. It includes areas of cooperation, specifically in higher education, and identifies several levels, which can be summarised as follows: cooperation between a university and a company, between a university and several companies, between a company and several universities, and between several companies and several universities. In any case, these are formal and continuous forms of collaboration over time.

Among the drivers that motivate firm-university collaboration, the report outlines the following (Healy et al., 2014):

An initial motivation involves different aspects of the staff. One aim is to ensure the recruitment of professionals with higher qualifications, either in terms of technical knowledge or the so-called "soft skills." Firm-university collaboration is also a source of recruitment and a channel of access to future employees, since it can attract more and better students. In addition, it offers the possibility of updating worker skills, which can also help retain staff and reduce turnover.

A second reason is the incorporation of new ideas into the organisation. The fact that the two areas are in contact allows the organisation to feed on the knowledge and experiences of students and supervisors. In addition to generating a relationship, it leads to the innovation and modernisation of company processes in order to adapt to change.

The third reason deals with more intangible aspects such as company image: collaborating with the university enhances prestige.

After this initial synthesis we will further examine each of the reasons mentioned, providing an additional literature review on the topic.

2.1. Collaboration as a source of recruitment, economic savings and increased productivity

Employee training

The university provides companies with staff (practitioners) either free of charge or at a low cost. These practitioners contribute economic savings for some time (Elijido-Ten & Kloot, 2015; Ferrández-Berrueco et al., 2016a; Siebert & Costley, 2013), since they work in the same or similar conditions to the rest of the staff. Bringing new knowledge to the company also covers employees' training needs (García Delgado, 2002; Guinart, 2005; Healy et al., 2014), which saves on training costs.

Other savings on collaboration are reported for extracurricular practices and involve sharing and reducing R&D expenses (Marzo et al., 2007).

Savings on candidate selection

Moreover, García Delgado (2002) considers that the system of granting internships is increasingly used as an efficient and economic form of workforce selection. Thus, during internships, the company can check the candidate's skills and whether or not they fit with the organisation.

Productivity gains

Other authors such as Basit et al. (2015) or Daley et al. (2016) consider that collaboration leads to increased productivity, which is vital for gaining a competitive advantage and was already pointed out by Dasgupta and David (1994) more than 25 years ago.

2.2. Collaboration as enhancement of corporate image

In previous works we found that companies collaborate in order to enhance their social image and prestige (Ferrández-Berrueco et al., 2016a, 2016b). We would highlight the fact that some companies choose to become "Employers of choice" or to achieve "Employer branding"— top companies where young people want to work. Generating this attractiveness of the brand as an employer is fundamental in order to attract the best candidates.

Thus, the case of the "good image" of Nestlé and Sheffield Hallam University, contributed by Daley et al. (2016), has other derived effects for the company: access to a greater source of candidates to recruit, a higher degree of commitment (loyalty) and a better alignment in the company's continuous training programmes.

A broader vision of the "image" concept would be included within Corporate Social Responsibility (CSR): the voluntary integration by companies of social and environmental concerns in their operations and relationships. CSR tends to be more closely linked to large companies. For most small and medium-sized enterprises, especially micro enterprises, the CSR process is likely to remain informal and intuitive (EC, 2011b).

As recognised by the European Commission (EC, 2011b), CSR is a multi-dimensional concept that, in addition to environmental issues and human rights, includes work and employment practices (including training), as well as the involvement of local communities and development. Development can be directly related to their role with universities.

Specifically, we find several authors (Daley et al., 2016; Ferrández-Berrueco et al., 2016a, 2016b; Marzo et al., 2007) who link collaborating with the university as a motivator to increase CSR, in terms of enhancement of corporate social image, reputation and prestige.

2.3. Collaboration as a source of transformation

Employee modernisation

In this area, we find arguments in favour of updating the organisation's employees (Basit et al., 2015; Felce, 2017; Ferrández-Berrueco, 2016a; Marzo et al., 2007; Whittington & Ferrández, 2007) through the new knowledge and innovations that students bring to the company (Antcliff et al., 2016; Geller et al., 2016; Guinart, 2005).

Marzo et al. (2007) indicate that pressure is now increasing for companies to continually improve their knowledge in order to prosper and ensure long-term survival. A few decades ago, this knowledge was produced within each organisation. Thanks to cooperation with universities, however, it has been possible to accelerate these processes and the parallel development of new technologies (Okubo & Sjoberg, 2000).

The involvement of students in companies is therefore justified from the point of view of their contribution: a new/different vision of problems, their motivation for the world of work after many years in the classroom, or their knowledge in some areas, such as technologies or languages (García Delgado, 2002).

Learning culture

Another benefit is the promotion of a learning culture within the organisation (Bolivar, 2007; Ions & Minton, 2012), which adds value to companies because it provides a better understanding of the problems (White, 2012) and is closely related to Senge's "learning companies" (1990).

Moreover, we found another type of factor associated with professional reflection in the sense that collaboration allows for a better acceptance of change and, to a certain extent, obliges mutual understanding (White, 2012), allowing the organisation to open up to change and not remain relegated to "what has always been done" (Ions & Minton, 2012; Whittington & Ferrández, 2007).

Assessing efficiency

We also found factors associated with assessment, since collaboration provides the company with a benchmark to assess its efficiency (Hegarty et al., 2011). At the same time, it is a way of evaluating employees' performance (Siebert & Costley, 2013), thus promoting a better qualification of current and future employees (Felce et al., 2016).

2.4. Collaboration as a business strategy

Identification of new professional profiles

Companies also collaborate with the university for strategic reasons. Thus, collaboration with universities and receiving students is now seen as a source of better qualified human resources more adapted to company needs and of the identification of new professional profiles (Daley et al., 2016; Elijido-Ten & Kloot, 2015; Felce, 2017; García Delgado, 2002, Marzo et al., 2007; Whittington & Ferrández, 2007).

Creating a network of contacts

However, business strategy also refers to the possibility of making good university contacts (Geller et al., 2016; Healy et al., 2014; Hegarty et al., 2011), since the university is a source of knowledge and technology for companies (Marzo et al., 2007).

3. Towards a company benefits framework. An empirical approach

After considering all the potential benefits reported by the literature, we concluded that some empirical analysis is needed to establish an initial framework that will help contextualise these benefits within the Spanish context.

A two-step survey[2] was conducted with companies collaborating in external placements with Spanish universities. The first step consisted of a series of open-question interviews, designed from the literature review, on a small sample of companies (N = 46) that reported the main benefits perceived (Ferrández-Berrueco & Sánchez-Tarazaga, 2019)[3]. For the second step, the content analysis of the previous interviews provided the information to design a Likert questionnaire[4] that

---

[2] The survey was carried out in 2018 and 2019 as part of the EMBI project (*University-Enterprise relationship. Motivators, Impact and Benefit.* (UJI-B2016-04)).

[3] The description of the interviews process was the first part of the project and it is published in English by the authors, we considered it was not necessary to describe it again as readers can access easily to the previous paper. (Please, see: Ferrández-Berrueco, Reina & Sánchez-Tarazaga, Lucía (2019). External placements from the perspective of collaborating companies. *Relieve*, 25(1), art. 5. doi: http://doi.org/10.7203/relieve.25.1.13189.)

[4] The questionnaire had good technical characteristics and very high reliability (Cronbach's alpha = 0.92), and Content validity was assessed positively by four experts from Finland, Austria and United Kingdom.

was delivered to a bigger sample (N = 922) (see the questionnaire and sampling distribution in Annex 1). The answers to this questionnaire (N = 159) allowed us to build the first framework approach.

The framework we propose is based on an exploratory Principal Components Analysis with oblique rotation (SPSS v.25), since no independence between factors was expected. The main statistical results are shown in Annex 2.

The initial solution showed excellent adequacy for factorisation and good values of explained variance in five dimensions: Innovation, Economy, Social Image, CSR and Strategic Planning (See Fig. 1).

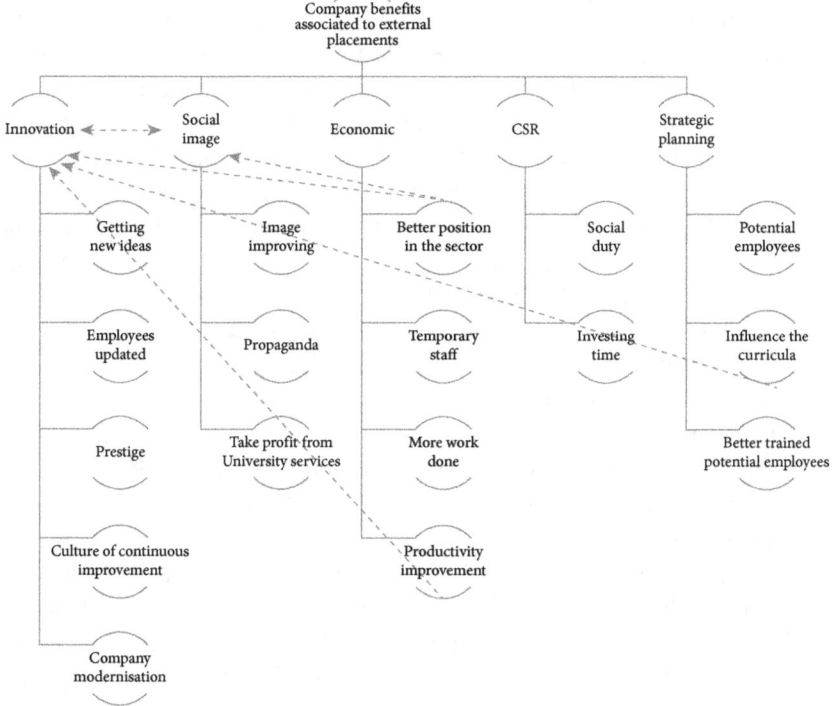

Fig. 1. Company benefits associated with external placements

- Dimension 1. *Innovation effects (40.98 % e.v.- of explained variance)*. The most relevant group of benefits. It consists of 5 items (12, 13, 18, 19 and 20) all of them with very high saturations between 0.73 and 0.88. That is, companies perceive that students bring new ideas (item 12), enabling them to sustain continuous modernisation (items 19 and 20) and become more updated organisations (item 13), thereby helping them to increase their prestige (item 18). This suggests that companies associate prestige with innovative traits rather than Social Image, as the experts predicted in the theoretical validation (though the analysis shows considerable saturation in that factor too).
- Dimension 2. *Economic effects (8.35 % e.v.)*. It consists of 4 items (1, 9. 10 and 17) with high and very high saturations ranging between 0.68 and 0.85. This second group of positive effects is connected to all the benefits relating to increased productivity and economic savings: Temporary staff (item 1); Get more work done (item 9); improvement of company's productivity (item 17). The inclusion of item 10 relating to the improvement of the company's position in the sector suggests that positioning is more connected to Economy than to Image, as could be expected.
- Dimension 3. *Social Image effects (6.58 % e.v.)*. This factor consists of 6 items (3, 4, 5, 6, 11 and 14) that saturates between 0.58 and 0.81. This dimension deals with the company's external (item 3) and modern image (item 5) and all the mechanisms implemented to advertise the company (item 4). In this sense, students become company ambassadors (item 11) and collaborating with the university becomes a social claim (items 6 and 14).
- Dimension 4. *Social Corporate Responsibility (5.41 % e.v.)*. This factor includes only two items (2 and 15) with medium saturation levels (0.65 and -0.51). It is the most independent and the only bipolar factor that includes the obligation to collaborate with the university (item 2) and saving time in staff selection (item 15) at the positive and negative extremes, respectively. Half of the items in the questionnaire sature negatively in this dimension and most of them are related to the economic factor. This finding suggests that companies understand the need to collaborate as a social duty, and this duty is seen as an investment rather than a saving.

- Dimension 5. *Strategic Planning (5.17 % e.v.)*. It is formed by items 7, 21 and 22 which show saturations between 0.53 and 0.84. This last group of benefits are related to long-term effects: recruiting (item 7) and training future employees. This last variable includes in-company training through an external internship (item 22), as well as training at university, and thereby influences curricular design (item 21).

Finally, the correlation between factors one and three (0.483) led us to perform a second order analysis. In this case, we obtained a four-factor solution where the dimensions Innovation and Social Image were combined in the same construct. As we predicted in the first analysis, from companies' perspective, that would confirm that social image relates more closely to innovation and modernisation effects than to CSR, as could be expected from the theory (Daley et al., 2016; Ferrández-Berrueco et al., 2016a, 2016b; Marzo et al., 2007).

4. Final remarks

There is still much work to do in Spain in adapting study programmes and developing a close collaboration with the labour market. Thus, although in a recent publication about the role of universities in Spain[5] (Fundación CYD, 2018), it is shown the perceived importance of the involvement of both the university and collaborating firms, reality shows it is more a statement of intentions than a fact, and many experts

---

5   This study is based on an annual survey addressed to a group of experts whose objective is to assess the importance of the role of universities in the Spanish economy and in society. The experts consulted are linked to three different sectors: the university system (rectors and presidents of social boards, among others), the business sector (representatives of chambers of commerce and business confederations and directors of Spanish companies) and the public administration (members of different ministries and general directors of universities in the autonomous communities, among others). The number of responses obtained in the last survey was 202, of which 72 % came from the university system and 22 % from the business sector.

agree that this collaboration should be encouraged (Álvarez & Osoro, 2014, Garín-Sallán et al., 2019). The new advances at an international level with Agenda 2030 (United Nations, 2015) and the adhesion of the Governing Board of Spanish Universities (CRUE, 2018) will hopefully prioritise strengthening the link between the university and other agents of society, from public administrations to social actors through companies and other groups.

This chapter has shown a way to strengthen such a relationship, and the relevant literature has pinpointed different benefits for companies. These benefits can be considered a claim to invoke partnership, but it is the educational institution which may take a first step forward to establish collaboration and set the rules. In fact, the empirical results of our survey have highlighted that the most important group of benefits for companies are related to Innovation and Economic savings, relegating CSR to the fourth place. From our point of view, this is a clear evidence that companies are not aware that the actual aim of students' internship is to reflect, to learn and to apply the knowledge acquired in the classroom. But far from establishing effective learning paths, they only look for the company's benefit. That is, students are somehow exploited as cheap or even unpaid workforce and if any, they learn the value of the experience (Zabalza, 2011).

Obviously, companies are not NGO's and the educational institutions have the responsibility to provide the companies with other benefits, benefits that, for example, make companies to feel listened in their needs. Moreover, this cooperation should go beyond external practices and give companies a more active role in curricular design. In this sense, there are several good examples in Europe (Austria, Finland, Germany, United Kingdom, etc.) that can help the Spanish system to develop such strategies (Ferrández-Berrueco et al., 2016a). In this way, companies and universities would move in the same direction with a common objective: to evolve from the simple collaboration to a real partnership (Whittington and Ferrández-Berrueco, 2007).

This active role would provide new benefits for Spanish companies—benefits reported by the literature but not mentioned by the companies in our survey—such as those related to the assessment or identification of new professional profiles, possibly because in Spain the most widespread type of networking is through external practices apart from R&D activities (Marzo et al., 2007).

Nevertheless, the survey should be considered as an initial approach to the topic. For more consistent results, we would need (1) a bigger sample that should include different educational levels in order to establish whether these benefits can be extended to them, or whether different levels report different effects for companies. (2) The survey should also include companies collaborating in different ways, not only in external placements. Finally, (3) new research should also take into account the international scope that helps clarify whether companies' expectations remain the same wherever the collaboration takes place.

1. With regards to the educational level, several employers' organisations[6] present the benefits for employers in engaging in Vocational Educational Training (VET) as higher productivity and innovation, increased customer satisfaction, better employee retention, knowledge transfer and risk management. When employers were asked about their motivators for cooperating with universities, the answers were not very different, as we have seen in this paper. In any case, we believe that the slightly divergent pictures between VET and HE may be seen as results of different summaries of motivators and expectations: medium- and long-term staff development, better knowledge transfer for innovation within the company, and filling the knowledge gaps within the company. The vanishing borderline between VET and HE increases the similarity of benefits for employers. Employers in Europe are increasingly involved in the development of vocational qualifications at upper secondary level (the traditional "place" for initial VET), as well as at a tertiary level (higher education). At higher levels of training, employers have played a specifically greater role since the mid-1990s, alongside a growing diversity of providers and programmes (Cedefop, 2019).

---

6   As edited in: https://soufflearning.com/en/benefits-of-vocational-training-for-employers/, 02.12.2019.

2. The second improvement deals with the idea that companies should collaborate both with external placements and curricular design, or by providing real cases. It is also relevant for further research, since demand from employers is not only defined by the qualifications provided. Employers and employers' organisations are steadily more engaged in VET and HE systems as development partners, and increasingly as financing partners in Europe. In higher education they are progressively becoming involved as partners in so-called "dual study programmes" (mainly in Germany, but also in Austria, the Netherlands, Sweden and the United Kingdom, where similar programmes are established). Few but good examples in Spain include the Instituto Máquina Herramienta, in the Basque Country.
3. Finally, it would be also interesting to discover how national structural context influences the motivations and benefits perceived by companies. Different countries have different traditions in partnerships between HE and the labour market. National regulations can force or reinforce the relationship between these two worlds. Europe has very good examples that highlight other ways of collaboration. For example, in Finland, at least 25 % of the curriculum in universities of applied sciences (*Ammattikorkealoulu*) must be agreed and planned with companies in the area. In the UK, programme planning is sufficiently flexible to encourage on-demand training. The question here is whether these structural variables promote new benefits or motivations for companies.

In this paper we have taken the first step. If we are able to respond to these additional issues, education providers will be in a position to establish mechanisms and strategies that will effectively improve relationships with employers, leading to a clearly defined partnership.

Annex 1. Questionnaire

Organisation name (optional but important for accurate response interpretation):

_____

Please mark the appropriate box with an 'X'.
Your previous relationship with this university

	Former student
	Teaching staff
	None
	Other (please specify)

Size of the organisation

	Fewer than 10 employees
	Between 10 and 50
	Between 51 and 250
	More than 250

Sector of activity

	Primary (agriculture and livestock)
	Secondary (Industry)
	Tertiary (services)
	Quaternary (technology, information management)

Type of activity

	Humanities (Library, Museums, Cultural Activities, etc.)
	Socio-Legal (Consultancy, Advice, Education, etc.)
	Health
	Science (Chemistry, Pharmacy, etc.)
	Engineering/architecture
	Other (please specify)

Ownership type

	Public
	Private
	Other (please specify)

Motivation for Collaboration. Please rate from 1 to 4 how important each of these statements is to you or your organisation in terms of why you chose to enter into a placement agreement (1 = Not at all important; 4 = Very important).	1	2	3	4
1. Need for temporary staff				
2. Collaborating with the university is a social duty				
3. Improve the company's image				
4. Publicise the organisation				
5. Modernise the company				
6. Make contacts at the university				
7. Know future graduates as potential employees				
8. Other (please specify)				
Benefits of Collaboration. Please rate from 1 to 4 the degree to which you believe your institution benefits from the following potential factors of collaborating with the university (1 = Strongly disagree; 4 = Strongly agree).	1	2	3	4
We get more work done				
10. The company is better positioned in the sector				
11. Students advertise the Company				
12. We obtain more new ideas				
13. Our employees are updated				
14. We benefit from the university's services				
15. It saves time in staff selection				
16. Other (please specify)				
Impacts of Collaboration. Please rate from 1 to 4 the overall long-term outcome you expect from this collaboration with the university (1 = strongly disagree/never/not at all important; 5 = Totally agree/always/very important).	1	2	3	4
17. It will improve the company's productivity				
18. The company will gain prestige				
19. A culture of continuous improvement will be established in the Company				
20. We will be a more modern Enterprise				

The interest of companies in participating 227

Motivation for Collaboration. Please rate from 1 to 4 how important each of these statements is to you or your organisation in terms of why you chose to enter into a placement agreement (1 = Not at all important; 4 = Very important).	1	2	3	4
21. The university will consider the needs of the company in the curricula				
22. Future employees will be better trained in the company's needs				
23. Other (please specify)				

Tab. 1. *Sample distribution according to the relevant variables (N) and responses (n).*

Variable	Category	N (%)	n (%)
Size	Large	96 (10.7)	15 (9.4)
	Medium	144 (16.1)	25 (15.7)
	Small	241 (26.9)	43 (27.0)
	Micro	414 (46.3)	75 (47.2)
	(Missing)		*1 (0.6)*
Production sector	Primary	4 (0.4)	1 (0.6)
	Secondary	103 (11.2)	22 (13.8)
	Tertiary	748 (81.3)	112 (70.4)
	Quaternary	67 (7.3)	23 (14.5)
	(Missing)		*1 (0.6)*
Academic sector	Arts and humanities	144 (15.6)	20 (12.6)
	Social sciences and law	408 (44.3)	78 (49.1)
	Formal sciences	195 (21.2)	37 (23.3)
	Health	73 (7.9)	12 (7.5)
	Engineering and architecture	83 (9.0)	6 (3.8)
	Others	19 (2.1)	6 (3.8)
Ownership	Public	129 (14.0)	19 (11.9)
	Private	793 (86)	136 (85.5)
	(Missing)		*4 (2.6)*
TOTAL		922	159 (17.2)*

(*) sampling error of 7 % for a 95 % representative sample.

Tab. 2. Questionnaire reliability

Cronbach's Alpha	Cronbach's Alpha based on standardised elements	No. of elements
,919	,919	20

Annex 2

Tab. 3. KMO & Bartlett test for factor adequacy

KMO		,887
Bartlett	Approx. Chi-square	1614,917
	Df.	190
	Sig.	,000

Tab. 4. Explained variance

Component	Initial Eigenvalues		
	Total	Variance %	Accumulated %
1	8.196	40.979	40.979
2	1.670	8.351	49.330
3	1.315	6.576	55.907
4	1.083	5.414	61.321
5	1.033	5.166	66.487

Tab. 5. Item saturation in factors

Structure Matrix

Item	1	2	3	4	5
1. Need for temporary staff	−.019	.730	.248	−.173	.419
2. Collaborating with the university is a social duty	.235	.184	.342	.650	.102
3. Improve the company's image	.235	.316	.768	.384	.242
4. Publicise the organisation	.379	.328	.805	.153	.389
5. Modernise the company	.516	.248	.759	−.008	.316
6. Make contacts at the university	.528	.321	.808	−.168	.198
7. Know future graduates as potential employees	.182	.455	.380	−.485	.526
9. Get more work done	.269	.853	.278	−.037	.116
10. Company is better positioned in the sector	.574	.687	.638	.020	.163
11. Students advertise the company	.542	.482	.584	.030	.142
12. Company obtains more new ideas	.736	.219	.431	.086	.281
13. Company employees are updated	.774	.346	.366	−.216	.227
14. We benefit from the university's services	.477	.306	.697	−.175	.134
15. It saves time in staff selection	.457	.446	.497	−.507	.001
17. It will improve the company's productivity	.551	.710	.320	.017	.263
18. The company will gain prestige	.763	.293	.663	.246	.249
19. A culture of continuous improvement will be established in the Company	.883	.317	.479	−.021	.224
20. We will be a more modern enterprise	.794	.323	.577	.072	.300
21. The university will consider the needs of the company in the curricula	.529	.260	.512	−.099	.610
22. Future employees will be better trained in the company's needs	.342	.262	.277	.063	.839

*Grey highlights denote items' factor affiliation

Tab. 6. First order factor correlation

Factor	1	2	3	4	5
1	1.000	.290	.483	−.016	.187
2	.290	1.000	.363	−.089	.235
3	.483	.363	1.000	.036	.262
4	−.016	−.089	.036	1.000	−.014
5	.187	.235	.262	−.014	1.000

Tab. 7. Second order factor saturation

	1	2	3	4
REGR factor score 1	.899	−.038	.164	.232
REGR factor score 2	.351	−.071	.242	.991
REGR factor score 3	.817	.095	.307	.439
REGR factor score 4	.003	.997	−.009	−.074
REGR factor score 5	.238	−.001	.998	.237

*Grey highlights denote items' factor affiliation

Biographical note

Reina Ferrández Berrueco. Is associate professor in the area of Research Methods and Diagnosis in Education, at the Universitat Jaume I (Castellon). She is a member of the IDOCE research group about innovation and development of competencies in education. Her main research interests are related to work-based learning as part of the University Social Responsibility. She has taken part as coordinator in different national and international projects about Work based learning and University Social Responsibility. For ten years, she was the director of the university quality office, designing developing the quality system in the Universitat Jaume I. Nowadays she is the Director of the department of Pedagogy and Didactics of Social Sciences, Language and Literature.

Stefan Humpl is managing director and partner of 3s Unternehmensberatung GmbH and chairman of 3s research laboratory. His main topics in research are labour market and education system studies, and supports the Austrian Public Employment Service through information about job and qualification trends via the AMS Skills Barometer, a labour market information and guidance tool that combines quantitative and qualitative information on the basis of a broad range of sources (meta-analyses). In international projects, he consults Cedefop. He is experienced project manager in national and EU research and development projects in the area of education and labour market. He is consulting in curriculum design and strategic development of educational institutions and public bodies concerned with VET and HE, but also quality improvement in education through evaluation and feasibility studies.

Lucía Sánchez-Tarazaga is PhD in Education from Universitat Jaume I and Business and Administration Management Degree in the same university. Assistant lecturer in the Department of Pedagogy and Didactics of the Social Sciences, Language and Literature. Her field of research focuses on teacher policy, initial teacher education and professional competences. She belongs to IDOCE research group, focused on innovation and development of competences in Education, with special focus on work based learning. She is also member of IAR-RED, participating in the training and seminars of reflective practice. She is Quality Coordinator in the Bachelor's Degree in Preschool Education. Previously, she has also worked for as a senior consultant in improvement projects and human resources management.

5. References

Álvarez, C., & Osoro, J. (2014). Colaboración Universidad-Escuela para el cambio escolar. Una investigación-acción en proceso. *Innovación Educativa*, *24*, 215–227. doi: https://doi.org/10.15304/ie.24.1483.

Álvarez, E., Iglesias, M. T., & García, M. S. (2008). Desarrollo de Competencias en el Practicum de Magisterio, *Aula Abierta*, *36* (1, 2), 65–78.

Aneas, A., & Vilá, R. (2018). Entornos de desarrollo y aplicación de las competencias en el Prácticum de grado en Pedagogía de la Universidad de Barcelona. *Revista Prácticum*, *3* (1), 1–19.

Antcliff, V., Baines, S., & Gorb, E. (2016). Developing your own graduate employees: Employer perspectives on the value of a degree apprenticeship. *Higher Education, Skills and Work-Based Learning*, *6* (4), 378–383. doi: https://doi.org/10.1108/HESWBL-052016-0032.

Barnett, R., & Coate, K. (2005). *Engaging the Curriculum in Higher Education*. The Society for Research into Higher Education and Open University Press, Maidenhead.

Basit, T. N., Eardley, A., Borup, R., Shah, H., Slack, K., & Hughes, A. (2015). Higher education institutions and work-based learning in the UK: Employer engagement within a tripartite relationship. *Higher Education. The International Journal of Higher Education Research*, *70* (1), 1003–1015. doi: https://doi.org/10.1007/s10734-015-9877-7.

Bolívar, A. (2007). *Los centros educativos como organizaciones que aprenden: Promesa y realidades.* Madrid: La Muralla.

Bruneel, J., D'Este, P., & Salter, A. (2010). Investigating the factors that diminish the barriers to university–industry collaboration. *Research Policy*, *39* (7), 858–868. https://doi.org/10.1016/j.respol.2010.03.006.

Cebrián, M., & Monedero, J. J. (2009). El e-portafolios y la e-rúbrica en la supervisión del prácticum. In M. Raposo, M. E. Martínez, L. Lodeiro, J. C. Fernández de la Iglesia and A. Pérez (Coords.), *El Prácticum más allá del empleo: Formación vs. Training* (pp. 369–380). Vigo: Imprenta Universitaria de Vigo.

Cedefop (2019). *The changing nature and role of vocational education and training in Europe. Volume 6: Vocationally oriented education and training at higher education level – expansion and diversification in European countries.* Luxembourg: Publication Office of the EU.

Clanchy, J., & Ballard, B. (1995). Generic skills in the context of higher education. *Higher Education Research and Development*, *14* (2), 155–166. https://doi.org/10.1080/0729436950140202.

CRUE (2018). Crue acuerda su contribución al Plan de Acción para la Agenda 2030 de la ONU [Press release]. Retrieved from http://www.crue.org/Comunicacion/Noticias/Las%20universidades%20acuerdan%20su%20contribuci%C3%B3n%20al%20Plan%20de%20Acci%C3%B3n%20de%20la%20Agenda%202030.aspx. (Accessed 2 December 2019).

Daley, J., Coyle, J., & Dwyer, C. (2016). Sheffield Hallam University and Nestlé: Developing future leaders with the Chartered Manager

Degree Apprenticeship – a partnership approach. *Higher Education, Skills and Work-Based Learning, 6* (4), 370–377. https://doi.org/10.1108/HESWBL-06-2016-0045.

Dasgupta, P., & David, P. (1994). Towards a new economics of science. *Research Policy, 23,* 487–522.

Devins, D., Ferrández-Berrueco, R., & Kekäle,T. (2015). Educational orientation and employer influenced pedagogy. *Higher Education, Skills and Work-Based Learning, 5* (4), 352–368. doi: http://dx.doi.org/10.1108/HESWBL-03-2015-0010.

EC (2003). *Commission recommendation of 6 May 2003 concerning the definition of micro, small and medium-sized enterprises* (DO L 124 de 20.05.3003). Retrieved from https://eur-lex.europa.eu/legal-content/EN/TXT/PDF/?uri=CELEX:32003H0361&from=ES. (Accessed 19 January 2020).

EC (2010). *Communication from the Commission Europe 2020. A Strategy for Smart, Sustainable and Inclusive Growth.* Retrieved from http://eurlex.europa.eu/LexUriServ/LexUriServ.do?uri=COM:2010:2020:FIN:EN:PDF. (Accessed, 19 January 2020).

EC (2011a). *Supporting growth and jobs – an agenda for the modernisation of Europe's higher education systems.* http://eurlex.europa.eu/LexUriServ/LexUriServ.do?uri=COM:2011:0567:FIN:EN:PDF. (Accessed, January, 19th 2020).

EC (2011b). *A renewed EU strategy 2011–14 for Corporate Social Responsibility.* https://eur-lex.europa.eu/legal-content/EN/TXT/PDF/?uri=CELEX:52011DC0681&from=ES. (Accessed, January, 19th 2020).

EC (2018). The State of University-Business Cooperation in Europe. https://www.ub-cooperation.eu/pdf/final_report2017.pdf. (Accessed 3 December 2019).

Egido, I. (2017). El prácticum como elemento clave en la iniciación al desarrollo profesional docente: debates y líneas de futuro. In H. Monarca and B. Thoilliez (Coords.), *La profesionalización docente: debates y propuestas* (pp. 133–146). Madrid: Síntesis.

Elijido-Ten, E., & Kloot, L. (2015). Experiential learning in accounting work-integrated learning: A three-way partnership. *Education +*

Training, 57 (2), 204–218. doi: https://doi.org/10.1108/ET-10-2013-0122.

Felce, A. (2017). The hub in a pub: University of Wolverhampton apprenticeship hub. *Higher Education, Skills and Work-Based Learning, 7* (1), 70–78. doi: https://doi.org/10.1108/ HESWBL-05-2016-0035.

Felce, A., Perks, S., & Roberts, D. (2016). Work-based skills development: A contextengaged approach, *Higher Education, Skills and Work-Based Learning, 6* (3), 261–276. https://doi.org/10.1108/HESWBL-12-2015-0058.

Ferrández-Berrueco, R., & Humpl, S. (2019). What are the companies looking for when collaborating with education? In F. Marhuenda and M. J. Chisvert-Tarazona (Eds.), *Pedagogical concerns and market demands in VET. Proceedings of the 3rd Crossing Boundaries in VET conference, Vocational Educationand Training Network (VETNET)* (pp.143–147). https://doi.org/10.5281/zenodo.2641090.

Ferrández-Berrueco, R., Kekäle, T., & Sánchez-Tarazaga, L. (2016a). Universidad y empresa. Experiencias europeas de currículum integrado. Interrogantes pendientes. *Revista Española de Educación Comparada, 27,* 151–171. doi: https://doi.org/10.5944/reec.27.2016.15973.

Ferrández-Berrueco, R., Kekale, T., & Devins, D. (2016b). A framework for work-based learning: Basic pillars and the interactions between them. *Higher Education, skills and work-based Learning, 6* (1), 35–54. https://doi.org/10.1108/HESWBL-06-20140026.

Ferrández-Berrueco, R., & Sánchez-Tarazaga, L. (2019). External placements from the perspective of collaborating companies. *RELIEVE, 25* (1), art. 5. doi: http://doi.org/10.7203/relieve.25.1.13189.

Fundación Conocimiento y Desarrollo (2018). *Barómetro CYD 2017, El papel de las universidades en España.* Retrieved from https://www.fundacioncyd.org/wp-content/uploads/2018/07/Barometro-CYD2017.pdf (Accessed 3 December 2019).

Gairín-Sallán, J., Díaz-Vicario, A., del Arco, I., & Flores, O. (2019). Efecto e impacto de las prácticas curriculares de los grados de educación infantil y primaria: la perspectiva de estudiantes, tutores y coordinadores. *Educación XX1, 22* (2), 17–43. doi: http://doi.org/10.5944/ educXX1.21311.

García Delgado, J. (2002). Lo que hemos aprendido en 20 años de prácticas en empresas. *Revista de Docencia Universitaria*, *2* (1). http://revistas.um.es/redu/article/view/11841/11421.

Geller, J., Zuckerman, N., & Seidel, A. (2016). Service-learning as a catalyst for community development: How do community partners benefit from service-learning? *Education and Urban Society*, *48* (2), 151–175. https://doi.org/10.1177 %2F0013124513514773.

Guinart, M. (2005). Diseño de contenidos atendiendo a la diversidad formativa. La relación universidad-empresa. Estudio de caso. *Revista de Universidad y Sociedad del Conocimiento*, *2* (2), 45–53.

Healy, A., Perkmann, M., Goddard, J., & Kempton, L. (2014). *Measuring the impact of University Business cooperation. Case studies*. Luxembourg: Publications Office of the European Union. https://www.eurashe.eu/library/mission-phe/NC0214337ENN_002.pdf. (Accessed 19 January 2020).

Hegarty, P. M., Kelly, H. A., & Walsh, A. (2011). Reflection in a workplace qualification: Challenges and benefits, *Journal of Workplace Learning*, *23* (8), 531–540. https://doi.org/10.1108/13665621111174889.

Ions, K., & Minton, A. (2012). Can work-based learning programmes help companies to become learning organisations? *Higher Education, Skills and Work-Based Learning*, *2* (1), 22–32. https://doi.org/10.1108/20423891211197712.

Kenessey, Z. (1987). The primary, secondary, tertiary and quaternary sectors of the economy. *The Review of Income and Wealth*, *33* (4), 359–385. doi: https://doi.org/10.1111/j.14754991.1987.tb00680.x.

Latorre, M. J. (2007). El potencial formativo del prácticum: Cambio en las creencias que sobre la enseñanza práctica poseen los futuros maestros. *Revista de Educación*, *343*, 249–273.

Latorre, M. J., & Blanco, F. K. (2011). El prácticum como espacio de aprendizaje profesional para docentes en formación. *Revista de docencia universitaria*, *9* (2), 35–54. doi: https://doi.org/10.4995/redu.2011.6157.

Marhuenda, F., Bernad, J. C., & Navas, A. (2010). Las prácticas en empresa como estrategia de enseñanza e inserción laboral: las empresas de inserción social. *Revista de Educación*, *351*, 139–161.

Marzo, M., Pedraja, M., & Rivera, P. (2008). Un modelo de relaciones empresa universidad. *Revista Europea de Dirección y Economía de la Empresa*, *17* (1), 3956. doi: https://doi.org/10.1016/j.redee.2013.09.003 N.

Mendoza, M., & Covarrubias, C. G. (2016). Competencias profesionales movilizadas en el Prácticum de los grados de Magisterio: Propuesta de un instrumento. *Revista de Pedagogía*, *37* (100), 161–185. Retrieved from www.redalyc.org/articulo.oa?id=659/65949681009. (Accessed 20 January 2020).

OECD (2012). *Fostering Quality Teaching in Higher Education: Policies & Practices*. Paris: OECD Publishing.

Okubo, Y., & Sjoberg, C. (2000). The changing pattern of industrial scientific research collaboration in Sweden, *Research Policy*, *29* (1), 81–98.

Ryan, G., Toohey, S., & Hughes, C. (1996). The purpose, value and structure of the practicum in Higher Education: A literature review. *Higher Education*, *31*, 355–377.

Sarceda-Gorgoso, M. C., & Rodicio-García, M. (2017). Escenarios formativos y competencias profesionales en la formación inicial del profesorado. *Revista Complutense de Educación*, *29* (1), 147–163. https://doi.org/10.5209/RCED.52160.

Senge, P. (1990). *The Fifth Discipline: The Art & Practice of The Learning Organization*. New York: Doubleday.

Serrano, R. (2013). *Identidad profesional, necesidades formativas y desarrollo de competencias docentes en la formación inicial del profesorado de secundaria*. Doctoral Thesis. Universidad de Córdoba, Córdoba.

Siebert, S., & Costley, C. (2013) Conflicting values in reflection on professional practice. *Higher Education, Skills and Work-Based Learning*, *3* (3), 156–167. https://doi.org/10.1108/HESWBL-07-2011-0032.

United Nations (2015). *Transformar nuestro mundo: la Agenda 2030 para el Desarrollo Sostenible* [Online Document]. Retrieved from: https://unctad.org/meetings/es/SessionalDocuments/ares70d1_es.pdf. (Accessed 20 January 2020).

Valle, J. M., & Manso, J. (2011). La nueva formación inicial del profesorado de Educación Secundaria: modelo para la selección de buenos centros de prácticas. *Revista de Educación*, 354, 267–290.

Verde, M. E. (2001). Análisis de los agentes del prácticum de las titulaciones de Maestro. In L. Iglesias, M. Zabalza, A. Cid and M. Raposo (Coords.), *VI Symposium Internacional sobre el Prácticum Desarrollo de Competencias Personales y Profesionales en el Prácticum*. (CD-ROM). Lugo: Unicopia.

Villa, A., & Poblete, M. (2004). Prácticum y evaluación de competencias. Profesorado. *Revista de currículum y formación del profesorado, 8* (2). Monográfico: Prácticum. Retrieved from http://www.ugr.es/local/recfpro/rev82ed.pdf. (Accessed 20 January 2020).

White, T. (2012). Employer responsive provision: workforce development through work-based learning. *Higher Education, Skills and Work-Based Learning, 2* (2), 6–21. https://doi.org/10.1108/20423891211197703.

Whittington, B., & Ferrández-Berrueco, R. (2007). From interaction to integration: Developing the relationship between higher education and the labour market. In B. Baugmartl, F. Mizikaci, y D. Owen (Eds.), *From Here to There: Mileposts of European Higher Education* (pp. 179–196). Viena: Navreme (AT) y Makedonska Riznitsa (MK).

Zabalza, M. A. (2008). El trabajo por competencias en la enseñanza universitaria. In I. Rodríguez, A. I. Caballero, M. Y. Fernández and M. C. Pérez (Coords.), *El nuevo perfil del profesor universitario en el EEES: Claves para la renovación metodológica* (pp. 79–113). Valladolid: Servicio de Publicaciones-Universidad Europea Miguel de Cervantes.

Zabalza, M. A. (2011). El practicum en la formación universitaria. Estado de la cuestión. *Revista de Educación, 354* (1), (21–43). doi: https://doi.org/10.4438/1988-592X-0034-8082-RE.

Zabalza, M. A. (2013). *El practicum y las prácticas en empresas en la formación universitaria*. Madrid: Narcea.

MARÍA JOSÉ CHISVERT-TARAZONA, JAVIER VILA-VÁZQUEZ,
ALICIA ROS-GARRIDO & DAVINIA PALOMARES-MONTERO

Does the dual VET bring curriculum improvements? A normative analysis in the Spanish context

Abstract: The recent introduction of dual vocational training (DVT) in Spain attempts to implement a new model of vocational training by replicating German DVT. The aim of this change in vocational education, as stated by the Spanish regulation, is to improve student learning and increase employability. The export of a model that has been successful in one country to another country does not seem to work properly in Spain because it is a country that does not have a tradition of this kind of training and its economic and social systems differ from those of the originating country. To measure the adequacy of a system, one parameter that may be used is the analysis of curricular improvements, since the curricular design seeks to respond to the needs of the labor market by adapting to the needs of companies. In Spain, the implementation of the DVT does not seem to guarantee the acquisition of new competencies but rather guarantees a null curriculum, that is, those competencies that are not taught but deserve to be taught.

Keywords: prescribed curriculum, dual vocational training, regulations,

1. Introduction

During the 60s and 70s of 20th century, the vocational education and training (VET) system in Spain was considered as an option marked by a strong social bias (Merino, 2013). It was established as a differentiated route from the academic. During the 90s, with the promulgation of the Organic law 1/1990 of General Planning of the education system, VET was, instead, concerned with the improvement of the production system. It started a process of social legitimation. In addition, workplace training became mandatory and helped to strengthen the relations between companies and schools. This law advanced in the integration of professional training within the education system, contributing to overcoming its consideration of secondary education. The mandatory practices in companies in all the VET system contributed to bring schools to companies, improving the employment of young people.

The current educational law in Spain, Organic Law 8/2013, for the Improvement of Educational Quality proposes a clear break from the comprehensive model of compulsory secondary education. The curriculum is divided into two modalities, one for the preparation of the baccalaureate and another for the preparation of access to vocational training. This law seeks in curriculum diversification solutions to school failure and deposits those solutions in VET (Merino, 2013). The students with the worst academic records are the ones that are usually oriented towards VET.

According to Cedefop (2019), in Spain, the 34,8 % of all students in upper secondary education was enrolled in VET in 2016 while the average in Europe was 49,3 %. The data provided by the Spanish Ministry of Education and Vocational Training (2019) reveal that students enrolled in Vocational Training, has increased almost 50 % from the 2007–2008 academic year to the 2017–2018 academic year, going from 451,541 students to 815,354 students.

Since the economic crisis in 2007, the European Union has considered dual learning to be the optimal model of vocational training (European Commission, 2012). This method is a formative modality where the alternance promotes practice learning within a productive and scholarly context to improve the transition to the labor market. The European institutional discourse has promoted the idea that countries that have little tradition in this modality study different models to assess and launch the dual system of VET. In some cases, as with the Spanish experience, the German system has received special interest, and the model has been exported without a deep analysis of the factors that will guarantee its successful dissemination. The social agents in Spain assumed the competences discourse in education as beneficial (Tejada, 2012). This contributed to introduce the dual model.

German dual vocational training (DVT) is a model that was developed in an industrial context, where huge and medium enterprises are numerous. It is, without a doubt, an appropriate model for economies with expansion trajectories (Marhuenda-Fluixà, Chisvert Tarazona, Palomares-Montero, & Vila, 2017). These particular characteristics generate reasonable doubts when considering the model's suitability in the Spanish context, which is characterized by a poorly articulated economy that is mostly dedicated to the service sector and mainly consists of small businesses. The manufacturing industry that is so relevant to German DVT has been significantly reduced in recent decades in Spain, as Díaz, Mosso and Torrent will show in Chapter 10. On the other hand, German curriculum development introduces competency-based frameworks (Gessler, 2017) that identify core occupational tasks (Mulder, 2017). Nore and Lahn (2019) argue that these frameworks "(...) are easy to identify for training establishments, but may be either too functional (no generic competencies), too restricted (no transversal or transferable skills) or too situational (restricted to a company-specific context and culture)" (p. 173). Therefore, an excessive focus on the teaching-learning processes for productive practice could make it difficult to learn certain specific relevant competencies that could be transferred to diverse work contexts. Access to learning in a productive environment rather than a pedagogical one could keep students from significant, relevant learning that would guarantee their qualifications. This issue is particularly a problem when companies prioritize their production (benefit) over the learning and qualification of the students, and the educational intentionality of the DVT is diverted, which makes the acquisition of all professional skills associated with the training cycle difficult.

The Spanish Ministry of Education and Vocational Training (2019) also highlights that, in the 2017–2018 academic year, 22,586 students were enrolled in Dual Vocational Training (information of Region of Murcia was not available). Therefore, only 2.77 % of VET students are enrolled in the dual system.

Under these circumstances, we analyze the curriculum configuration and the evaluation of DVT in Spain. In this sense, the chapter is concerned with the following research question: Does the prescribed curriculum provided by the regulations at the state level and in the regions for the DVT improve the VET model?

The objective is to generate a space for reflection on the prescribed DVT curriculum in the Spanish context that is available in the state and regional regulations. We consider it relevant to analyze whether the decisions of the legislators in relation to the curriculum proposal for DVT present benefits, damages and/or uncertainties in the training and learning process.

The paper is organized as follows. The following section presents the relevance of the VET curriculum and analyzes the alternance produced in the dual modality between the productive context and the school. The methodology section presents the phases applied in the content analyzes of the regulations. The results and discussion section provides the most significant results with regard to curricular development and evaluation. The results are discussed in relation to previous studies to go deeper into the analyzes. The conclusions section provides comments and some final remarks.

2. The curriculum of vocational training: Does DVT introduce novelties?

We agree with Gimeno-Sacristán (2010) that the curriculum is a cultural content that educational institutions try to disseminate in their students and it causes importants effects in them. In the theory of curriculum research it could be differentiated diverse types of curricula and their functions. In this chapter we highlight the prescribed curriculum.

The VET curriculum fulfills an organizing function and introduces limits through a structure of meaning that seeks to respond to the qualification needs of the labor market. The regulations establish prescriptions to help organize the curricular system and are used as a starting point for the delimitation of content and control of the system.

The Organic Law, 8/2013, for the Improvement of Educational Quality states that society's interest in vocational training shows that it is the first choice for a training itinerary. A year before, the same state government introduced a new form of vocational training, DVT, in relation to the training and learning contracts regulated by Royal Decree 1529/2012. However, this regulation has not allowed Spain to move towards a coherent regulatory framework that integrates modalities and explicitly makes a single model. Since educational competencies in Spain are decentralized, the different regions regulate and develop diverse models of DVT (Echeverría, 2016). The variability in the dual models among the certified trades, and especially between regions, suggests independence in development and a lack of centralized governance in the VET system in Spain. This fact implies that the regulatory norms of DVT in Spain belong to different legal fields. There are several departments responsible for establishing training policies that require effective coordination (Echeverría, 2016).

Several authors maintain that after many attempts to export the DVT model to countries without this kind of tradition, the result has generally not been satisfactory (Rego-Agraso, Barreira-Cerqueiras, & Rial-Sánchez, 2015; Valiente, Scandurra, Zancajo, & Brown, 2015). We wish to consider this in the Spanish context and assess whether the prescribed curriculum in the regulations of the DVT could improve the current VET model.

In fact, previous studies maintain that 50.6 % of VET teachers perceive that the curriculum of the training cycle is not sufficiently adapted to dual training, and 41.9 % of VET teachers argue that companies are not consulted about the contents of the DVT program that they are to carry out (Pineda-Herrero, Ciraso-Calí, & Arnau-Sabatés, 2019).

The prescribed curriculum creates a barrier by setting and limiting the knowledge to be taught, and it defines limits to the universe of the thinkable (Bourdieu & Passeron, 1995). The technical approaches of the curriculum, either political or pedagogical, are considered in VET. These approaches hide cultural, epistemic and political options under technical arguments that do not discuss the underlying conflicts (Gimeno-Sacristán, 2010). The curriculum is considered, by many authors, to be a battlefield that showcases different disputes: corporate, political, economic, religious, identity, and cultural (Apple, 2000). For this reason, to achieve the harmonious integration of teaching and the learning process, it is necessary to be aware of the fundamental curricular issues. Real curriculum is a possibility, an alternative. It is a conceivable product that is open to change. It is not neutral, universal or unchangeable. On the contrary, it is a controversial space where decisions are made, different options can be pursued, and diverse orientations can guide actions (Gimeno-Sacristan, 2010). Defining the curriculum and its ability to change should acknowledge different options with respect to diverse interests and models of society, knowledge worth and sharing responsibilities.

3. Methodology

We use content analysis, an important social science research technique. Content analysis considers data as representations not of physical events but of texts, images, and expressions that are created to be seen, read, interpreted and acted on (Krippendorff, 2018). We need to define a unit of analysis, encompassing three possible types: sampling units (included selectively), context units (text that identifies the information used to describe recording units), and recording units (separately described, recorded, transcribed or coded). In this paper, the units of analysis are the state and regional regulations on education matters; the context units are the two modalities of VET that we want to compare: DVT and VET itself; the recording units are the subjects we are interested in: DVT Curriculum development, evaluation system in DVT and organizational issues. Fig. 1 describes the content analysis theoretical and practical approach.

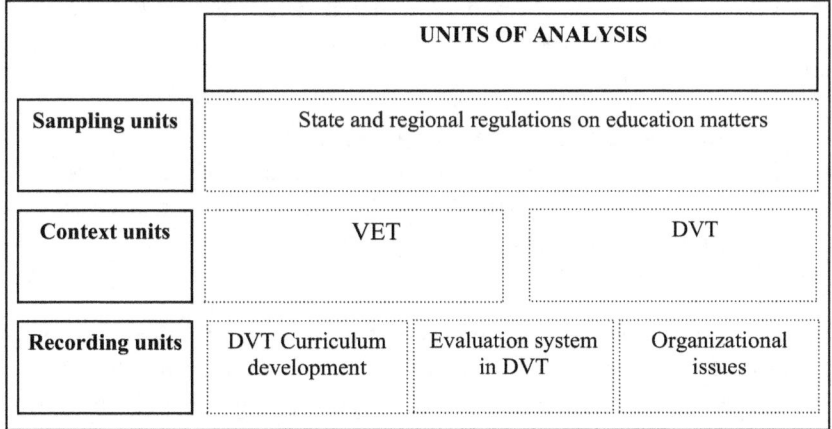

Fig. 1. Theoretical and practical framework of content analysis of regulations.

We conducted a categorization process to organize and classify our recording units based on analogy and differentiation criteria through the process of transforming raw data (regulation on education matters) into useful information. This process provides a corpus of material that enables identification of a list of indicators for each recording unit. The number of indicators is refined according to equivalence and similarity criteria to obtain a final list that includes straightforward indicators of curricular development (curricular aspects and the percentage of training hours in the training center and in the company), evaluation system (degree of responsibility of the school and company tutors and the mechanisms of coordination and evaluation of the student evaluation process) and organizational issues.

We carried out the content analysis of the regulations in two phases. In the first phase, we reviewed the scientific literature regarding DVT analysis in Spain. We focused on the literature that compared the system in Spain with the German dual system because that system has been used as a paradigmatic reference to the OECD (Hoeckel & Schwartz, 2010) or the European Business Conference (BUSINESSEUROPE, 2012). These international institutions have tried to promote DVT in countries with a more scholarly VET, as in the Spanish case. Bibliographical research allowed the revision of VET representation in the academic context and an analysis of the focus of these studies. In this phase, we also performed an exhaustive search of Spanish DVT regulations. We followed the five preparatory steps recommended by Krippendorff (2018):

- Locating and sampling the relevant texts
- Ascertaining stable correlations in the contexts of these texts
- Preparing the text in method-specific and context-sensitive ways
- Adopting standards or criteria
- Allocating resources

In the second phase, the content analysis of the regulations allowed us to move from primary documents to secondary documents (Bardin, 1986). The evidence highlighted what regulates the curricula in Spanish legislation and the differences between the regions in curricular development, in the evaluation system and in organizational issues. In this phase, we fulfilled the three aspects highlighted by Pope, Ziebland and Mays (2000): much time and work has been devoted to the rigorous analysis of all of the regulations, the regulations have been inductively analyzed using content analysis to generate categories and explanations that are shown in this chapter, and the analysis of the qualitative data was performed by experts with more than 10 years of experience in research from different areas of knowledge (legal, pedagogical and sociological).

In short, in both phases, the discourse analysis implies the use of language that is understood not only as an individual activity but also as a social action (Hake, 2005). The content analysis of the regulations involves an explanation of the relationships between the prescribed state curriculum in Spain and the prescribed regional curriculum in the different regions and compares the differences between the two levels of curricular concreteness.

4. Results and discussion

The academic literature on VET, in a general sense, shows that the similarities between DVT and VET that have been developed to date in the Spanish context are relevant (Echeverria, 2016; Marhuenda-Fluixá, Chisvert Tarazona, Palomares-Montero, & Vila, 2017, Marhuenda-Fluixá, Chisvert Tarazona, Palomares-Montero, 2019); both develop work-linked training, the source of the curriculum for both is the National Catalogue of Professional Qualifications (CNCP), the training space is common (even the classrooms in which they are taught are mixed, including students of both models), the teachers of both curricula have the same profile and requirements for acquiring their teaching position, and the methodology used and evaluation systems are identical for both. However, the same authors present some differences between both VET models. It is worth highlighting the value that is given to the practice environment of the company, which becomes more relevant in DVT. Pragmatic knowledge promotes learning by doing, and the inductive method responds to the logic that regulates this training. The model in which the curriculum was developed was, for the most part, the business environment. However, there is no reference in the regulations to differentiated requirements in the companies that participate in this training. The results obtained from the units of analysis are shown below to reveal the extent to which the curricular proposals of DVT improve VET.

4.1 Curriculum development and evaluation in DVT

DVT in Spain is defined in RD 1529/2012 as training initiatives that qualify workers through actions that combine work activity in a company with training activity received in a school.

This regulation describes the curricular requirements that a company must meet in order to provide DVT: specifying the contents, activities, teaching staff, form and assessment criteria. For their part, the regions explicit state in their regulations that in order to carry out DVT in their territories, the contents, activities, resources, methodology, evaluation and learning outcomes must be detailed in a training program. However, the commitment of the students who will participate in the program is required, which is revealed especially in the detailed schedule of permanence and the teaching of each subject in both the school and in the company. In this sense, an individualized training program for each student must be developed in each school, which is not possible on a large scale.

A priori, the training activity responds to the contents stipulated in the title of the professional training or the certificate of professionalism related to the effective work to be performed. DVT does not introduce curricular or evaluative variation in relation to traditional VET beyond a basic regulation of an organizational nature, which clarifies the collaboration and participation of companies in the training. The regulations include five modalities for the development of DVT in article 3 of the state rule (Fig. 1): (a) training at a school exclusively, making the alternance compatible between training in the work activity carried out in the company; (b) training with the participation of the company, which consists of the company providing training centers with spaces, facilities or experts to provide all or part of certain professional modules or training modules; (c) training in an authorized or accredited company and in a training center, which consists of the delivery of complementary professional modules or training modules in the company in addition to those taught in the training center; (d) shared training between the school and the company, which involves coparticipation in different proportions in the teaching and learning processes in both contexts; and (e) training at the company exclusively. The regulations seem to emphasize modalities of training that affect the context from which total or partial responsibility for the training is assumed.

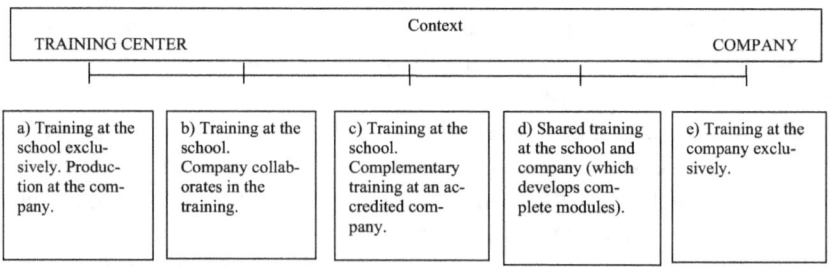

Fig. 2. DVT modalities in Spain.

This chapter reflects on the distribution of time in the two training environments, on the coordination and training of agents, and on the evaluation of learning outcomes and how they affect the development of the prescribed curriculum.

4.1.1. State versus regional regulations

In most of the regions' regulations, models of DVT are not mentioned, and what is stated in the real state decree is assumed. In fact, only four of the seventeen regional regulations refer to this dual modality. The regulations in Andalusia, Valencia and Balearic Island fully reproduce them. Cantabria is the only region that has regulated this question to adapt it to its educational context. Thus, Order ECD/84/2013 establishes the possibility of developing three DVT models of the five regulated in the royal decree, excluding the two models in which the development of training is allowed exclusively in the company or in the school. Subsequently, Order ECD/20/2017 in Cantabria establishes that DVT will be developed only in the training modality with the participation of the company.

In contrast to the previous case, most territories do not regulate curricular aspects and are subject to state regulations[1]. Only four regions explicitly regulate these aspects: Canarias (Resolution of March 14, 2018), Valencia (Decree 74/2013), Extremadura (Decree 100/2014) and Murcia (Resolution of March 14, 2016.) These four regions state that the training programs will be agreed upon with the company and will collect the learning outcomes noted in the national law for qualifications and in the autonomic decrees of each curriculum. These programs will also collect the contents that must be taught in the company and in the VET school. These contributions continue to be very vague and superficial, although at least they explicitly state the necessary participation of the companies in curricular design and their adaptation to the environment in which the training takes place. Therefore, there are two parallel processes. The first is the development of training content regulation, and the second is the design of the corresponding framework curriculum for the school-based part. The latter is the task of

---

1   Territorial legislation is very abundant and has been thoroughly analyzed and is included in the reference section. To facilitate reading, references have been avoided when results refer to aspects that are common in all territories.

the regions, which requires coordination between the global prescribed curriculum and its development in the regional framework. In practice, this coordination is not happening (Echeverria, 2016).

4.1.2. Relationship between learning outcomes and access requirements

We would like to highlight Cantabria's case with Order ECD/20/2017. The rules in this Order explicitly require that the learning outcomes of DVT are only those that provide for the FCT (a workplace training program that is mandatory in Spanish VET). Thus, what is the DVT's added value if the required learning results are the same for both modalities? This regulation reflects what implicitly occurs in most of the regions, which is the integral assumption of the traditional VET curriculum in dual training. The reality contrasts with the students' access difficulties to the dual modality. In principle, in the dual path, the state and employers collaborate in order to meet the training goals for the professional skills required for the labor market. However, the firms in dual VET select the apprentices. Consequently, not every student gets access to in-firm training. In Switzerland, Germany and Denmark, governments develop measures that try to make their dual VET systems more inclusive but are limited to the extent to which firms are expected to play an active role in those systems (Bonoli & Wilson, 2019). The main requirement to access DVT is a student's academic record. In fact, this record is the unique element that is taken into account in 11 regions where it is normative to establish this criterion. Under these circumstances, it is easy to assume that only those with the best academic records can access DVT. An exception occurs in País Vasco, Decree 83/2015, where the capacity for teamwork, innovation and creativity are also taken into account in the selection of students. In short, the requirements for access to VET are identical in both modalities but give priority to those with the best academic records. However, the effects are different due to the number of places at each modality. In Germany, which is the reference pattern for Spanish DVT (Echeverría, 2016), the curricular specification of dual training is included in the work contract and involves specifying the curricular content that will be developed in the company and school, mainly the training program for each specific position. The curriculum specifies the skills to be acquired and their timing, as well as the space in which that knowledge will be acquired in addition to the tests that the apprentice must pass to obtain his certificate of professionalism (Todolí, 2015). Spanish Royal Decree 1529/2012 establishes the basis of the DVT regulations that develop the contract for training and learning. Paradoxically, this contract is hardly ever used. In their 3-year programs, País Vasco and Castilla & León (Law 4/2018 and Decree 2/2017, respectively) offer the possibility of including training that is complementary to the state and autonomic regulations in order to adapt the training to the needs of the student or to allow the specialization required by the company or productive sector. However, it is important to note that this formula increases the cost for the students and the education system. At the same time, it is very beneficial for companies with qualified professionals, making a low outlay even if an apprenticeship contract is signed.

4.1.3. Challenges in curricular content concision

With regard to the curricular content, Marhuenda-Fluixá, Chisvert-Tarazona, Palomares-Montero, Gil, and Vila (2015) point out that the design of the training curriculum is one of the most complex parts of a DVT modality. However, we have seen that no new content or skills are introduced in these proposals and can therefore ask whether there is any progress or improvement in the achievement of the learning outcomes in DVT. The normative analysis reveals that the curriculum in DVT is the same as the curriculum in VET. Also, it is more difficult to guarantee that the curriculum is taught in an alternance modality. In this sense, some studies confirm that company participation in the definition of these projects is considered scarce by teachers (Marhuenda-Fluixá, Chisvert-Tarazona, Palomares-Montero, Gil, & Vila, 2015; Pineda-Herrero, Ciraso-Calí, & Arnau-Sabatés, 2019). It is also difficult to guarantee similar training content, regardless of the company in which students develop learning, especially because of the small size of Spanish companies (Echeverria, 2016). There is not always a link between curriculum from the academic disciplines and the productive process, which has an effect on subjects that do not generate the expected learning. The productive processes at companies could replace value knowledge and create a space for the null curriculum (Torres, 2005). In addition, an important percentage of teachers agree on the difficulties that students of DVT and traditional VET may have. Therefore, it is a challenge to adapt the contents to each profile (Valiente, Scandurra, Zancajo, & Brown, 2015) not only at schools but also at companies. Curricular and organizational issues could be contained in the state rules or in their regional development. However, this has not been considered.

4.1.4. Curricular timing in schools and companies

The state regulations establish that the minimum hours of training that must be given in companies should be 33 % of the curriculum, which is a percentage that can be expanded according to the characteristics of each subject and the participating company. The disparity of these situations increases within territorial regulation. Only the territorial laws in Asturias, Extremadura, Valencia and Murcia introduce the same minimum number of training hours in the company as the state regulations. However, many more regions differ in the manner in which they distribute the teaching load that should be shared between the VET school and the company. There are some regions with greater business involvement in terms of the percentage of training given at the company. Aragón proposes that 90 % of the curriculum can be taught in a shared manner between the company and the VET school. In contrast, other territories leave the development of this aspect of their DVT projects to the schools. Each school has the freedom to establish the terms of the agreement with the company in view of the five modalities of dual vocational training (Fig. 1). Schools and enterprises decide the subjects and the number of teaching hours that will be taught in the company because the regulations do not provide a guide on specific subjects or characteristics of the subjects that can or cannot be taught in each space. It is important to clarify, as has been pointed out before, that in a VET classroom, there are students from the DVT modality and students from traditional VET. Therefore, students from both models attend the same class during different hours and sometimes, depending on the contract with the company, with alternance in different periods of time. These circumstances affect teaching in the school context and require a high level of coordination with the company, which must adapt the curriculum to each student according to the study program. This flexibility can be a problem for the system given the poor pedagogical training of the companies' tutors (Marhuenda-Fluixá, Chisvert Tarazona, Palomares-Montero, & Vila, 2017), since there could be a weakening of knowledge, skills and competencies if the productive is prioritized over the pedagogical. If the productive is prioritized, students could be limited to certain work and tasks without any economic risk to the company, or the kind of responsibilities could be reduced based on the productive needs of the company.

In short, the curriculum regulations in Spain are identical in both VET modalities. In fact, this outcome has been established in the normative analysis of every professional training and in the state and regional regulations of DVT. Schools, and their contracts with companies, will be essential in making the curriculum concise. In addition, the standard about the time when the company training is to be accessed should have been made more clear. The DVT curricular benefits are relevant in reference to this factor. Billett (2001) shows that increased time in the workplace benefits student learning and that students become more independent, have the opportunity to do routine tasks and have access to other more complex tasks, and develop better comprehension at work. This is not a banal matter. As Billett (2014) and Eiríksdóttir (2018) have advised, the time at which the student starts his or her training in the company determines how beneficial to the student or the company it will be. If training at the company starts at the end of the last course, the pedagogical benefit will be smaller and the productive benefit will be larger.

4.2 Evaluation system in DVT

In Spain, the grades for the subjects that are taught totally or partially in the company are the responsibility of the school tutor, although feedback from the tutor at the company will be taken into consideration. Although the alternance has been introduced, this circumstance shows how the system is basically still scholarly. Both of the tutors evaluate the process, but only the school tutor grades the student.

On the other hand, there is not a formal coordination mechanism between the company and the school or the administration in any of the territories.

Paradoxically, in Aragón, which is the territory where more hours of training are taught in the companies, the evaluation depends exclusively on the teaching staff of the VET school, which is especially significant in view of the differences between the types of knowledge accessed at each location. The knowledge that is principally theoretical and propositional is accessed in the formal context of a school, while more practical and tacit knowledge is accessed in the companies.

Rules are clear in FCT and DVT. In both cases, the school is responsible for the evaluation. The reaching staff must qualify the student while taking into account the report provided by company tutors.

Marhuenda-Fluixá et al. (2015) reveals that the competency assessment in Spanish DVT, which first considers the result and then the process, is the least used but seems the most appropriate for assessing the learning of skills that are fundamental in DVT.

In contrast, the evaluation in the dual German system is conducted by joining the implied agents. According to Todolí (2015), in Germany, it is the state that determine whether students have achieved professional qualification through bodies such as chambers of commerce. The evaluation is carried out throughout the period that the student is in the company and focuses on the productivity of workers and not on their employability. The evaluation's objective is the acquisition of the skills necessary to perform a job that will lead to a qualification.

VET schools and other organizations, professionals or social agents are fundamental in the German system because they are the coordination mechanisms and guarantee the relationship with the company. In Spain, state regulations do not establish a mechanism for the coordination and evaluation of the projects. Without a doubt, this is a substantial difference with respect to the German system, which arose through a complex historical process and was capable of building a coordinated teaching and learning context, "a connected whole" (Gessler & Howe, 2013). A monthly meeting between the school tutor and the company tutor regarding the follow-up of the student is the only mechanism for coordination that exists.

4.3. Organizational solutions to curricular problems

Spanish state and regional regulations establish the framework for preparing the curriculum for all official qualifications. Despite asking the business sector to weigh in on the suitability of proposed curricular content, small and medium-sized enterprises (SMEs) have serious difficulties participating in these definitions. In fact, Fariñas and Huergo (2015) confirm that the business fabric of Spain is principally composed of micro-enterprises, which, together with SMEs, account for 99 % of the total number of companies that offer work. SMEs offer 40 % of the country's employment, while large companies account for 23 % of the job offers. In this context, micro- and medium-sized enterprises do not always know how to face pedagogical objectives if they lack suitable training personnel or if their particular specialization does not allow them to cover all of the training content themselves. In the same way, if evaluation is considered a curricular component, the companies' tutors have little responsibility in the evaluation process. They have a role in content development (what is going to be learned by students in the company); however, this role is not explicitly recognized and validated at the evaluation. The German context is different. German DVT implementation was developed in the tradition of more diverse social agents that allow DVT to develop at companies with few employees. In fact, 49 % of companies with 1–9 workers are authorized to perform DVT, although the companies with more than 500 workers are those that are most involved in DVT (91 % of them are authorized) (IESE, 2014). This statistic proves that the German business fabric affects DVT independent of the business size. However, small and medium enterprises must also work harder to participate in the dual system in Germany. Hensen-Reifgens & Hippach-Schneider (2014) consider various initiatives to solve these problems. For example, Germany offers inter-company vocational training centers (überbetriebliche Berufsbildungsstätten, ÜBS). These centers are designed to supplement in-company training. Educational institutions offer training at these companies that is often sponsored by autonomous bodies in the relevant sectors of industry. The German Federal Ministry of Education supports sponsors with investment subsidies. Spain also has vocational training centers for employment, but they are exclusively used for the continuous training of working people or for training unemployed people. Perhaps this participation is not redundant if we consider that the school has difficulties developing this training. In fact, the schools could better adjust the training to meet the company's requirements and extend responsibility and decision making in curricular matters to the company.

German companies are also organized to benefit from participating in the dual training system (Ausbildungsverbünde). They use four formulas that could be transferred to the Spanish context: (1) lead enterprise with partners (Leitbetrieb mit Partnerbetrieben), where one enterprise takes the lead and bears the overall responsibility for training, and some parts of the training are conducted in specialized partner enterprises; (2) training to order (Auftragsausbildung), where some training takes place outside of the regular enterprise, perhaps in a nearby large enterprise with a training workshop, on the basis of an order; (3) training consortium (Ausbildungskonsortium), where several small and medium-sized enterprises sign a cooperation agreement and work together on equal footing and take on apprentices and train them independently, and if an enterprise cannot cover a specific content area, the apprentice moves to another enterprise (rotation principle); and (4) training association (Ausbildungsverein), where some enterprises establish an organization that exclusively takes over administrative tasks such as contracts, etc., while other enterprises conduct training. Association structures are usually comprised of a general meeting and an honorary committee.

The transfer of any of these proposals to the Spanish context could be useful. In Spain, there are some antecedents that would facilitate the adoption of these measures. The Spanish business culture has relevant collaborative references in the context of cooperative companies that are prepared to take on these challenges; however, other productive contexts are less likely to establish collaborative ties to facilitate training processes.

This organizational effort requires a change in business organizations in the Spanish context. An awareness of the relevance of their participation in the training processes of DVT students is necessary. Moreover, it is necessary to analyze the differences or the new requirements that a workplace training module would represent in VET. In fact, company tutors do not have an official accreditation because the state and regional regulations do not require it, which is proof of the lack of pedagogical and formative culture in Spanish companies regarding the alternance training. In this context, the following question arises regarding the DVT: is the company tutor in Spain trained for the development of the curriculum in the professional environment?

The lack of a training structure that prepares and recognizes company tutors in Spanish DVT differs from the German DVT system that supports in-company trainers in the acquisition of pedagogical and technical/professional competence, where the chambers and other educational providers offer different types of courses. The Federal Institute for Vocational Education and Training (BIBB) recommends taking a 115-hour course to prepare for the AEVO examination (Hippach-Schneider & Huismann, 2019). According to the Vocational Training Act, Berufsbildungsgesetz BBiG, (BMBF, 2005), only in-company trainers who possess pedagogical and professional aptitude are eligible to train. This mechanism could be transferable to the Spanish context and could be progressively adopted to ensure a cultural change in companies in relation to their training responsibilities.

5. Conclusions

The objective of DVT in the legal regulations is to improve the skills of young people and reduce youth unemployment, but the evidence seems to indicate that the students of VET and DVT acquire the same competencies according to the curricular regulation of both modalities. However, it is worrying to observe how the dual system in Spain transfers the responsibility of the development of part of the curricular content (even though they have a limited role in evaluation tasks) beyond measuring their productivity in an occupation proper according to the professional qualifications in which they are being trained. The difficulties that the model must overcome in response to the curriculum are diverse given that the school cannot provide the entire prescribed curriculum. The curriculum that is not taught to these students in the school is transferred to the company without being certain of the treatment of the curriculum (changing part of the prescribed curriculum to a null curriculum because it is not developed in the specific company) in many cases. Neither the coordination mechanisms nor the evaluation system nor the formation of the company tutor is guaranteed in the current dual system. If DVT aims to facilitate the transition to the labor market and provide students with skills that improve their employability, the curriculum will no doubt be affected. According to our study, there is no evidence of improvement in the curriculum in DVT, and we cannot affirm that students improve their skills despite spending long periods of time in the company with this type of training. In addition, the current dual system cannot guarantee that the content taught in the company in DVT programs cannot be addressed in the school and can only be learned in the workplace.

In conclusion, DVT does not provide curricular improvements at a regulatory level compared to those that have already been introduced by traditional VET in Spain. It will be necessary to continue investigating on the other levels of curricular creation, particularly on the practice component, to determine whether curricular improvements occur.

Biographical notes

María José Chisvert-Tarazona and Alicia Ros-Garrido are assistant professors in the Department of Didactics and Scholar Organization in the Faculty of Philosophy and Sciences of Education at the University of Valencia (Spain), and Davinia Palomares-Montero is a tenured professor in the same department. They are all members of the research group 'Transitions to the working world in at-risk populations' (TRANSICIONS). Javier Vila-Vázquez is a VET teacher.

María José Chisvert-Tarazona holds a Ph.D. in Philosophy and Educational Sciences. Her areas of research are related to the accreditation of professional qualifications, vocational training and guidance and social entrepreneurship. She has been the main researcher on a project concerning the accreditation of qualifications in vulnerable groups, which is financed by the University of Valencia (2013–2014).

Javier Vila-Vázquez is a graduate in Labour Sciences and has a Masters of Management of Educational Institutions. He is a vocational training and guidance and entrepreneurship teacher. His areas of research are related to soft skills in VET students and dual vocational training.

Alicia Ros-Garrido has a Ph.D. in Pedagogy. Her research interests focus on continuing vocational education, the accreditation of learning, and how to bring these issues into the education of vocational education and training teachers and trainers. Before entering university, she was a vocational trainer as well as a counselor.

Davinia Palomares Montero holds a Ph.D. in Sociology from the University of Valencia. She is interested in the study of higher education curriculum design, vocational training and the analysis of multidisciplinary innovation for social change.

References

Apple, M. (2000). *Official Knowledge*. London: Routledge (first published March 25th 1993).
Billett, S. (2001). *Learning in the Workplace: Strategies for Effective Practice*. Crows Nest: Allen & Unwin.
Billett, S. (2014). Integrating learning experiences across tertiary education and practice settings: A socio-personal account. *Educational Research Review*, *12*, 1–13. https://doi.org/10.1016/j.edurev.2014.01.002.
BMBF (2005). Die Reform der beruflichen Bildung: Berufsbildungsgesetz 2005. Bonn: Bundesministerium für Bildung und Forschung. https://www.gesetze-im-internet.de/bundesrecht/bbig_2005/gesamt.pdf.

Bonoli, L., & Wilson, A. (2019). Bringing firms on board. Inclusiveness of the dual apprenticeship systems in Germany, Switzerland and Denmark, *International Journal of Social Welfare*, *28*(4), 369–379.

Bourdieu P., & Passeron, J. C. (1995). *La Reproducción. Elementos de una teoría del sistema de enseñanza*. París: Fontamara.

BUSINESSEUROPE (2012). *Creating opportunities four youth. How to improve the quality and image of apprenticeships?* Brussels: Social Affairs Department. Downloaded https://www.businesseurope.eu/publications/creating-opportunities-youth-howimprove-quality-and-image-apprenticeships.

Cedefop (2019). *Spotlight on VET – 2018 compilation:vocational education and training systems in Europe*. Luxembourg: Publications Office. Retrieved from http://data.europa.eu/doi/10.2801/540310.

Echeverría, B. (2016). Transferencia del Sistema de FP Dual a España. *Revista de Investigación Educativa*, *34*(2), 295–314. DOI: http://dx.doi.org/10.6018/rie.34.2.249341.

Eiríksdóttir, E. (2018). Variations in implementing the dual VET system: Perspectives of students, teachers, and trainers in the certified trades in Iceland. In S. Choy et al. (Eds.), *Integration of Vocational Education and Training Experiences*, Technical and Vocational Education and Training: Issues, Concerns and Prospects, 29 (pp. 145). https://doi.org/10.1007/978-981-10-8857-5_8.

European Commission (2012). Communication from the Commission to the European parliament, the council, the European economic and social committee and the committee of the regions. Rethinking Education: Investing in skills for better socio-economic outcomes. COM/2012/0669 final. Estrasbourg: Comisión Europea. https://www.cedefop.europa.eu/files/com669_en.pdf.

Fariñas, J. C., & Huergo, E. (2015). *Demografía empresarial en España: tendencias y regularidades*. Estudios sobre la Economía Española. 2015-24. FEDEA. Retrieved from http://documentos.fedea.net/pubs/eee/eee2015-24.pdf.

Gessler, M. (2017). Areas of learning: The shift towards work and competence orientation within the School-based Vocational Education in the German Dual Apprenticeship System. In Martin Mulder (ed.), *Competence-based Vocational and Professional Education* (pp. 695–717). Cham: Springer International Publishing.

Gessler, M., & Howe, F. (2013). The German dual vocational system-the origin of the current arquitecture-. *Bulletin of Institute of Technology and Vocational Education Nagoya University, 10*, 17–28.

Gimeno-Sacristán, J. (Comp.) (2010). S*aberes e incertidumbres sobre el currículum.* Madrid: Morata.

Hake, B. (2005). Fragility of the "employment agenda", flexible life courses and the reconfiguration of lifelong learning in The Netherlands. In: A. Bron, E. Kurantowicz, H. S. Olesen and L. West (Eds.), *'Old' and 'New' Worlds in Adult Learning* (pp. 234–253). Wroclaw: Wydawnictwo Naukowe.

Hensen-Reifgens, K. A., & Hippach-Schneider,U. (2014). Germany. VET in Europe – Country report 2014. Cedefop.

Hippach-Schneider, U., & Huismann, A. (2019). Vocational education and training in Europe: Germany. Cedefop ReferNet VET in Europe reports 2018. Retrieved from http://libserver.cedefop.europa.eu/vetelib/2019/ReferNet_Germany_VET_in_Europe_2018.pdf.

Hoeckel, K., & Schwartz, R. (2010). *Learning for Jobs. OECD Reviews of Vocational Education and Training.* Germany: OECD Publishing. Downloaded de http://www.oecd. org/germany/45668296.pdf.

IESE (2014). La formación profesional dual como reto nacional. Una perspectiva desde la empresa. Navarra: IESE. Retrieved from http://www.iese.edu/research/pdfs/ST-0362.pdf.

Jovanic, T. (2019). Regional development agencies within the governance structures for regional development in the countries of the Former Yugoslavia. *Lex Localis-Journal of Local Self-Government, 17*(3), 771–808.

Krippendorff, K. (2018). *Content Analysis: An Introduction to Its Methodology.* Singapore: Sage publications (4ª Ed.).

Marhuenda-Fluixá, F., Chisvert-Tarazona, M. J., Palomares-Montero, D., Gil, G., & Vila, J., (2015). *La implantación de la Formación Profesional Dual en España: Certezas e incertidumbres.* Universidad de Valencia.

Marhuenda-Fluixá, F., Chisvert-Tarazona, M. J., Palomares-Montero, D., & Vila, J. (2017). D as in dual: Research on the implementation of dual training in the Spanish vocational education system. *Educar*, *53*(3), 285–307.

Marhuenda-Fluixá, F., Chisvert-Tarazona, M. J., & Palomares-Montero, D. (2019). The implementation of dual VET in Spain: An empirical analysis. In F. Marhuenda-Fluixà (Ed.), *The School-Based Vocational Education and Training System in Spain.* (pp. 205–222). Singapore: Springer.

Merino, R. (2013). Las sucesivas reformas de la formación profesional en España o la paradoja entre integración y segregación escolar. *Archivos Analíticos de Políticas Educativas*, *21*(66). Recuperado [data]. http://epaa.asu.edu/ojs/article/view/1222.

Ministerio de Educación y Formación Profesional (2019). Informe "Estadística del alumnado de formación profesional curso 2017–2018". Retrieved from https://www.educacionyfp.gob.es/dam/jcr:a461da71-8247-4442-9ab1-e0401fff8039/nota-17-18.pdf.

Mulder, M. (2017). Competence and the alignment of education and work. In *Competencebased Vocational and Professional Education* (pp. 229–251). Springer: Cham.

Nore, H., & Lahn, L. C. (2019). How can apprentices learn and develop professional competences through ePortfolios? In F. Marhuenda-Fluixá & M. J. Chisvert-Tarazona (Eds.), *Pedagogical concerns and market demands in VET. Proceedings of the 3rd Crossing Boundaries in VET conference, Vocational Education and Training Network (VETNET)* (pp. 171–175) https://doi.org/10.5281/zenodo.2641862.

Pineda-Herrero, P., Ciraso-Calí, A., & Arnau-Sabatés, L. (2019). La FP dual desde la perspectiva del profesorado: elementos que condicionan su implementación en los centros. [Dual VET from the teachers' perspective: the elements that condition its implementation in schools]. *Educación XX1*, *22*(1), 15–43. doi: https://doi.org/10.5944/educXX1.21242.

Pope, C., Ziebland, S., & Mays, N. (2000). Qualitative research in health care: Analysing qualitative data. BMJ: *British Medical Journal*, *320*(7227), 114.

Rego-Agraso, L., Barreira-Cerqueiras, E. M., & Rial Sánchez, A. F. (2015). Formación Profesional Dual: Comparativa entre el sistema alemán y el incipiente modelo español. *Revista Española de Educación Comparada*, 25, 149–166. Retrieved from http://dx.doi.org/10.5944/reec.25.2015.14788.

Tejada, J. (2012). La alternancia de contextos para la adquisición de competencias profesionales en escenarios complementarios de educación superior: marco y estrategias. *Educación XXI*, 15(2), 17–40.

Todolí, A. (2016). La formación dual alemana y el contrato para la formación y el aprendizaje: ¿Diferente legislación o diferentes controles de calidad? *Relaciones Laborales y Derecho del Empleo*, 3(4), 224–267.

Torres, J. (2005). *El curriculum oculto.* Madrid: Morata.

Valiente, O., Scandurra, R., Zancajo, A., & Brown, C. (2015). Un model de formació professional dual per a Catalunya? Reptes en el disseny i implementació de la reforma. Fundació Jaume Bofill. Retrieved from http://www.fbofill.cat/sites/default/files/607.pdf.

DÍAZ-CHAO, ANGEL, MOSO-DIEZ, MÓNICA, AND TORRENT-SELLENS, JOAN

VET, value generation and firm results: An empirical exploration from Spanish industrial firms

Abstract: The aim of this paper is to analyse the business strategies of Spanish firms in terms of Vocational Education and Training (VET), identifying and studying the general characteristics of Spanish manufacturing firms and their differences based on human resources employed with vocational qualifications from the Initial VET system. This analysis is developed quantitatively, within the framework of the Business Strategies Survey of SEPI Foundation, which is an annual panel survey, aimed at industrial manufacturing firms based in Spain. The survey referred to 2016 will incorporate, for the first time, some items related to VET, being surveyed 1800 industrial firms. This analysis is developed from a business strategic approach for competitive advantage as well as from a human capital approach in terms of human capacity and organisational building and the contribution of VET in firm results. The contribution that this research makes to the field lies in its novel comparative approach and in the quantitative scale of the sample. Nevertheless, as the research is exploratory, it requires further analysis in this significant scientific field.

Keywords: VET and qualifications, business strategies, manufacturing industry, productivity,

1. Introduction

In this era of globalisation and digitalisation, countries face the constant challenge of achieving the competitiveness, sustainability and inclusiveness they need to respond to an ever-changing, interconnected and uncertain reality. The fourth industrial revolution is under way and will profoundly transform European industry which requires to create competitive capacities to take advantage of this window of opportunity (Schwab, 2016). The European Union (EU) recommends the European industry, as well as countries that should review key issues for this transformation such as: professional skills, change of business model, sectors and clusters collaboration, regulatory and technological shared standards, climate change and sustainability of resources, and specially much more market-oriented research and development (R&D) and innovation (Smit, Kreutzer, Moeller and Calberg, 2016). By the end of 2020 European industry's contribution is targeted to be raised to 20 % of Gross Domestic Product (GDP)—one of the targets set by the EU 2020 growth strategy. Overall, it is meeting its target as European manufacturing industry's Gross Value Added (GVA) as a proportion of the total European economy rose to 20.1 % in 2018. In Spain, however, this remains a distant goal since the country is still more than 4 points below the European average, being a profound challenge for Spanish manufacturing industry and economy in general (Ministerio de Industria, Comercio y Turismo-MICT, 2019). In this context Spanish manufacturing firms need to think and rethink about their competitive advantages and about the most appropriate strategies to achieve added value, especially since the last world economic crisis in 2008.

The literature on business strategies has been profuse since the 1960s (Ansoff, 1965), proposing different analytical frameworks and typologies in this firm domain. A characteristic shared by most of the literature on business strategies is that a firm's competitive advantage is the result of a combination of different strategies, that evolve over time, depending on structural and contextual conditions, as well as on the nature of the firm, its positioning in the value chain and sector. However, the nature and prioritisation of the strategies are diverse (and even divergent), among which are related to cost, quality, differentiation, specialisation/diversification, design, innovation, quality, processes, organisation, etc. (Utterback and Abernathy, 1975; Porter, 1980; Schuler and Jackson, 1987; etc.).

With the emergence of the concept of industry 4.0, coined in 2011 in Germany and with a rapid international expansion thereafter (Schroeder, 2016), innovation in both technological and organisational level, requires greater relevance in the search for competitiveness by the manufacturing industry. As a sector there are two main strategies, also called the 'dual strategy,' to be a provider of technologies 4.0 or to be a consumer of technologies 4.0 (Smit et al., 2016). This dual strategy implies a new business opportunity window for both providers and consumers of technologies 4.0., given that for the former is a new market niche and for the latter, accelerate their ability to adapt to new market demands and even to transform their business model. Most of the firms are potential 'consumers' and the speed with which they take on this new role will depend on their capacity to absorb new technologies at process, organisational, human and relational level. In this sense, technological innovation and learning capacity building are drivers of the current transformation of the manufacturing sector, and increasingly human capital, mainly in terms of skills, is understood as an enabling key for both efficiency and innovation. This implies changes to a large extent to existing qualifications to meet the demand for professional skills (Lorenz, Rübmann, Strack, Lueth and Bolle, 2015). We understand that human capital refers to the values, attitudes, skills, abilities, knowledge and experiences of the personnel who work in the firm, held by people, and whose catalyst are the professional competences (technical and transversal). Planning and investment in training, appropriate qualifications and new forms of learning (alternation, online, specialisation programmes, etc.) is required in close collaboration with the vocational education and training system.

While business strategies theoretical and empirical analysis have been prolific in the scientific community, the analysis of the contribution of VET to the competitiveness of enterprises has been more recent and less profuse (Toner and Woolley, 2016). In this sense, some empirical studies indicate that a positive of value creation (Alba-Ramirez, 1994; Aragón-Sánchez, 2003; Huerta et al., 2006; Konings, 2008; Cedefop, 2011; Wolter and Mühlemann, 2015), although the parameters of analysis are diverse and heterogeneous and require further development. There are some studies that focus specifically on the influence of skills on firm results, mainly in terms of productivity (Becker, 1994; Card, 1999) and, in particular in their role in boosting the capacity of firms to absorb innovations (Hermann and Peine, 2011). The paper studies the business strategies of Spanish firms according to the VET qualification of the workers, following the International Standard Classification of

Education (ISCED 3 and ISCED 5)[1] from the United Nations Educational, Scientific and Cultural Organization (Unesco).

The main research question is: 'What are the differences in strategies and results between Spanish manufacturing firms to their employees' VET qualification?'

2. Context

In this section we briefly present the Spanish context. The aim is to set out the main characteristics and challenges of both manufacturing sector and VET system, which will help to understand the results of the survey.

2.1. At industry level

In Spain, the contribution made by industry—which includes energy but excludes construction—to the economy is below the eurozone average and is significantly lower than that of countries like Germany, where industry managed to maintain its contribution to Gross Domestic Product (GDP[2] over 2000–2018 (MICT, 2019)).

---

[1] In this chapter we use the code 'employees or workers with VET' referring to those workers that hold an official and formal training qualification (in terms of attainment of ISCED 3 and ISCED 5 levels from the Unesco). In the same way, we refer to workers who do not have and ISCED 3 or 5 qualification as 'employees or workers without VET.'

[2] Gross domestic product (GDP) is the standard measure of the value added created through the production of goods and services in a country during a certain period. As such, it also measures the income earned from that production, or the total amount spent on final goods and services (less imports). It is usually used on annual basis (OECD, 2019a).

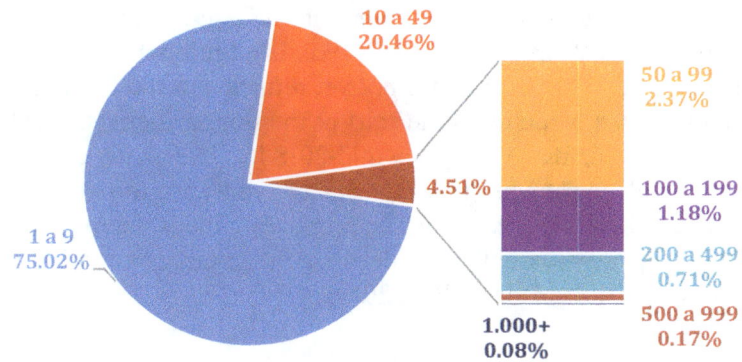

Fig. 1. Manufacturing firms by number of employees in Spain (2018)

Source: (Spanish Statistical Office-INE, 2019a)

As Fig. 1 shows small and medium-sized enterprises (SMEs) (from 1 to 249 employees) account for more than 99 % of companies in Spain. It is noteworthy the large presence (95.48 %) of small firms (from 1 to 49 employees) in the Spanish economy that partially explains its productivity gap, as their productivity do usually go significantly behind that of larger firms (INE, 2019a). In this context, the most important Spanish industrial sector is manufacturing, reaching the 82 % of total production in October of 2019. The following subsectors are the main ones in percentage terms with respect to total industrial production: food products (12 %), abricated metal products, except machinery and equipment (9 %), chemicals and chemical products (6 %), motor vehicles, trailers and semi-trailers (6 %); other non-metallic mineral products (5 %); rubber and plastic products (4 %); machinery and equipment (4 %), basic metals (4 %); and beverages (4 %) (INE, 2019, 3Q). In 1980, Spanish manufacturing industry's GVA[3] stood at 25.9 %. Today

---

3   Value added reflects the value generated by producing goods and services and is measured as the value of output minus the value of intermediate consumption. Value added also represents the income available for the contributions of labour and capital to the production process. Value added by activity shows the value added created by the various industries (such as agriculture, industry, utilities, and other service activities). The indicator presents value added for an activity, as a percentage of total value added (OECD, 2019a).

it is just 14 %. Moreover, its contribution to GDP has fallen to 12.6 % compared to 17.8 % in 2000 (INE, 2019b). In addition, manufacturing's contribution to overall GVA has not yet returned to the level recorded in 2008 (14.5 %), which was the start of the financial crisis. Weakness in the manufacturing sector since mid-2018 has had an adverse impact on equipment investment growth, which is expected to bottom out in 2019. In October 2019, the industrial production index decreased (1,3 % year-one-year in seasonally), evidencing the complex situation of the Spanish industrial sector (MICT, 2019).

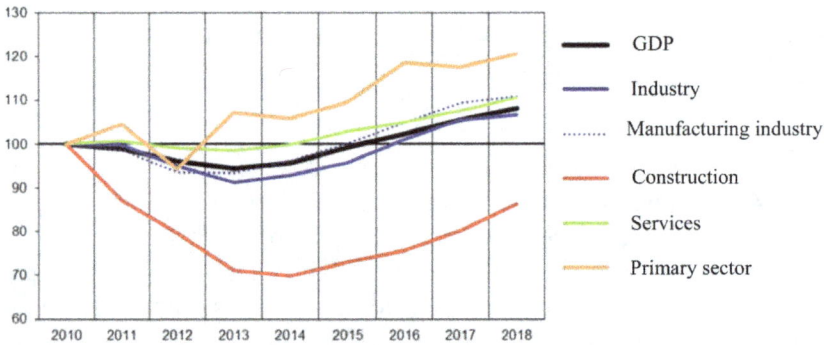

Fig. 2. Evolution of GDP by sectors (2010–2018). Volume index (2010 = 100)

Source: MICT (2019)

The Fig. 2 shows the evolution of the GDP by the main sectors, also including the manufacturing industry, indicating that the crisis has affected all sectors, although unevenly. For instance, the construction sector was the most affected, and with less capacity for recovery, while the manufacturing industry has been recovering above the general industry and the DGP average. That points out a higher capacity to adapt to the post-crisis scenario than the rest of the industry, although in a very moderate way.

Fig. 3. *Evolution of Industrial Production Index (2008–2019)*

Source: Bankia (2019) (corrected and seasonally adjusted data from INE)

In the Fig. 3 the evolution of the Industrial Production Index (IPI) is represented from Quarter 3 of 2008–2019 (Q3). That economic indicator measures levels of production by the manufacturing sector, mining—including oil and gas field drilling services—and electrical and gas utilities. It also measures capacity, an estimate of the production levels that could be sustainably maintained; and capacity utilisation, the ratio of actual output to capacity. Fig. 3 shows that IPI is far from the situation before the crisis (2008) and seems to be difficult to achieve it according to the latest data from the Spanish institute of statistics (INE, 2019b).

Tab. 1 shows the evolution of significant indicators when observing the progress of the Spanish economy, as well as its industry and, specifically, its manufacturing industry. These indicators are GDP, employment and productivity. The data show that since 2014 the manufacturing industry has shown a significant growth in its added value. However, this growth in activity has also been accompanied by notable growth in employment, which has restricted the dynamics of productivity.

Tab. 1. GDP, GAV, employment and productivity (1) (2005–2018). (Constant values corrected by season and data. Interannual variation rate, %)

	All Economy				Industry				Manufacturing Industry			
	GDP	Employment	Productivity	GAV	Employment	Productivity	GAV	Employment	Productivity	GAV	Employment	Productivity
2005	3.7	3.6	0.1	3.8	-0.2	2.4	1.8	-0.4	2.3			
2006	4.2	3.7	0.5	4.3	-1.5	4.6	3.2	-1.8	5.1			
2007	3.8	3.2	0.5	3.0	-1.5	3.4	1.4	-1.9	3.4			
2008	1.1	0.2	0.9	0.7	-1.0	0.2	-2.1	-1.0	-1.1			
2009	-0.4	-6.1	2.7	1.7	-11.5	1.7	-10.9	-12.4	1.8			
2010	0.0	-2.6	2.7	1.1	-3.0	6.7	0.0	-4.0	4.1			
2011	-1.0	-2.8	1.8	2.1	-3.5	3.3	-1.3	-3.8	2.6			
2012	-2.9	-4.8	2.0	3.7	-6.9	2.2	-5.2	-7.4	2.3			
2013	-1.7	-3.4	1.8	1.5	-4.5	0.6	-0.2	-4.8	4.8			
2014	1.4	1.0	0.3	2.6	-1.2	3.3	3.0	-1.3	4.2			
2015	3.6	3.3	0.3	2.7	2.8	0.1	4.2	3.1	1.1			
2016	3.2	3.0	0.1	1.0	4.0	1.6	4.7	4.2	0.4			
2017	3.0	2.9	0.1	1.8	3.5	0.9	4.4	3.8	0.5			
2018	2.6	2.5	0.1	2.0	1.0	0.1	1.4	1.1	0.3			

(1) Equivalent full-time employment

Source: MICT (2019).

Regarding innovation, in the last country profiles studies of the European Innovation Scoreboard (EIS)[4], Spain is ranked 19th out of 28 in the EU innovation ranking[5] (with 2017 as the reference year) (Hollanders et al., 2019). In that framework Spain is classified as a 'moderate innovator' according to the innovation performance of her national innovation system. Most of Spain's economic indicators are closely above or below the EU average, except for the indicator measuring small and medium-sized enterprises (SMEs) innovation performance. The innovation indicator for SMEs in Spain stands at 45 % of the EU28 average. The result of Spanish SMEs is low in the three indicators that make up the dimension: product/service innovations (39 %), organisational/marketing innovations (66 %) and internally innovative SMEs (31 %).

To conclude it is relevant to note the recommendation made by the EU to Spain to improve skills shortages and mismatches, as they are understood a critical barrier to the development and use of advanced technologies. In this sense, stronger cooperation between educational and business actors is recommended to boost the diffusion of knowledge and help increase the presence of innovative firms and a competitive industry (European Commission, 2019).

---

[4] The European innovation scoreboard provides a comparative analysis of innovation performance in EU countries, other European countries, and regional neighbours. It assesses relative strengths and weaknesses of national innovation systems and helps countries identify areas they need to address. (European Commission, https://ec.europa.eu/growth/industry/innovation/facts-figures/scoreboards_en).

[5] Member States fall into four performance groups; 'innovation leaders' (above 120 % of the EU average), 'strong innovators' (between 90 % and 120 % of the EU average), 'moderate innovators' (between 50 % and 90 % EU average) and 'modest innovators' (below 50 % of the EU average). That measurement framework distinguished between four main dimensions; framework conditions, investments, innovation activities, and employment and sales impacts (Hollanders, Es-Sadki & Merkellback, 2019: 8).

2.2. At vocational education and training level

Spanish VET system includes two different subsystems: Initial Vocational Education and Training (IVET) and the Continuous Vocational Education and Training (CVET).

- Initial Vocational Education and Training

IVET aims at helping young people gain qualifications that are accredited by the respective diplomas. It is overseen by the Ministry of Education and Vocational Training (MEFP) and by the governments of Spain's autonomous communities. Lower secondary education is the second and final phase of compulsory education (from 12 to 16 years) and after graduation, learners can access high school (general upper secondary education, ISCED 3) or intermediate VET (vocational upper secondary education, ISCED 3). Students who do not get graduated of compulsory school receive an official certificate of compulsory education, which details the years studied and they can work or access to basic VET[6]. Those students that obtained their graduation of general/vocational upper secondary school, could access Higher VET programmes (ISCED 5). Education authority VET was reformed in 2012 and basic, intermediate and higher VET qualifications are offered from 2014/15 (Cedefop, 2015). Programmes last two years (2,000 hours), with training in a firm (minimum 20 %) and at a VET school (maximum 80 %). The reform also allows to acquire IVET qualifications through dual track schemes (with or without a labour contract). In such cases, duration could be up to three years. VET programmes are based on learning outcomes with a focus on work-based learning, following ECVET guidelines.

As Tab. 2 shows, enrolment in VET programmes have grown intensively since the 2007–2008 academic year, almost doubling, especially in the case of Higher VET.

---

6   The 2013 education reform introduced an alternative vocational path (Basic VET) open to low secondary students aged 15 years, who meet certain age and academic requirements (Cedefop, 2019).

Tab. 2. Evolution of number of students enrolled on VET programmes

Programmes	2007–2008	2012–2013	2017–2018	2018–2019	2019–2020*
Basic VET	0	0	72,180	74,009	74,947
Intermediate VET (ISCED 3)	239,559	332,495	344,266	350,820	358,657
Higher-level VET (ISCED 5)	222,933	328,552	398,908	413,935	428,302
Total	462,492	661,047	815,354	838,764	861,906

* Forecast for 2019/2020 academic year.

Source: Compiled in-house using MEFP data (2019a, 2019b).

According to the European Commission report published in the first half of 2019, Spain has yet to address the following challenges. Firstly, it is recommended to increase access to VET. While enrolment rates have increased considerably in recent years (see Tab. 2), there is still room for improvement, uptake of which is half the EU-23 average.

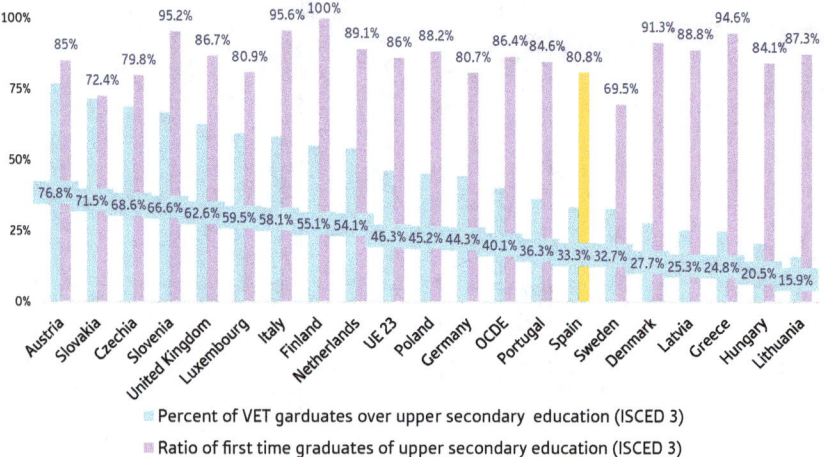

Fig. 4. Percentage of people holding upper secondary qualifications and percentage holding VET qualifications. EU countries. 2017.

Source: MEFP (2019a: 25). Adapted from Organisation for Economic Co-operation and Development (OECD) data (2019b).

Secondly, it is recommended to increase the proportion of vocational graduates. As Fig. 5 shows in Spain, 33 % of first-time upper secondary graduates held a vocational qualification in 2017, compared to the OECD (2019b) average of 40 % and the EU23 average of 46 %.

Thirdly, it is recommended to reduce the school dropout rate. The potential for growth in VET student numbers is connected to the early school-leaving rate among Spaniards aged 18–24. This rate is the highest (17.9 %) in the EU-28 (10.6 %) and although it has fallen in recent years it remains a major challenge for the Spanish education system, since the EU has set the goal of achieving no more than 10 % dropout throughout the European Union by 2020.

In respect to dual VET, first of all should be noted that there are two modalities. The first one is called 'training and apprenticeship contracts,' in which the learning can be part of the education or employment systems. The second modality is related to dual VET projects offered within the education system and implemented by the regions. In 2017 the total number of both modalities of training and apprenticeship contracts raised up to 48,317, which is an emerging increase slightly exceeding 2 % in 2017. In this sense, boosting dual VET is one of the strategies included in the first Spanish Strategic Plan on Vocational Education and Training (MEFP, 2019c), the design of which was presented in November 2019. The objective is for the dual VET modality to grow in quantitative and qualitative terms, promoting a larger number of apprentices in firms, which seeks to be a way to bring the educational and business worlds closer together.

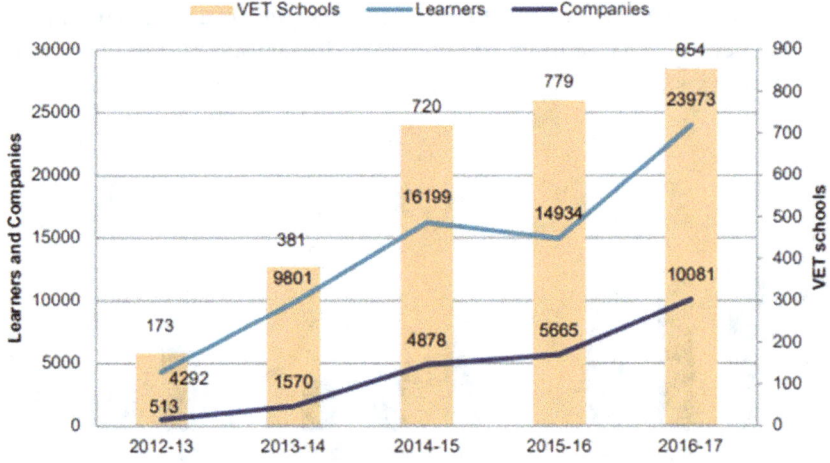

Fig. 5. Dual VET in the education system, 2012–2016

Source: Sancha y Gutiérrez (2019: 24).

Fig. 5 shows the growing evolution of dual VET in Spain since regulations made it possible in 2012. On one side, there is a strong increase in the participation of both learners and vocational training schools in absolute terms, but in relative terms it is low, given that it accounts for 3 % of those currently enrolled in vocational training (with 2018 as the year of reference). On the other side, the increase was unequal as it was more intense in the first three courses than in the last ones. The literature points to various reasons for this situation, such as lax regulation and uncoordinated implementation, a rigid supply system, a weak guidance system, scarce explicit incentives and funding for both education and business stakeholders, the lack of a business culture of training, the nature and structure of sectors, the small size of companies and so on (Olazaran y Brunet, 2013; Echeverría and Martínez, 2018; Navarro et al., 2018; Marhuenda-Fluixá, Chisvert-Tarazona and Palomares-Montero, 2019).

- Continuous Vocational Education and Training (CVET).

As a starting point of this section, it is interesting to begin by presenting the level of educational attainment of Spanish society which is quite polarised in terms of 'tertiary education' and 'preprimary, primary and lower secondary education' in respect to the average of the OECD and EU countries.

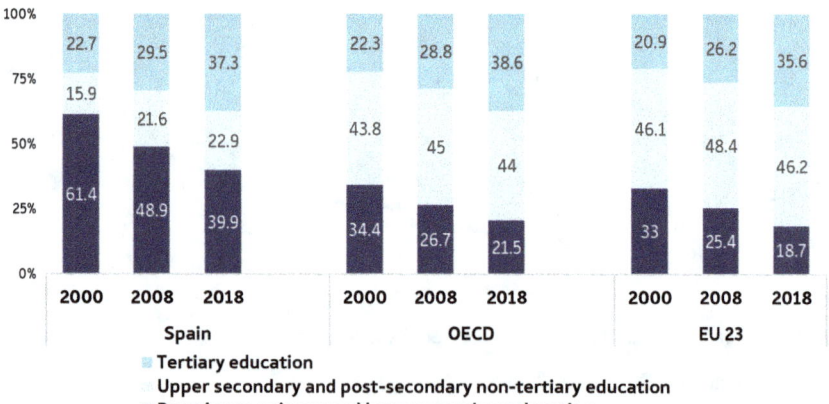

Fig. 6. Trend in educational level of the adult population (25–64 years old) from 2000 to 2018.

Source: MEFP (2019b: 6).

As Fig. 6 shows the percentage of Spain's adult population holding qualifications up to upper secondary or initial vocational education and training (IVET) level (39.9 %) is roughly twice that of both the EU-23 and the OECD (Fig. 7). Although this situation has steadily improved over the last decade, the level in 2018 was still hugely higher than the international averages (18.7 % for the EU-23 and 21.5 % for the OECD). The situation is the reverse for the population with qualifications above upper secondary or IVET level (22.9 %) and is practically half the EU-23 (46.2 %) and OECD (44 %) averages. In this sense, there is a field of improvement to increase upper secondary and post-secondary non-tertiary education, where Vocational Training is integrated. Although it is necessary for young people to be more oriented towards VET studies (as we have seen in the previous section), it is also important that adults can continue to be trained and qualified through training for employment.

CVET aims to upgrade people's skills and acquire formal qualifications from either the education or labour awarding entities. The source of finance can be private (from firms or employees) or public (from labour public policies) and they are oriented to both active workers and the unemployed. Main authorities are the Ministry of Employment, Migration and Social Security and the governments of Autonomous Communities, being connected to the Spanish National Catalogue of Vocational Qualifications. From the CVET subsystem a wide range of courses skill profiles are offered by public or private institutions accredited as providers for professional certificates and other accredited VET training centres (Cedefop, 2015). Training modalities are articulated in three types of training initiatives. The first modality is the 'offering training' that includes 'training plans for employed' and 'training actions for unemployed.' The second modality is the 'on-demand training' that integrates the 'training in Firms' and 'individual permits.' The last one is the 'work-linked training' which brings together the 'theoretical training of contracts for training' and the 'employment and Training Programmes.' According to the basic indicators of the FPE, presented by the State Employment Public Service (Sepe), supply training initiatives are those with the highest proportion of the budget (59 %); specifically, those managed by Sepe, State Foundation for Vocational Training (Fundae) and the autonomous communities for the employed and unemployed. Demand initiatives have a 36 % budget and a large participation, exceeding four million participants. The remaining budget is for work-linked training initiatives, which account for 5 % of the budget.

The main challenges faced are as follows: to increase skills training and to reduce the mismatch between skills supply and demand, particularly as regards advanced technologies (European Commission, 2019). The EU has set the goal of having 15 % of the population aged 25–64 participating in skills training by 2020. In 2018, the European average stood at 11.1 % and the Spanish average at 10.5 %. The figures for the various EU countries vary extremely widely, with highest participation being recorded in the Nordic states (Sweden, 29.2 %; Finland, 28.5 %; and Denmark 23.5 %) (MEFP, 2019b).

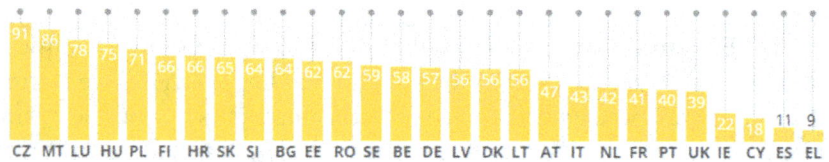

Fig. 7. EU skills matchmaking (2018)

Source: European Skills Index-ESI (2019)

Even though, Fig. 7 shows that Spain is almost in the average of the European target, it is badly positioned in terms of matching skills according to the ESI (2018). Within that index skills matching *'represents the degree of successful utilisation of skills, the extent to which skills are effectively matched in the labour market. This can be observed in the form of jobs and mismatches which include unemployment, shortages, surpluses or underutilisation of skills in the labour market. Sub-pillars are included to distinguish unemployment and skills mismatches.'* (ESI, 2019).

To sum up, from the Spanish context key questions are raised to that will directly influence both the manufacturing sector and educational system such as *'to foster innovation and resource efficiency in firms (specially, on small and medium sized firms), to promote skills and employability, to promote job quality, to invest further on digitisation and skills, to enhance stronger cooperation between educational and business actors in order to contribute to the diffusion of knowledge and lifelong learning, etc.'* (European Commission, 2019). All those challenges are closely related to the assets that make up a company's capital (human capital, structural and/or organisational capital and relational capital) and its underlying strategies.

3. Methodology

In this chapter the business strategies of Spanish firms are studied according to the qualification of the workers in terms of vocational education and training. First, it aims to identify and study the general characteristics of Spanish manufacturing firms and their differences based on human resources employed with professional training. Second, the aim is to analyse the differences mains strategies underlying the obtained results such as productivity, export and import intensity, gross operating margin and inverse rate.

The research questions are[7]:

- What are the differences in business strategies between Spanish manufacturing firms according to their employees' VET qualification?
- What are the differences in results between Spanish manufacturing firms according to their employees' VET qualification?

This analysis is developed quantitatively within the framework of the Business Strategies Survey, which is an annual panel survey, aimed at industrial manufacturing firms based in Spain. Firstly, value elements and outcomes are analysed, paying special attention to human resources and employment, technology and innovation, and productivity and

---

7   This analysis is part of a collaborative research project between the SEPI Foundation and the Bankia Foundation for Dual Training to gather information in relation to the professional training of workers in the manufacturing sector.

competitiveness. For this analysis, data from the Business Strategies Survey (BSS) conducted by the SEPI Foundation (2016 edition) is used. This survey has been in operation since 1990 between the Ministry of Industry and the SEPI Foundation, having an annual average of 1800 industrial companies been surveyed using a questionnaire with 107 questions and more than 500 specific fields, and which also includes information on the firms' balance sheet together with their profit and loss statements[8].This survey is designed to obtain information about industrial firms' strategies. Strategies are understood as the decisions that firms make with regard to the variables that comprise their competitive levers, including both those that are most flexible or modifiable in the short term (e.g. pricing or product promotion) and those that take longer to realign (e.g. choices within the product space or R&D) (Fundación SEPI, 2018). The BSS's population of reference is composed of firms with 10 or more employees within the manufacturing industry. Tab. 3 below shows the universe of Spanish manufacturing industrial firms obtained for the 2016 from the Central Business Register (CBR) that joins together all Spanish enterprises, including their local units situated within the country, into one single information system (INE, 2016).

---

8 The SEPI Foundation preserves the consistency and quality of the time series and produces the corresponding 'Annual Report and Statistical Tables.'

Tab. 3. Total number of manufacturing industrial firms by area of activity and size (2016)

Area of activity	≤ 200 workers	> 200 workers	Total
Meat processing	3,766	44	3,810
Foodstuffs and tobacco	18,946	169	19,115
Beverages	5,136	29	5,165
Textiles and clothing	14,679	24	14,703
Leather and footwear	4,732	6	4,738
Wood industry	10,181	10	10,191
Paper	1,706	34	1,740
Graphic arts	13,801	12	13,813
Chemicals and pharmaceuticals	3,795	143	3,938
Rubber and plastic	4,527	59	4,586
Non-metallic minerals	8,541	61	8,602
Ferrous and non-ferrous metals	1,173	59	1,232
Metal products	34,126	67	34,193
Agricultural and industrial machinery	756	2	758
Computing and electronics	2,442	21	2,463
Electrical equipment and machinery	6,079	90	6,169
Motor vehicles	1,621	115	1,736
Other transport equipment	724	31	755
Furniture	12,453	12	12,465
Other manufacturing	10,061	13	10,074
TOTAL	159,245	1,001	160,246

Source: INE (2016)

The geographical scope of reference is the Spanish economy, and the survey uses yearly variables. Moreover, the sample is taken from the directory of Social Security contribution accounts. The units surveyed were selected by combining comprehensiveness and random sampling criteria according to the number of firm employees. Firms with between 10 and 200 workers are selected by stratified, proportional (with restrictions) and systematic sampling with a random starting point. The sample strata are defined by cross-referencing the National Classification of Economic Activities (CNAE) activity groups at two-digit level against the 10–20, 21–50, 51–100, 101–200 and 201+ employee ranges. The Business Strategies Survey aims to delimit and maintain a representative sample of Spain's manufacturing firms. One of the most relevant characteristics of the BSS is its representativeness[9]. Tab. 4 below shows the sample of firms obtained for the 2016 Business Strategies Survey. Within the sample it is noted that most of firms surveyed were industrial SMEs, with less than 200 workers (80.9 %). Although large industrial enterprises make up a significant proportion (19,1 %), above the average for the sample universe, the proportionality was maintained between the samples of SMEs and large industrial enterprises (BSS data, 2016).

Tab. 4. Number of firms participating in the Business Strategies Survey by area of activity and size (2016)

Area of activity (CNAE)	≤ 200 workers	> 200 workers	Total
Meat processing	70	16	86
Foodstuffs and tobacco	189	55	244
Beverages	32	8	40
Textiles and clothing	102	7	109
Leather and footwear	66	0	66
Wood industry	52	1	53
Paper	67	10	77
Graphic arts	68	3	71
Chemicals and pharmaceuticals	83	43	126
Rubber and plastic	93	16	109
Non-metallic minerals	93	22	115
Ferrous and non-ferrous metals	27	24	51
Metal products	205	25	230
Agricultural and industrial machinery	88	27	115
Computing and electronics	28	7	35
Electrical equipment and machinery	43	13	56
Motor vehicles	39	39	78
Other transport equipment	17	15	32
Furniture	68	8	76
Other manufacturing	34	5	39
Total	**1,464**	**344**	**1,808**

Source: Díaz-Chao y Torrent-Sellens (2019)

---

9 The initial selection was carried out combining exhaustiveness and random sampling criteria. Those firms with more than 200 employees were included in the first category. The second category was composed by firms employing 10-to-200 workers. These firms were selected through a stratified, proportional and systematic sampling with a random seed (Díaz-Chao and Torrent-Sellens, 2019).

BSS is oriented towards capturing information about firms' strategies including information about (1) 'activity, products and manufacturing processes,' (2) 'customers and suppliers,' (3) 'costs and prices,' (4) 'markets,' (5) 'technological activities,' (6) 'foreign trade,' (7) 'accounting data' and (8) 'employment' The last variable includes the number of employees working in the firm, its structure according to the type of contracts, their professional categories and qualifications, as well as other information needed to calculate the effective work-time during the year.

The survey referred to 2016- incorporates, for the first time, some items related to VET, as a result of this piece of collaborative research between both foundations. The design of the 'VET' items was elaborated for both foundations and the survey and statistical treatment was done by Sepi Foundation (Díaz-Chao and Torrent-Sellens, 2019). The analysis of the data is developed by both foundations combining a business strategic approach (Schuler and Jackson, 1987) for competitive advantage as well as from a human capital theory in terms of capacity building and the contribution of VET in firm results (Becker, 1994; Card, 1999; Hermann and Peine, 2011). The dependent variable is the level of attendant in VET (ISCED 3, ISCED 5), and an associative analysis is made with the results of the firms in terms of productivity, export and import intensity, gross operating margin and the inverse rate, and identifying the underlying business strategies.

From a statistical approach the results of the survey are considered valid, as for the 2016 Business Strategies Survey 69.9 % of the questionnaires were valid (in the case of the panel, this figure exceeded 92 %). In total, 1,808 firms participated and incidents affecting 20 firms in the live sample (panel plus new recruits) were recorded. Moreover, from the sector structure perspective, data obtained responds to the criteria of diversification, and therefore Spanish manufacturing industry is reflected in the data of the survey data.

The contribution of this research makes to the field lies in its novel comparative approach and in the quantitative scale of the sample. Nevertheless, we are aware that the research has its limitations and that it is necessary to continue study in this significant scientific domain.

4. Results and discussion

4.1. An overview of manufacturing firms and their workforce according to VET

The analysis of the survey data has been according to the educational attainment of workforce of manufacturing firms in terms of vocational education and training, following the ISCED classification. As Tab. 4 shows the results of the survey show that almost 22 % of staff employed in Spanish manufacturing firms hold a VET qualification (ISCED 3 and/or ISCED 5) and 14.5 % have a university qualification (ISCED 6, 7 and/or 8). The remaining 63.6 % have either a school-leaving certificate (ISCED 1 and/or 2) or no qualifications at all. Consequently, most of Spanish manufacturing industry's employees do not hold any vocational ISCED qualifications from the Initial VET system, and this is the first and most important finding of the survey. This situation is 17 points above the average for large firms.

Tab. 5. *Percentage of* employees working in Spanish manufacturing industry with VET qualifications (2016)

ISCED levels		
	Workers with a University qualification (ISCED 6, 7, 8)	14.5 %
	Workers with a VET qualification (ISCDE 3, 5)	21.9 %
	Workers with a low qualification (ISCED 1, 2)	63.6 %
	Total	100 %

Source: Own elaboration based on BSS data (Fundación Sepi, 2018)

This situation of low qualification in the manufacturing industry is aligned with the educational level of the Spanish population. Specifically, the population between 25 and 64 years of age has a very low level of vocational training qualifications in relation to other countries (as shown in Fig. 7). Practically 40 % of the population has a low qualification. But if we move to higher age groups, this increases to 60 %, which corresponds in large part to the profile of workers in the manufacturing industry. Moreover, it should be noted that although this population is not qualified by the IVET system, they may have knowledge derived from experience, informal training and other types of employment training, which is not analysed in this chapter, but which would be of interest for future analyses.

The second finding points out that the size of the companies influences the level of qualification of the employees, that is to mention, in the hiring of them according to educational levels. The larger the manufacturing enterprise (with over 200 employees), the greater the proportion of workers with VET qualifications is (29.5 %); nonetheless, the low qualified workers are almost half of the total workface of large firms (see Tab. 5).

Tab. 6. *Percentage of* employees working in Spanish manufacturing industry with VET qualifications by firm size (2016)

Educational Classification	Educational level	SMEs	Large Enterprises
ISCED levels	Workers with a University qualification (ISCED 6, 7, 8)	13 %	21 %
	Workers with a VET qualification (ISCDE 3, 5)	20.4 %	29.5 %
	Workers with a low qualification (ISCED 1, 2)	66.6 %	49.5 %
	Total	100 %	100 %

Source: Own elaboration based on BSS data (Fundación Sepi, 2018)

This situation is more dramatic in the case of manufacturing SMES since at least two-thirds of its workers are low-qualified, and only 20.4 % of their workers hold a vocational qualification (ISCDE 3 and ISCED 5), more than 9 points below large firms. When the distribution is analysed, comparing the means, the results indicate that 80.5 % of firms hire workers, but with an unequal distribution. The fact that Spanish SMEs have two thirds of low-skilled staff, and that these in turn account for more than 95 % of all manufacturing firms (see Fig. 1), shows the extent of this situation and it can be said that most Spanish companies have a challenge in terms of qualifications. Although this situation has been improving in recent years as well as in society (see Fig. 7), there is still a long way to go.

The third finding points out that certain branches of activity tend to have more skilled workers than others. It is noteworthy that the first six sub-sectors concentrate more than half of the firms with employees in professional training with respect to the total of the Spanish manufacturing industry[10]: 'metal products,' 'foodstuffs,' 'chemicals and pharmaceuticals,' 'agricultural and industrial machinery,' 'rubber and plastic' and 'non-metallic minerals.' However, the relevance of the subsectors changes when it is analysed in relation to the total of subsector, and not to the total of the manufacturing industry. In particular, it is found that only two manufacturing subsectors match between the first 6 ('Chemicals and pharmaceuticals' and 'Agricultural and industrial machinery').

Inversely, other subsectors such as 'other industrial subsectors' are significantly distant from the sub-sectoral average, followed by the subsectors of 'wood,' 'leather and footwear' and 'textile and clothing' industries, in all of which employees with VET qualifications make up less than 70 % of their workforce.

This could be partially explained because some branches of manufacturing activity are more knowledge-intensive than others, both because of their product and/or service and because of the structure of the value chain in which they are immersed (due to customer quality requirements or for reasons of occupational and/or environmental safety and so on) (Porter, 1980; Zwick, 2006). In any case, these results show a first approach that would require further research to investigate the causes of this situation.

---

10   However, this issue should be further analysed as it is noted a high presence of both metal products subsector and foodstuffs subsector in the sample of companies used.

Tab. 7. Percentage of firms employing workers with VET qualitications (ISCED 3 and %) by subsectors

Proportion of firms employing workers with VET qualification			
Compared to manufacturing industry overall		**Compared to the total of each subsector**	
Manufacturing subsectors	**%**	**Manufacturing subsectors**	**%**
1. Metal products	13.3	1. Motor vehicles	95.8
2. Foodstuffs	12	2. Chemicals and pharmaceuticals	94.2
3. Chemicals and pharmaceuticals	8.1	3. Ferrous and non-ferrous metals	93.2
4. Agricultural and industrial machinery	7.4	4. Agricultural and industrial machinery	92
5. Rubber and plastic	6.5	5. Computing and electronics	91.4
6. Non-metallic minerals	6.3	6. Electrical equipment and machinery	90.4
7. Textiles and clothing	5.3	7. Other transport equipment	88.9
8. Motor vehicles	4.9	8. Beverages	87.5
9. Meat processing	4.3	9. Rubber and plastic	85.7
10. Furniture	4	10. Metal products	83.3
11. Paper	3.8	11. Non-metallic minerals	80.6
12. Graphics arts	3.7	12. Furniture	75.7
13. Electrical equipment and machinery	3.4	13. Graphics arts	75.4
14. Leather and footwear	3	14. Other manufacturing industry	74.4
15. Ferrous and non-ferrous metals	3	15. Foodstuffs	72.8
16. Beverages	2.5	16. Paper	72.6
17. Wood	2.3	17. Meta processing	72
18. Computing and electronics	2.3	18. Textiles and clothing	69.2
19. Other manufacturing industry	2.1	19. Leather and footwear	64.1
20. Other transport equipment	1.7	20. Wood	62.7

Source: Own elaboration based on BSS data (Fundación Sepi, 2018)

4.3 Business strategies of Spanish manufacturing firms according to VET

According to the set of differential results obtained, deductively we have identified a first comprehensive approach according to the strategic focus that can aggregate different business strategies. Finally, we have decided to use a three-dimensional typology, which encompasses the focus on efficiency, learning capacity and innovation, which we have been partially following the typology of Schuler and Jackson (1987). Those researchers proposed a typology of business strategies that analysed the competitive advantage considering the following strategies: innovation, cost reduction and quality enhancement. We have introduced some variations to the typology, replacing the dimension of quality enhancement by that of learning enhancement. On one side, we understand that the quality assurance and management has been interiorised organisational and culturally in the manufacturing sector, becoming a hygienic condition in firm direction and management. Therefore, the quality strategy does currently offer little margin for strategic differentiation. On the other side, learning is increasingly understood as key factor in terms of human and relational capital, which allows both adaptation and leverage of strategies related to efficiency and innovation. In particular Senge's studies about adaptative capacities of industries showed how firms are increasingly being challenged not only to leverage learning, but also to articulate it as a business strategy in order to become a learning organisation (Senge, 990).

1st. Strategic focus: Efficiency

The efficiency improves outcomes with the same level of resources. In this sense, we have analysed the main business indicators related to productivity, including also workers conditions as they influence optimisation results (Tab. 8). Firstly, the variable of 'employee with VET' has been crossed by the total Gross Added Value (GAV) and productivity per hour (GAV per hour) and results show that is more than 12 points higher in those firms that contract employees with VET qualifications.

Tab. 8. Characterisation of significant differences of effort in efficiency strategies by 'workforce with/without VET'

Strategic focus	Strategies identified	Business indicators crossed by the presence of formal qualified workers in VET	Firms without VET	Firms with VET
Efficiency	Optimisation	Gross value added in total	2.145.107	13.912.148
		Gross value added per worker	42.6	63.5
		Gross value added per hour	24.2	36.3
	Human resources conditions	Proportion of full-time permanent workers	78.6	83.7
		Proportion of temporary workers	12.1	10.6
		Personnel cost per worker (€)	31,800	44,600

Source: Own elaboration based on BSS data (Fundación Sepi, 2018)

Secondly, when workers conditions are analysed in terms of stability (salaried staff on permanent full-time contracts or temporal contracts), research results show that those employees who hold VET qualifications have a greater job stability. Finally, it is noteworthy that personnel cost per worker is higher in the category 'employees with VET,' implying better wages. As it is shown in Tab. 9, those firms that hire more workers with vocational qualifications are positively associated with better results in terms of efficiency.

- 2nd. *Strategic focus: Learning capacity*

The capacity of learning has been analysed by the effort on training, foresight and vocational and technological collaborations. The emergence and socialisation of new technologies in the manufacturing business environment implies new efforts on training and this is more evident in firms with workers that hold VET qualifications, as their both internal expenditure per employee (€81.40) and external expenditure per employee (€106.60) are clearly higher than in firms without workers with vocational qualifications (€22.9 and €24.3 respectively). Concerning technology foresight, the percentage of firms that systematically carry out technology assessments is much higher in the case of VET-qualified personnel. In the same way, the proportion of firms with VET that develop collaborations with vocational schools is much higher (13.6 %) than the other firms; nonetheless, this type of collaboration is less intense than those maintained with providers (17.1 %) and universities (20.1). With respect to the role of apprentice-training firm, it is found that Spanish manufacturing firms are far from having it assumed in their organisations, given the very low average of both apprentices with contract (0.23) and students in alternation with scholarships (0.21) present in the firms. Moreover, there is no significant differentiation according to the category of firms with/without VET.

Tab. 9. Characterisation of significant differences of effort in learning capacity strategies by 'workforce with/without VET'

Strategic focus	Strategies identified	Business indicators crossed by the presence of formal qualified workers in VET	Firms without VET	Firms with VET
Learning capacity	Training (up/re-skilling)	Internal training costs per worker (€)	22.9	81.4
		External training costs per worker (€)	24.3	106.6
	Technological foresight	Technological change evaluation (% of firms)	1.3	20.1
	Collaborations & partnerships	Collaboration with VET schools (% of firms)	0.8	13.6
		Technological collaboration with providers (% of firms)	1.2	17.1
		Technological collaboration with universities and research institutes (% of firms)	1.9	20.4

Source: Own elaboration based on BSS data (Fundación Sepi, 2018)

As it is shown in Tab. 9, those firms that hire more workers with vocational qualifications promote more learning capacities in terms of investing in human capital (internal and external training costs per worker), as well as of both making a greater organisational effort to evaluate technological change and promoting relational capital in the educational and innovation environment

- 3rd. *Strategic focus: Innovation*

Firstly, it is noteworthy the fact that one fifth of firms that employ workers with VET qualifications count with an innovation plan, which show that innovation strategy is explicit and systematised at organisational and managerial level. Secondly, regarding types of innovation, research findings show that it is more intense among firms with workforce with VET qualifications, highlighting the intensity in process innovation (33,9 %), followed by organisational innovation (18.7 %), sales and marketing innovation (16 %) and product innovation (13.6 %).

Tab. 10. Characterisation of significant differences of effort in innovation strategies by 'workforce with/without VET'

Strategic focus	Strategies identified	Business indicators crossed by the presence of formal qualified workers in VET	Firms without VET	Firms with VET
Innovation	Innovation	Product innovation activities	1.2	13.6
		Process innovation activities	4.6	33.9
		Organisational innovation activities	1.8	18.7
		Marketing innovation activities	2.1	16
		A firm Innovation Plan	1.3	19.8
	Research and development	Development of R&D activities (% of total firms)	2.4	30.2
		Only internal R&D activities (% of subtotal firms)	7.4	92.6
		Only external R&D activities (% of subtotal firms)	10	90
		Both internal and external R&D activities (% of subtotal firms)	7.1	92.9
		No R&D activities (% of subtotal firms)	25.3	74.7
		Personnel with R&D experience	0.2	6.3

Source: Own elaboration based on BSS data (Fundación Sepi, 2018)

The fact that there is a greater proportion of firms innovating in processes can be deduced that Spanish manufacturing firms prioritise the improvement of their production processes and their capacity to adapt to the new technologies and methodologies that are being consolidated in the market. From these data it could be inferred that firms have a role more as users of new technologies than as suppliers of the same, given that their effort to innovate in products is more than 20 points lower. In addition, this innovation intensity is aligned to the systematisation of this strategy through an innovation plan, as almost 20 % of manufacturing firms have got one.

Finally, other relevant difference among firms that employ staff with vocational qualifications is their greater propensity to develop R&D activities as 30.2 % of manufacturing firms carry out and/or subcontract R&D, highlighting a difference of more than 27 points with respect to those who do not have such qualifications among their workers. It is noteworthy the data on where the R&D activities are carried out, internally and/or externally, as it will be the firms with VET those with the greatest internal and external development. Specifically, those that carry out both external and internal activities account for 92.9 % of the total. However, most of the firms (74.7 %) do not develop R&D activities which is quite meaningful.

As it is shown in Tab. 10, those firms that hire more workers with vocational qualifications promote more innovation promoting further their research and innovation capital through both specific innovation and R&D activities, and qualified people. With regard to innovation, there are two noteworthy issues: firstly, the innovation most developed is that related to processes, which tends to be of a greater incremental nature; and secondly, there is a greater organisational understanding of innovation through having specific and explicit innovation plans.

4.4 Business results of Spanish manufacturing firms according to VET

The first finding is that Spanish manufacturing firms with staff with vocational qualifications achieved better business results in terms of productivity (VAB per worker and per hour), sales (export and import intensity) and operating profits. Moreover, the potentiality for future investments is larger. Therefore, data show that outcomes are associated with the employment of workers with VET qualification in a positive way. It is relevant to indicate that this greater efficiency and competitiveness is reflected in firm profit and, gross operating margin stood at 8.6 % in 2016, significantly above the figure achieved by firms that did not employ staff with VET qualifications (5.1 %). Moreover, these higher profits were carried over into the business in the form of higher investment. Thus, the investment ratio among industrial firms that employ VET graduates stood at a significant 10.2 %, more than four percentage points above the ratio for firms that do not have staff with vocational qualifications on their workforce (6.1 %).

Tab. 11. Result indicators crossed by the presence of formal qualified workers in VET

Type of Results	Indicators	Firms without VET (%)	Firms with VET (%)
Productivity	VAB per worker (thousand euros)	42.6	63.5
	VAB per hour (euros)	24.2	33.9
Trade Intensity	Export intensity (% total sales)	14.6	28.2
	Import intensity (% total sales)	6.5	11
Operating profits	Gross operating margin (%)	5.1	8.6
Potential Investments	Inverse rate (%)	6.1	10.2

Source: Own elaboration based on BSS data (Fundación Sepi, 2018)

As it is shown in Tab. 11, those firms that hire more workers with vocational qualifications have better business results (in terms of productivity and trade intensity), higher operating profits and better investment prospects (potential investments). Finally it could be established that those firms that contract employees with VET qualifications tend to be more competitive than those that do not.

5. Conclusions

In the current business environment, where the economic weight of Spanish manufacturing industry has decreased considerably in recent decades, accounting for one-sixth of Spain's GDP, it is necessary to review its business capacities to maintain and, as far as possible, improve its competitiveness in the global market.

From the perspective of the **human capital** that makes up Spanish manufacturing firms, this research shows the low qualification of its workers, given that two thirds of workers in Spanish manufacturing industries do not have any professional or university qualifications. However, those firms that have more professionally qualified personnel obtain better business results in terms of efficiency, sales, profits and investment capacity. This association between the qualification and the competitiveness of firms implies reviewing the hiring, employment and human resources policies of firms to improve the results of Spanish manufacturing firms. This is of special relevance as skills shortages and mismatches are another important barrier to the development and use of advanced technologies. From the research findings could be inferred that two of the challenges for Spanish firms are, firstly, to hire workers with higher educational levels, especially vocational training; and secondly, to qualify and requalify (up-skilling and re-skilling) current workers with low educational levels. In this sense, it is especially SMEs that have the greatest challenges, which is of great significance because they represent the majority of industrial firms in Spain. From a sector perspective, while all sub-sectors should work in this direction, those with the greatest challenge are those related to metal products, foodstuffs, rubber and plastic and non-metallic minerals, given their weight on the total manufacturing industry. In this sense, in future research it would be relevant, on the one hand, to analyse subsectors in greater depth; and, on the other hand, to analyse other types of formal qualifications (certificates of professionalism) or informal experience to complement their findings with those of this study.

From the perspective of **business strategies**, the most highlighting differences between those hiring or not qualified employees in VET are identified in strategies related to efficiency, learning and innovation.

The analysis of the strategies, through the aggregation of associated indicators, shows that those firms with higher qualifications make a greater strategic effort. By implementing a value-generation process that makes more intensive use of human capital, technology, R&D and innovation, industrial firms that employ VET graduates could also be expected to perform better.

Firstly, they stand out for optimising resources both at the process level and at the human capital level, which is especially reflected in their productivity, both hourly and per worker and indirectly is connected to their high proportion of innovation in process. This greater propensity for efficiency, which is normally connected to a culture of quality and improvement in European manufacturing industry, is clearly associated with having both intermediate and higher vocational qualifications. In this sense, it could be stated that the professional qualification of manufacturing industries is one of the factors promoting efficiency in the Spanish manufacturing industry.

Secondly, firms with vocational qualified employees differ in that they promote more intensively learning through training (both internal and external), technology assessment, as well as their collaborations with external agents in terms of training and/or technological collaborations (with VET schools, suppliers and/or universities). However, the role of the apprentice training firm is practically non-existent, so it could be inferred that it is not still integrated into the learning strategies of Spanish manufacturing firms. From the findings analysed, it can be inferred that firms with qualified employees in vocational training are more committed to increasing business capacities in terms of learning, both by promoting new skills or improving existing ones, and by generating a relational capital of knowledge with the spheres of vocational training, firms and their own sectoral? value chain. However, there is still a great margin for manufacturing firms to acquire the role of apprentice training firm, which is one of the levers to be used to achieve the qualifications and skills needed to increase their competitiveness.

Thirdly, the propensity for greater innovative intensity on firms with vocational qualified workers reflects a differential strategic approach. On one side, strategic systematisation is greater when it is formalised and managed through specific innovation plans of the firms, which demonstrates an explicit culture and managerial praxis.

On the other side, these firms with higher qualifications develop greater innovation activities, especially from the processes, which is associated with a vision of technological adaptation to production processes and the capacity to absorb new technologies. This characterisation of innovation also shows a less effort in product innovation, from which it can be deduced that firms prioritise more a strategy of technological absorption than the creation of new products or technologies; in other words, they would be more consuming of new technologies than generating them. This is also reflected in the fact that a significant proportion of these firms do not carry out R&D, which is the most sophisticated stage of innovation. Although they carry out more R&D than firms with lower qualifications, only one third of them do so. This shows a timid attitude towards the generation of new products, technologies, etc., which is aligned with Spanish national accounting data regarding the generation of new technologies, patents, etc. To sum up, to invest new further on efficiency, learning and innovation capacities of Spanish manufacturing firms in order to boost competitiveness should be aligned to investment on qualifications and skills.

From the perspective of **business results**, the business differences according to VET qualifications of their employees are clear. By implementing an employment and human resources policy according to VET qualifications, Spanish manufacturing industries performs and achieves better business results from which it could also be expected to compete better. Therefore, it is important that firms internalise it and reflect their strategy and operations, but also that they have a structural environment, both educational, vocational and technological, favourable to develop it in the most efficient and innovative way possible, which allows to shorten the absorption cycles of new technologies in terms of incremental innovation.

The contribution of this research makes to the field lies in its novel characterisation and association analysis approach and in the quantitative scale of the sample. Nevertheless, we are aware that the research has its limitations and that it is necessary further research on the causal relationships, that of predictive capacity on the direct and indirect effects of VET on the business results. We understand that it is relevant to continue study in this significant scientific field.

Acronyms

BSS: Business Strategies Survey
CBR: Spanish Central Business Register
CEDEFOP: European Centre for the Development of Vocational Training
CNAE: Spanish National Classification of Economic Activities
CVET: Continuous Vocational Education and Training
EIS: European Innovation Scoreboard
ESI: European Skills Index
EU: European Union
FUNDAE: Spanish Foundation for Continuous Vocational Training
GDP: Gross Domestic Product
GVA: Gross Added Value
INE: Spanish Statistical Office
ISCED: International Standard Classification of Education
IVET: Initial Vocational Education and Training
MEFP: Spanish Ministry of Education and Vocational Education
MICT: Spanish Ministry of Industry, Trade and Tourism
OECD: Organisation for Economic Co-operation and Development
R&D: Research and Development
SEPE: Spanish Employment Public Service
SEPI: Spanish State-owned Industrial Holding Company
SMEs: Small and Medium-sized Enterprises
UNESCO: United Nations Educational, Scientific and Cultural Organization
VET: Vocational Education and Training

Biographical notes

Dr. Angel Díaz-Chao is the Managing Director of the SEPI Foundation and Professor of Applied Economics Department at Rey Juan Carlos University. His research is linked to statistics and econometrics and has focused on productivity and labour market and technological innovation, having published in journals such as Journal of Business Research, Journal of Travel Research, Journal of Medical Internet Research and Social Indicators Research.

Dr. Mónica Moso-Díez is the Head of the Centre for Knowledge and Innovation at Bankia Foundation for Dual Training. Her research interests focus on 'regional VET systems'? VET governance and research and innovation agendas and business strategies. She has 20 years of research and innovation experience.

Dr. Joan Torrent-Sellens is Full Professor of Economics at Faculty of Economics andBusiness at Open University of Catalonia (UOC) and group leader of ICT Interdisciplinary Research Group (i2TIC). He has 25 years of teaching and research experience. Dr. Torrent-Sellens specialises in the analysis of digitisation, automation, productivity and competitiveness; the knowledge economy; the future of work; eLearning and eHealth subjects.

References

Alba-Ramirez, A. (1994). Formal training, temporary contracts, productivity and wages in Spain. *Oxford Bulletin of Economics and Statistics*, *56*(2) (pp. 151–70).

Ansoff, H. I. (1965). *Corporate Strategy*. New York: McGraw-Hill.

Aragón-Sánchez, A., Barba-Aragón, I., and Sanz-Valle, R. (2003). Effects of training on business results. *International Journal of Human Resource Management*, 14, (956–980).

Bankia Estudios (2019). Panorama (2019, November 30). Retrieved from: https://www.bankiaestudios.com/recursos/doc/estudios/20191202/diciembre/ipi-oct19.pdf.

Becker, G. (1994). *Human Capital*, third edition. Chicago: University of Chicago Press.

Card, D. (1999). *The Causal Effect of Education on Earnings. Handbook of Labour Economics 3* (pp. 1801–1863).

Cedefop (2011). The impact of vocational education and training on company performance. *Research paper* (19). Luxemburg: Publications Office of the European Union. Retrieved from: https://www.cedefop.europa.eu/files/5519_en.pdf.

Cedefop (2015). *Spotlight on Vet: Spain.* Luxemburg: Publications Office of the European Union. Retrieved from: https://www.cedefop.europa.eu/files/8104_en.pdf.

Cedefop (2018). *Spotlight on VET -2018 compilation: Vocational education and training systems in Europe.* Luxemburg: Publications Office of the European Union.

Díaz-Chao, A., and Torrent-Sellens, J. (2019). Formación profesional y empresa industrial en España: Efectos sobre la generación de valor y los resultados de la actividad empresarial. En Díaz-Chao, A., Moso-Diez, M. and Torrent-Sellens, J. (Eds.). *Formación Profesional en la empresa industrial española.* Madrid: Fundación Bankia por la Formación Dual. Retrieved from: https://www.dualizabankia.com/recursos/doc/portal/2019/07/08/formacion-profesional-empresa-industrial-espanola.pdf.

Echeverría, B., and y Martínez, P. (2018). Estrategias de mejora en la implantación de la Formación Profesional Dual en España. *Ekonomiaz-Revista de Economía*, 94 (pp. 178–203).

European Commission (2019). Communication from the commission to the European parliament, the European Council, the Council, the European Central Bank and the Eurogroup 2019 European Semester: *Assessment of progress on structural reforms, prevention and correction of macroeconomic imbalances, and results of in-depth reviews under Regulation* (EU) No 1176/2011, COM(2019) 150 final.

European Innovation Scoreboard (2019). *Report Country-Spain.* Brussels: European Commission Publications.

European Skills Index- EIS (2919). Skills Panorama: Country Spain (2019, October 12). Retrieved from: https://skillspanorama.cedefop.europa.eu/en/countries/spain.

Fundación Sepi (2018). Survey on Business Strategies. (2019, June 18). Retrieved from: http://www.fundacionsepi.es/investigacion/esee/en/spresentacion.asp.

Grant, R. M. (1996). Toward a knowledge-based theory of the firm, *Strategic Management Journal*, 17 (pp. 109–122). Retrieved from: https://doi.org/10.1002/smj.4250171110.

Herrmann, A., and Peine, A. (2011). When 'national innovation system' meet 'varieties of capitalism' arguments on labour qualifications: On the skill types and scientific knowledge needed for radical and incremental product innovations. *Research Policy*, 40 (pp. 687–701).

Hollanders, H., Es-Sadki, N., and Merkelback, I. (2019). *European Innovation Scoreboard 2019*. Luxembourg: Publication Office of the European Union.

Huerta, M. E., Audet, X. L., and Peregort, O. P. (2006). In-firm training in Catalonia: Organizational structure, funding, evaluation and economic impact. *International Journal of Training & Development*, 10 (pp. 140–163).

INE (2016). Directorio Central de Empresas (2019, July 17). Retrieved from: https://www.ine.es/dynt3/inebase/es/index.htm?padre=54&capsel=3920.

INE (2019a). Directorio Central de Empresas (2019, July 15). Retrieved from: https://www.ine.es/dynt3/inebase/es/index.htm?padre=54&capsel=3920.

INE (2019b). Industrial Production Indices (2019, November 30). Retrieved from: https://www.ine.es/dyngs/INEbase/en/operacion.htm?c=Estadistica_C&cid=1254736145519&menu=ultiDatos&idp=1254735576715.

Konings, J. (2008). The impact of training on productivity and wages: Evidence from Belgian firm level panel data. LICOS, *Discussion Paper Series*, 197.

Leiponen, A. (2000). Competencies, innovation and profitability of firms. *Economics of Innovation and New Technology*, 9(1) (pp. 1–24).

Lorenz, M., Rübmann, M., Strack, R., Lueth, K. L., and y Bolle, M. (2015). Man and Machine in Industry 4.0, How will technology transform the industrial workforce through 2025? Boston: The Boston Consulting Group. Retrieved from: http://englishbulletin.adapt.it/wp-content/uploads/2015/10/BCG_Man_and_Machine_in_Industry_4_0_Sep_2015_tcm80-197250.pdf.

Mahlberg, B., et al. (2009). Firm productivity, workforce age and vocational training in Austria. In: Kuhn, M. and Ochsen, C. (Eds.). *Labour Markets and Demographic Change*. Wiesbaden: VS Verlag (pp. 58–84).

Marhuenda-Fluixá, F., Chisvert-Tarazona, M. J., and Palomares-Montero, D. (2019). The implementation of dual VET in Spain: An empirical analysis. In F. Marhuenda-Fluixà (Ed.), *The School-Based Vocational Education and Training System in Spain*. Singapore: Springer (pp. 205–222).

MEFP (2019a). *Panorama de la Educación. Indicadores de la OCDE. Informe español*. Madrid: Ministerio de Educación y Formación Profesional. Retrieved from: https://www.educacionyfp.gob.es/dam/jcr:b8f3deec-3fda-4622-befb-386a4681b299/panorama%20de%20la%20educaci%C3%B3n%202019.pdf

MEFP (2019b). *I Plan Estratégico de Formación Profesional del Sistema Educativo 2019–2022*. Madrid: Ministerior de Educación y Formación Profesional. Retrieved from: http://todofp.es/dam/jcr:163978c0-a214-471e-868d-82862b5a3aa3/plan-estrategico--enero-2020.pdf.

MEFP (2019c). *Datos y Cifras Curso escolar 2019/2020*. Madrid: MEFP. Retrieved from: http://www.educacionyfp.gob.es/dam/jcr:b998eea2-76c0-4466-946e-965698e9498d/datosycifras1920esp.pdf.

MICT (2019). *Informe Anual 2018. Evolución reciente de la economía española y de los sectores competencia del ministerio de industria, comercio y turismo*. Madrid: Ministerio de Industria, Comercio y Turismo.

Moso-Diez, M. (2019). El valor de la Formación Profesional para la Industria 4.0. En Díaz-Chao, A., Moso-Diez, M., and Torrent-Sellens, J. (Eds.). *Formación Profesional en la empresa industrial española*. Madrid: Fundación Bankia por la Formación Dual.

Murray, A., and Steedman, H. (1998). Growing skills in Europe: The changing skill profiles of France, Germany, Netherlands, Portugal, Sweden and the UK. *CEPDP* (399). London: London School of Economics and Political Science.

Navarro, M., Albizu, M., Egaña, J., Egurbide, I., Retegi, J., and y Vázquez, R. (2018). *La formación profesional de Navarra. Hacia un nuevo modelo de centro y el reto de la FP dual*. Madrid: Fundación Bankia por la Formación Dual. Retrieved from: https://www.dualizabankia.com/recursos/doc/portal/2019/07/08/fp-navarra.pdf

Nonaka, I., and Takeuchi, H. (1995). *The knowledge-creating firm: How Japanese firms create the dynamics of innovation*. Oxford: Oxford University Press.

OECD (2019a). National Accounts of OECD Countries. 2019(2). Paris: OECD. Retrieved from: htpps://doi.org/10.1787/g2g9ff01-eng.

OECD (2019b). *Education at a Glance 2019: OECD Indicators*. Paris: OECD Publishing. https://doi.org/10.1787/f8d7880d-en.

OECD (2019c). *OECD Economic Outlook*, 2019(1). Paris: OECD Publishing. Retrieved from: https://doi.org/10.1787/b2e897b0-en.

Olazaran, M., and y Brunet, I. (Ed.) (2013). *Entorno regional y formación profesional*. Bilbao: Servicio Editorial de la Universidad del País Vasco y URV publicaciones.

Porter, M. E. (1980). *Competitive Strategy: Techniques for Analyzing Industries and Competitors*. New York: Free Press.

Sancha, I., and Gutiérrez, S. (2019). *Vocational Education and Training in Europe: Spain*. Cedefop ReferNet VET in Europe reports, 2018. http://libserver.cedefop.europa.eu/vetelib/2019/Vocational_Education_Trainin g_Europe_Spain_2018_Cedefop_ReferNet.pdf.

Schroeder, W. (2016). *Germany's Industry 4.0. strategy. Rhine capitalism in the age of digitalisation*. London: FES.

Schuler, R. S., and Jackson, S. E. (1987). Linking competitive strategies with human resources management practices. *The Academy of Management Executive*, 1(3) (pp. 207–219).

Schwab, K. (2016). *The Fourth Industrial Revolution*. Geneva: World Economic Forum.

Senge, P. M. (1990). *The Fifth Discipline: The Art and Practice of the Learning Organization*. New York: Doubleday/Currency.

Smit, J., Kreutzer, S., Moeller, C., and y Carlberg, M. (2016). *Industry 4.0*. Brussels: Directorate-General for Internal Policies.

Toner, P., and y Woolley, R. (2016). Perspectives and debates on vocational education and training, skills and the prospects for innovation. *Revista Española de Sociología*, 25(3) (pp. 319–342).

Utterback, J. M., and Abernathy, W. J. (1975). A dynamic model of process and product innovation. *Omega*, 3, 639–656.

Wolter, S. C., and Mühlemann, S. (2015). *Apprenticeship Training in Spain – A Cost-Effective Model for Firms?* Gütersloh: Bertelsmann Stiftung.

Zwick, T. (2006). The impact of training intensity on establishment productivity. *Industrial Relations: A Journal of Economy and Society*, 45(1) (pp. 26–46).

studies in vocational and continuing education

edited by
philipp gonon & anja heikkinen

The aim of this series is to present critical, historical and comparative research in the field of vocational and continuing education and human research development, seen from a pedagogical, organisational, economic and societal perspective. It discusses the implications of latest research to contemporary reform policies and practices. One central issue reflected in all publications is gender. A basic feature of all volumes is their cross-cultural approach.

The series has a firm basis in the international research network "VET and Culture" (Vocational Education and Training and Culture; www.peda.net/veraja/uta/vetculture) and the editors invite distinguished researchers from Europe and other continents to contribute to the series. Studies in vocational and continuing education include monographs, collected papers editions, and proceedings.

Vol. 1   Antony Lindgren & Anja Heikkinen (eds)
         Social Competences in Vocational and Continuing Education
         2004. 256 S. ISBN 3-03910-345-8 / US-ISBN 0-8204-7013-9

Vol. 2   Liv Mjelde
         The Magical Properties of Workshop Learning
         2006. 230 S. ISBN 3-03910-348-2 / US-ISBN 0-8204-7014-7

Vol. 3   Liv Mjelde & Richard Daly (eds)
         Working Knowledge in a Globalizing World
         From Work to Learning, from Learning to Work
         2006. 406 S. ISBN 3-03910-974-X / 0-8204-8364-8

Vol. 4   Philipp Gonon, Katrin Kraus, Jürgen Oelkers & Stefanie Stolz (eds)
         Work, Education and Employability
         2008. 324 S. ISBN 978-3-03911-294-4

Vol. 5   Olav Eikeland
         The Ways of Aristotle
         Aristotelian Phrónêsis, Aristotelian Philosophy of Dialogue,
         and Action Research
         2008. 560 S. ISBN 978-3-03911-471-9

Vol. 6   Vibe Aarkrog & Christian Helms Jørgensen (eds)
         Divergence and Convergence in Education and Work
         2008. 441 S. ISBN 978-3-03911-505-1

Vol. 7   Anja Heikkinen & Katrin Kraus (eds)
         Reworking Vocational Education. Policies, Practices and Concepts
         2009. 230 S. ISBN 978-3-03911-603-4

Vol. 8   Markus Weil, Leena Koski & Liv Mjelde (eds)
         Knowing Work. The Social Relations of Working and Knowing
         2009. 252 S. ISBN 978-3-03911-642-3

Vol. 9   Philipp Gonon
         The Quest for Modern Vocational Education – Georg Kerschensteiner
         between Dewey, Weber and Simmel
         2009. 278 S. ISBN 978-3-0343-0026-1

Vol. 10 Thomas Deissinger, Josef Aff, Alison Fuller & Christian Helms Jørgensen (eds)
         Hybrid Qualifications: Structures and Problems in the Context of
         European VET Policy
         2013. ISBN 978-3-0343-1059-8

Vol. 11 Stefanie Stolz & Philipp Gonon (eds)
         Challenges and Reforms in Vocational Education.
         Aspects of Inclusion and Exclusion
         2012. 260 S. ISBN 978-3-0343-1068-0

Vol. 12 Markus Maurer & Philipp Gonon (eds.)
        The Challenges of Policy Transfer in Vocational Skills Development.
        National Qualifications Frameworks and the Dual Model of Vocational Training
        in International Cooperation
        2014. 363 S. ISBN 978-3-0343-1536-4

Vol. 13 Gabriele Molzberger & Manfred Wahle (eds.)
        Shaping the Futures of (Vocational) Education and Work.
        Commitment of VET and VET Research
        2015. 240 S. ISBN 978-3-0343-1617-0

Vol. 14 Esther Berner & Philipp Gonon (eds.)
        History of Vocational Education and Training in Europe.
        Cases, Concepts and Challenges
        2016. 599 S. ISBN 978-3-0343-2120-4

Vol. 15 Fernando Marhuenda-Fluixá (ed.)
        Vocational Education beyond Skill Formation.
        VET between Civic, Industrial and Market Tensions
        2017. 439 S. ISBN 978-3-0343-2806-7

Vol. 16 Janis Vossiek
        Collective Skill Formation in Liberal Market Economies?
        The Politics of Training Reforms in Australia, Ireland and the
        United Kingdom
        2018. 230 S. ISBN 978-3-0343-2969-9

Vol. 17 Vesa Korhonen & Pauliina Alenius (Eds.)
        Internationalisation and Transnationalisation in
        Higher Education
        2018. 314 S. ISBN 978-3-0343-2776-3

Vol. 18 Philipp Eigenmann, Philipp Gonon & Markus Weil (eds.)
        Opening and Extending Vocational Education
        2021. 130 S. ISBN 978-3-0343-3487-7

Vol. 19   María José Chisvert-Tarazona, Mónica Moso-Diez & Fernando Marhuenda-Fluixá (Eds.)
Apprenticeship in dual and non-dual systems
Between tradition and innovation
2021. 310 S ISBN 978-3-0343-4305-3

www.ingramcontent.com/pod-product-compliance
Lightning Source LLC
LaVergne TN
LVHW021951060526
838201LV00049B/1662